CAMBRIDGE CONCISE HISTORIES

A Concise History of Germany

CAMBRIDGE CONCISE HISTORIES

This is a new series of illustrated 'concise histories' of selected individual countries, intended both as university and college textbooks and as general historical introductions for general readers, travellers and members of the business community.

First titles in the series:

A Concise History of Germany
MARY FULBROOK

A Concise History of Greece
RICHARD CLOGG

A Concise History of France
ROGER PRICE

A Concise History of Britain, 1707–1795
W. A. SPECK

A Concise History of Portugal
DAVID BIRMINGHAM

A Concise History of Italy
CHRISTOPHER DUGGAN

A Concise History of Bulgaria
RICHARD CRAMPTON

A Concise History of South Africa
ROBERT ROSS

A Concise History of Brazil
BORIS FAUSTO

A Concise History of Mexico
BRIAN HAMNETT

A Concise History of Australia
STUART MACINTYRE

Other titles are in preparation

A Concise History
of Germany

SECOND EDITION

MARY FULBROOK

CAMBRIDGE
UNIVERSITY PRESS

CAMBRIDGE UNIVERSITY PRESS
Cambridge, New York, Melbourne, Madrid, Cape Town, Singapore, São Paulo,
Delhi, Dubai, Tokyo

Cambridge University Press
The Edinburgh Building, Cambridge CB2 8RU, UK

Published in the United States of America by Cambridge University Press, New York

www.cambridge.org
Information on this title: www.cambridge.org/9780521540711

First published 1991
Reprinted eight times
Second edition 2004
Eighth printing 2009

Printed in the United Kingdom at the University Press, Cambridge

A catalogue record for this publication is available from the British Library

ISBN 978-0-521-83320-2 hardback
ISBN 978-0-521-54071-1 paperback

CONTENTS

ILLUSTRATIONS

MAPS

PREFACE

A book such as this is infinitely easier to criticise than to write. The attempt to compress over a thousand years of highly complex history into a brief volume will inevitably provoke squeals of protest from countless specialists, who see their own particular patches distorted, constrained, misrepresented, even ignored. Yet a brief history of such a large topic can make no attempt at comprehensiveness. At best it can provide an intelligent guide to the broad sweep of developments.

These limitations are indeed partly inherent in the nature of historical writing, which cannot be a simple matter of recounting an agreed narrative, but rather must be a process of imposing an order on the mass of material – and on the interpretations of that material – which comes to us from the past. But it is particularly the case for a concise history of Germany that some brutal decisions about selection and omission have had to be made. While readers will all have their own views on the matter, the author has had to make particular choices. In terms of space devoted to different periods, the book operates on the landscape principle: things nearer to the observer loom larger, are perceived in closer detail, than the mistier general views of the distant horizons. Thus chapters generally deal with progressively shorter periods of time as the present is neared. Within the general landscape surveyed some features appear more important than others. The problem of 'teleology' is well known to historians: there is a tendency to notice particularly features pointing towards the present, explaining developments partly in terms of their consequences (whether or not participants were aware of their 'contributions' to historical 'progress'), and to ignore turnings that led nowhere. While there has been a healthy reaction against this in recent historical writing, it is still the case that certain developments appear more important from the point of view of current concerns than do others. And all authors inevitably have their own particular interests, enthusiasms and blind spots, however hard they try to be balanced and objective in coverage. There is also the particular problem, in relation to the history of 'Germany', of the limits of what is held to be its proper subject matter. In this volume the history of Austria has had to be considered only insofar as it was an integral part of 'Germany' at different times, or interrelated with the history of modern Germany since 1871. Austria, while perhaps the most obvious, is not the only area to suffer in this way: the boundaries of 'Germany' have been extremely changeable over the centuries.

A wide-ranging work such as this must rely heavily on researches undertaken by others, and represent a synthesis of existing knowledge and often quite conflicting views, while yet developing a coherent overall account. The author is painfully aware of gaps and inadequacies in the present analysis, but hopes at least that in presenting a broad framework which spans the centuries two useful purposes will have been accomplished. This book may present a basis and stimulus for subsequent more detailed exploration of particular aspects; it may also serve to locate existing knowledge and interests of readers within a wider interpretive framework. The book is intended as a form of large-scale map which can be used as a context for finer investigation of details along the way.

I am tremendously grateful to my colleagues and friends who have read and made valuable comments on parts of the manuscript, saving me from factual errors and inappropriate interpretations. I would like in particular to thank the following for their painstaking efforts to improve the text: David Blackbourn; Ian Kershaw; Timothy McFarland; Rudolf Muhs; Hamish Scott; Bob Scribner; Jill Stephenson; Martin Swales. Obviously, I alone am responsible for the inadequacies which remain. The work benefited from a small grant from the UCL Dean's Fund enabling me to spend some time combing libraries, museums and archives for suitable illustrative

material. The choice of appropriate illustrations was almost as difficult as the construction of the text, and raised as many problems of
selection, interpretation and omission. Discerning readers will notice
that illustrations of personalities and familiar sights have generally
been demoted in favour of representation of broader themes and
more remote periods or places. Finally, I would also like to thank
my husband and my three children for being willing to spend innumerable summers wandering around central Europe in search of
aspects of the German past.

PREFACE TO THE UPDATED EDITION (1992)

First of all, I would like to thank Dr Werner Schochow of Berlin for
pointing out to me some errors of detail which crept unnoticed into
the first edition, and for suggesting certain amendments to the index.
I am extremely grateful to him for his close and careful reading of
the text, and the trouble he took in providing detailed comments
and suggestions.

I have also taken the opportunity to put discussion of West
Germany into the past tense (East Germany having already suffered
that fate at the time of the first edition). While much of what was
'West Germany' has of course passed over into the enlarged Federal
Republic after unification in 1990, nevertheless united Germany is
a new entity, and it would be prejudging its development in a quite
a-historical fashion to suggest that what was true of the pre-1990
Federal Republic will continue to obtain in the new, rather lop-sided
united Federal Republic, which faces both new domestic challenges
and a changed European context.

Mary Fulbrook
London, October 1991

PREFACE TO THE SECOND EDITION (2004)

For the Second Edition, I have made a number of minor changes
throughout the text, to reflect the changing viewpoints of the
present, and the implications of recent scholarship. A new chapter

has been added on Germany since 1990. The bibliography has been drastically pruned and substantially updated. But I have chosen not to tinker dramatically with the main body of the book, which has now proved its usefulness as an accessible overview for a wide range of readers across the English-speaking world and in a number of foreign translations.

Mary Fulbrook
London, March 2003

I

Introduction: the German lands and people

In a famous and much-quoted verse, those two most renowned German writers, Goethe and Schiller, posed the question which has been at the heart of much German history: 'Deutschland? aber wo liegt es? Ich weiss das Land nicht zu finden.' ('Germany? But where is it? I know not how to find the country.') They went on to put their finger succinctly on a further problem of the Germans: 'Zur *Nation* euch zu bilden, ihr hoffet es, Deutsche, vergebens; / Bildet, ihr könnt es, dafür freier zu Menschen euch aus.' ('Any hope of forming yourselves into a *nation*, Germans, is in vain; develop yourselves rather – you can do it – more freely as human beings!') Between them, these quotations encapsulate perhaps the most widespread general notions about Germany and the Germans – although of course Goethe and Schiller could hardly foresee, let alone be held responsible for, what was to come. A belated nation, which became unified too late, and a nation, at that, of 'thinkers and poets' who separated the freedom of the sphere of the spirit from the public sphere and the powers of the state; a nation which, notoriously, eventually gave rise – whatever its contributions in literature and music – to the epitome of evil in the genocidal rule of Adolf Hitler. A nation with an arguably uniquely creative culture and uniquely destructive political history; a nation uniquely problematic, tormented, peculiar, with its own strange, distorted pattern of history. And a nation uniquely efficient, in every transformation becoming a 'model' of its kind.

As with all platitudes, there is some element of truth in these generalisations; and as with all generalisations, there is much which is oversimplified, misleading, and downright wrong. Perhaps the most misleading aspect of all these statements is the underlying assumption that there is some simple entity, the 'Germans', who have an enduring national identity revealing itself over the ages in all the twists and turns of a tortuous national history. The realities are infinitely more complex. There is a geographical complexity, with a range of peoples speaking variants of the German language across a central European area, in which over the centuries there has been a great diversity of political forms, which have for most of 'Germany's' history included also non-German-speaking peoples. There is a historical complexity, with as much contingency and accident as predetermined drive along any evolutionary path to a pre-ordained end. And there is the complexity inherent in the nature of reconstructing and writing a history of a shifting entity, itself constituted in the light of current concerns and interest. For many people, recent times will appear infinitely the most interesting; remoter periods will remain – for all but the few, fascinated by a far-removed culture – by way of a 'background', a setting of the scene, to know what the situation was 'when the story began'. Even a decision about the latter, the starting point, is to some extent arbitrary. All reconstructed history is a human construction from the perspective of certain interests, conscious or otherwise.

For most English-speaking people until 1989, 'Germany' would have meant the Federal Republic of Germany, or West Germany, with its capital in Bonn. To others, the German Democratic Republic, or East Germany, would be included, created as it was out of the ruins of defeated Nazi Germany. Most people today would not even think of Austria, let alone Switzerland, as candidates for being included in 'Germany'; yet it was only in 1871 that Austria was excluded from the unified 'small Germany', under Prussian domination, of Imperial Germany. German-speaking Switzerland separated, even from the 'Holy Roman Empire of the German Nation', many centuries earlier. And, of course, there are other areas in central Europe which were either previously included in some German states – as, for example, those former German territories now in Poland and Russia – or where there were or are substantial German-speaking minorities under other governments. For some historians, Germany's politically and geographically insecure and contested central European location – *mitten in Europa* – has indeed been

Plate 1. Kloster Grüssau in Silesia. Since 1945 part of Poland, Silesia was a province of Habsburg Austria until it was seized by Prussia in 1740–42. Central European boundaries have been very fluctuating over the centuries.

elevated to a central interpretive factor in 'German' history and identity. It certainly makes a clear definition of the subject of study more complex than is the case for many 'national' histories. While the ultimate landing stage of this book will be the united Germany formed in 1990 from the two Germanies of the late twentieth century – the German Democratic Republic and the Federal Republic of Germany – much else will need to be considered along the way, with a flexibility of focus and boundary.

The areas covered by Germany in the twenty-first century include many striking regional variations, based partly in topography and geography, partly in historical differences. Topographically, the German lands stretch from the sandy coasts of the North Sea and Baltic Sea, with their trading ports, through the heathy North German plain; then, broken by the hillier country of the Central German Uplands (as in the Harz mountains, or the Erzgebirge), down through the gentle undulations of southern Germany to the foothills of the Alps on the borders with Austria and Switzerland. The climate varies from the mild, wet Atlantic climate of the north and west to a drier, more continental climate, with cold, snowy winters and hot summers punctuated by frequent thunderstorms, in the south and east. Natural resources are variable: there are considerable deposits of the inferior lignite (brown coal) in eastern Germany, which produces about a third of the world's total production, whereas in western Germany bituminous coal is mined in greater quantities, particularly in the Ruhr area. Germany has small amounts of natural gas and oil, insufficient for current energy needs, and is reliant also on controversial nuclear power production. There are variable, but not extensive, mineral deposits (iron ore, lead, zinc, potash salts). Soils and farming conditions vary: in many areas, the land is left as heath or forest rather than being put to grain production or pasture. In the 1980s, the population of West Germany was slightly over 61 million, while that of East Germany was somewhat under 17 million; in 1990, the population of united Germany was 78.3 million.

Historically, formed as they are of regions which had their own existence as independent provinces or principalities in the past, the German lands show striking regional variations based more in political, cultural and socioeconomic history than in geography. What will strike the visitor to Germany are the results of human occupation, human use of the environment, human beliefs, practices and social relationships: mediaeval walled towns and castles, great baroque churches and monasteries, princely palaces, different styles of farm house, burgher house, or industrial slum. Regional stereotypes abound: Prussian Protestant asceticism, militarism and conservatism is often contrasted with Hamburg liberalism or with the more expansive mode of the Catholic, beer-swilling, unintelligible Bavarians. There is a great variety of regional accents and cultures still to be found in the more cosmopolitan and centralised Germany of the late twentieth century. Even those with only a casual acquaintance will be aware of differences between the Rhineland, with its castles and vineyards, the industrial Ruhr (no longer belching the smoke and fumes it used to do before the shift to high-tech industries in south-western Germany), the forests, streams and cuckoo-clock attractions of the Black Forest, or the lakes and Alpine pastures of Upper Bavaria. Fewer casual tourists will be familiar with the northern coasts, the Frisian islands or the lakes and waters of Schleswig-Holstein, although they may have visited Bremen, Hamburg and Lübeck; most will have sped through the rolling Westphalian hills

Plate 2. A crucifix near Jachenau, in southern Bavaria. With its carved wooden 'curtains', this is a particularly splendid example of Catholic popular piety. In some predominantly Protestant areas of Germany, such as Württemberg, small patches of territory rich in crucifixes testify to a long-distant past when they might have been, for example, fiefs of the Catholic Austrian Habsburgs.

on a fast autobahn, bypassing the Lüneberg heath to the north or the mediaeval attractions tucked away in the Harz mountains; very few will have explored the forgotten communities in the Bohemian border country and the Bavarian forest on the Czech border, or be aware of quite local differences between such regions as the Spessart, the Kraichgau or the Odenwald. Many will know the major urban centres, particularly cities such as Munich, Nuremberg, Frankfurt, Stuttgart, Cologne, but will have little idea about the reasons for the decentralised nature of pre-1990 West German urban life (with its capital, Bonn, so easily dismissed as 'a small town in Germany'); before the revolutionary events of autumn 1989, very few western visitors would have penetrated further into East Germany than a day trip to its capital, East Berlin. Eastern Germany, although smaller than the western areas of Germany, evinces a comparable regional variation: from the sand dunes of the Baltic coast in the north, through the sparsely populated lake country of Mecklenburg, down to the varied regions of the hillier southern areas, including industrial centres such as Halle, Leipzig, Erfurt and Chemnitz, major cultural centres such as Dresden and Weimar, and tourist attractions in Saxon Switzerland, the Thuringian forest, or the Harz mountains. All these regions differ for a multitude of reasons beyond purely topographical factors such as proximity to rivers, sea or mountains. Economically, they have been developed and exploited in different ways and become involved as different elements in wider economic systems. Culturally, the differences between Catholic and Protestant areas in the confessionalised states of post-Reformation Germany endured and had a profound impact over the centuries. Politically, the histories of the different regions experienced a myriad of forms, a veritable laboratory for the historically oriented political scientist. All these varied influences have left their imprint on the more homogenised industrial Germany of today.

For most visitors before 1989, it would have been almost impossible to imagine away what was perhaps the most striking feature of the two Germanies: the fiercely guarded frontier running down between the Germanies from the Baltic to the Czech border with southern Germany, dividing not only East and West Germany but also East and West Europe, communism and capitalism, democratic centralism and liberal democracy, symbolising the international rifts of the second half of the twentieth century – in Churchill's phrase,

Plate 3. The view towards Alexanderplatz in East Berlin in the 1980s. At the end, the television tower dwarfs the Marienkirche; on the left, the rebuilt Cathedral faced the new East German 'Palace of the Republic', built on the site of the former Royal Palace, on the right.

the 'Iron Curtain'. This border not only snaked down along miles of frontier between the two Germanies, with a no-man's land dividing formerly close communities, cutting them off from natural hinterlands; it also cut right through the very heart of that former magnificent metropolitan centre, the erstwhile capital of Prussia and of Imperial, Weimar and Nazi Germany, and now again of Germany since 1990: Berlin. Heavily armed guards monitored the highly restricted flow of traffic at the limited crossing points and ensured that no East German citizen left without permission. West Berlin, economically dependent and highly subsidised by the West German government, was also a city of self-advertising capitalism: vast department stores, bright lights, extravagant cultural performances, international conference centres, patronage of the arts. The old, turn-of-the-century slums, built as the Imperial capital rapidly expanded, by the 1980s housed not only the still surviving working-class Berliners, but also a large number of foreign 'guest workers' as well as a range of groups cultivating 'alternative' life styles in a variety of ways. In amongst all this, there was the inevitable pervasion of military presence – Berlin was still formally a city under four-power control – and even when escaping to the remarkable natural resources of the lakes and forests in West Berlin, there was the omnipresence of the Wall. Only a few yards away, across the Wall, there was a very different Berlin: 'Berlin, capital of the GDR', as was so proudly proclaimed on every signpost. Less empty of traffic than in earlier decades, East Berlin covered the heart of the old Imperial capital: new East German public buildings, as well as mass-produced apartment blocks, jostled with the crumbling splendours of the old political and cultural centres. Whatever the East German attempts to promote a comparably – but differently – attractive image to that of the west, in areas such as the modern Alexanderplatz, much of East Berlin had a drab, dusty, old-fashioned air. The two Berlins, in extreme forms, epitomised and symbolised many of the strengths and weaknesses of the two socioeconomic and political systems for which they served as representatives.

And, in a dramatic fashion, the opening of the Berlin Wall in November 1989 symbolised the passing of an era. With the revolutionary changes in the Soviet Union and Eastern Europe in the late 1980s, the 'Iron Curtain' began to crumble. As communist rule collapsed in the East, economic and political pressures combined to produce the unexpectedly rapid, unprecedented unification of two very different systems and societies in October 1990. For observers of the new, united Germany of the early twenty-first century, history takes on a new significance, as once again – as so many times over the centuries – the issue of Germany's character, form, and role in Europe and the world gains prominence. Yet with the end of the Cold War the character of world alignments and tensions changed too. With international terrorism and new conflicts, the 'German problem' came to be seen in a very different light.

So much for initial appearances and observations. There is much more to German history, society, culture and political life than can be gained from travelling impressions. There are, too, many aspects of the German past which have been neglected, repressed, transformed, or simply ignored. We must now begin to explore the broad outlines of the twists and turns of German history which have led to the Germany we see today.

2

Mediaeval Germany

The area now known as Germany shows evidence of settlement since prehistoric times: Neanderthal man is a well-known archaeological find, and there are traces of stone, bronze and iron-age settlements right across central Europe. The Roman Empire extended across the western and southern parts of what is now known as Germany, and there are Roman foundations and remains in many German towns, such as Trier, Augsburg, Mainz, Cologne, Regensburg and Passau. A frontier fortification (essentially a ditch and bank) known as the *limes* can still be seen between the rivers Main and Danube. The Roman Empire had considerable impact on those parts which it occupied. Beyond it lay what the Romans called 'barbarians' (meaning foreigners). The Roman author Tacitus (c. AD 55–116) gives us an intriguing, if not entirely reliable, glimpse of the Germanic tribes in his *Germania*. He describes their social and political organisation, their modes of warfare, concepts of crime and punishment, styles of housing, dress and hairstyle, their marriage practices, funerals, agricultural techniques, and habits of drinking, banqueting, quarrelling and sloth. Apart from praise for the chastity of German women, Tacitus' description of Germany and the Germans is not entirely flattering: the Germans must be a native people, not immigrants from elsewhere, for 'who would . . . [want] to visit Germany, with its unlovely scenery, its bitter climate, its general dreariness to sense and eye, unless it were his home?' There are more qualified descriptions of differences among the individual Germanic tribes, ranging from the Swabians with their intricate hairdos, through the relatively civilised Hermunduri who traded with the Romans, to the far-flung Fenni (living in what became Lithuania) who are characterised as 'astonishingly wild and horribly poor. They eat grass, dress in skins, and sleep on the ground.'

By the beginning of the fifth century AD the Roman Empire was in crisis. While the causes of its collapse are various, the fall of the western part was precipitated by the invasions of barbarian tribes – Visigoths, Vandals and Huns (whose names have become enduring concepts) – across already weakening and overstretched frontiers. Those Germans who settled on Roman land tended to abandon tribal gods and convert to Christianity. In the sixth and seventh centuries, a new Romanised form of Germanic society emerged in the west.

The first settled Germanic communities were under the Franks: Clovis defeated the last Roman governor in Gaul in 486, and established the Merovingian monarchy. This Frankish empire united certain Germanic tribes, and eventually included the so-called Alemanni, Saxons and Bavarians. It was ruled by a certain partnership – replete with tensions – between king, nobility and church. From the sixth century onwards, monasteries were founded, and churches built in the countryside, frequently founded by and dependent on the nobility. The majority of the population lived in a servile status on the land, although there were distinctions between free peasants and serfs, as well as differences between manorial estates in the west and the farms in areas which had not been under Roman occupation. In 751 the Merovingians were deposed and the Carolingian king Pepin elected; he was also anointed by Frankish bishops, to lend religious legitimacy in place of royal blood, thus inaugurating the tradition of kingship as an office conferred by God, although under his successors this continued to be associated with heathen notions of blood-right. While at the beginning of the Merovingian period the total land under cultivation in what was to become Germany had been perhaps 2 per cent, with the rest left as thick forests or swampy marshes, the Carolingian period saw some increase in population, with the clearing of forests to establish new villages.

When does the history of 'Germany' proper begin? Different historians give different answers. Some operate with a wide perception of German history as European history, and are flexible about origins. Others start with the re-foundation of a 'Roman' empire in the west by Charlemagne. Charlemagne had become king in 771, and had extended Frankish power with the annexation of Lombardy, Bavaria and Saxony, and the creation of border 'marches' in the south-east, with the establishment of Austria. He had assumed certain imperial rights, such as coinage, before his formal coronation as Roman Emperor on Christmas Day in AD 800. The emperorship was firmly distinguished from the kingship; while the latter could be divided among heirs, the former was supposedly indivisible. There were however continuing difficulties in the course of the ninth century concerning the unity or partition of the Empire. An apparent solution was produced in the Treaty of Verdun in 843. Squabbling heirs agreed to terminate their battles and divide their inheritance between eastern, western, and middle kingdoms, laying the foundations for the separation of future French and German states. But with further partitions, and the aspirations of non-Carolingian nobles to monarchical status, it began to appear that the Empire would collapse. Of the five independent kingdoms that had emerged by the later ninth century (West Francia, East Francia, Upper and Lower Burgundy and Italy), only East Francia remained in Carolingian hands. Even here, central authority was diminishing. In a situation of virtual civil war combined with external threats of invasion (Vikings in the north, Arabs in the south and Magyars in the east), new forms of political organisation began to emerge. The so-called 'stem duchies' of Franconia, Saxony, Bavaria, Swabia and Lorraine (or Lotharingia) began to develop in the East Frankish realm, in which strong local leaders who could effectively rally their tribes and defend their territories against invasion became more important than the weak king. In 911, the east Carolingian line died out. For some historians, the election of the first German king, Conrad I, Duke of Franconia, marks the real beginning of the history of 'Germany'. Conrad's somewhat ungracious attempts to suppress the stem duchies which had elected him ended in failure. On his death in 918, Duke Henry of Saxony was elected as his successor, indicating the dominance of election over blood-right as the principle of succession. His own

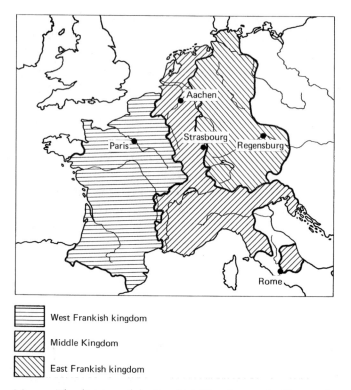

West Frankish kingdom

Middle Kingdom

East Frankish kingdom

Map 1. The division of the Frankish Kingdom at the Treaty of
Verdun, 843

designation of his second son as his successor broke the tradition of
partibility of monarchical inheritance, a further factor of importance
in the development of a specifically German polity.

Other historians are sceptical about the existence of a 'kingdom of
Germany' at this early date. As Gillingham points out, Henry I's effective rule was limited to the duchies of Saxony and Franconia; his
authority elsewhere was very fragile. It was not until the eleventh
century that the term 'regnum Teutonicum' was used. Other historians, such as Fleckenstein, argue that there was nevertheless a
growth in the sense of a 'German identity' before the label, and that
the reigns of Henry I and his son Otto I marked decisively the character of the emerging kingdom. Yet even by the later middle ages,
there are grounds for doubting whether the German-speaking lands

constituted a single polity. In the middle of the fourteenth century, the plural *deutsche Lande* (German lands) was much more common than the singular *Deutschland*; and throughout the middle ages there were inconsistencies and fluctuations in the name used, with *regnum Alamannae, regnum Germaniae* or *Teutonicae* or *Romanorum* prevailing at different times. A further complication is the relationship between German kingship and the emperorship, on which more below. It should also not be forgotten that Germany is probably unique among modern European states in having a name derived not from a tribe or territory, but from a spoken language.

These debates about terminology and dating the beginnings of 'German history' derived essentially from the political complexity of the history of the German peoples. Whatever view one holds on when the story should legitimately start – and what should be considered as 'background' rather than 'history' – an attempt can be made to recount the details of its complexity.

GERMANY IN THE EARLY AND HIGH MIDDLE AGES

Mediaeval Germany under the Saxon (or Ottonian) and Salian dynasties, from the accession of Duke Henry of Saxony in 919 to the death of Henry III in 1056, was characterised by the feudal organisation of society and politics, with the dominance of a military aristocracy; the development of what was to become the 'Holy Roman Empire of the German Nation'; and by relatively harmonious relations of church and state. When recounting the structures of high politics and religion, the general condition of the vast masses of the population must be constantly borne in mind. At the end of this period, in the mid-eleventh century, the total population of the German lands was probably around 5 or 6 million. (Population estimates must remain tentative for pre-modern times.) The majority of people lived in very small villages, hamlets, or isolated farmsteads surrounded by small agricultural clearings amid vast forests. Houses were in the main very primitive huts: only royal palaces, castles, churches and monasteries were built to last. Life for most people was, in Hobbes's famous phrase, 'nasty, brutish and short'. Average life expectancy was little over thirty years: more in the higher classes, less in the lower. Following a very high death rate among infants, most people died between the ages of fourteen and forty. While alive, their experiences were generally of illness, hunger and periodic famine. They were at the mercy of the seasons, of unpredictable events, of human violence; even when nominally Christianised, many pagan elements (charms, superstitions, magic) remained in the attempt to appease evil spirits or ward off misfortune. Most people lived within a restricted compass, a limited locality of work, trading, intermarriage; a pilgrimage might form the longest outing of a lifetime. Only members of the aristocracy travelled great distances and had ties of kinship across wide areas. During the period from 750 to about 1050, Old High German and Old Saxon dialects were spoken, and there were probably rich traditions of oral poetry, although few works of vernacular literature have survived. Literacy was largely confined to the clergy, who wrote in Latin.

For all its apparent primitiveness, this was no longer a purely tribal society. Feudalism was developing as the major pattern of sociopolitical organisation. This complex system may briefly be defined at the political level as an asymmetrical, reciprocal relationship of service, fidelity, protection and support. The vassal would swear an oath of allegiance to the lord, who would in turn agree to protect the vassal – a relationship symbolised by the vassal placing joined hands between those of the lord in the act of commendation. Vassals were given grants of land, known as fiefs, which were legally distinct from their own property (*Eigen*, or allodial land). This system arose in the course of the invasions, feuding and violence of the eighth century; it gradually developed, spread and changed in subsequent centuries. Great magnates with large fiefs were able to grant smaller fiefs to their own vassals. The royal bureaucracy also became feudalised. Over time, there was a tendency for fiefs to become heritable; there was also a tendency for vassals to start holding fiefs from several lords, in which process the vassals gained in power in relation to the lords. Feudalism as a political system was a useful means of ensuring connections between a distant centre, via a network of subordinate ties, down to quite personal local relationships. It partially displaced the clan or tribe as the principle of political organisation, although the family – or dynasty – continued to be of major importance.

The term 'feudalism' is also used by some historians to refer to economic relationships, and in particular to lord–peasant relationships on the land. Unfree peasants (serfs) were subjected to a lord to whom they owed labour services and dues, in contrast both to free property-owning peasants and to the capitalist relationship where formally free wage-labourers (whether working on the land or, later, in proto-industrial or industrial enterprises) sold their labour power for wages on the market. There were of course also political elements in this narrower economic definition: peasants, whether free or unfree, performed military service in return for 'protection' from violence over which they had no control, in the service of causes from which they could hardly hope to benefit. It should also be noted in this connection that the concept of feudalism has given rise to extensive debates, not only over definition (with certain historians seeking to extend it more widely) and location (was it uniquely European, or found elsewhere in the world, for example in pre-modern Japan, aiding Japan's path to modernity?), but also over its implications. For feudal Europe, in contrast to the civilisations of ancient China and India, for example, was uniquely dynamic and gave rise to modern capitalist industrial society with all its implications for world history. We shall return to these wider questions again.

By the eleventh century, there was a struggle in Germany between sub-vassals, with non-heritable fiefs, and major vassals. In 1037 a feudal law-code (the *Constitutio de feudis*) was issued, which gave legal sanction to the inheritance of small fiefs. The small knights began to emerge as a class between the higher nobility and the peasants. The so-called *ministeriales*, a group of legally unfree serving-men, also rose as a new lower nobility, whose status as a legally defined class or 'estate' was codified in a 'law of services'. As Karl Leyser has pointed out, by the end of the eleventh century Germany had a much more immobile social hierarchy and was a more 'caste-ridden' aristocratic society than either England or France. The German aristocracy indulged in endless feuding, with families tearing each other apart over disputed rights of succession, attempting to maintain parity of status at the same time as dividing inheritances. It was a society in which the nobles, perpetually contending for wealth, power and status, set limits on the potential power of their *primus inter pares*, the elected king.

The Ottonian and early Salian kings were nevertheless remarkably successful, viewed in early mediaeval terms. Henry I asserted monarchical control over the church and over the stem duchies, also incorporating Lorraine (after its initial turning to the West Frankish realm). In 936 Otto I was elected and crowned in Aachen, symbolising his role as successor to Charlemagne. Otto made use of the church as a counterweight to the dukes: since the king could determine elections to bishoprics, and since church property could not become the object of dynastic inheritance, the new episcopate could to some degree be relied on as more faithful servants of the king than were the secular magnates. Church properties provided useful places for the king and his retinue to stay on their perpetual travels – for it was only by visiting different parts of the realm in person that a monarch could express and sustain his authority. (Some young noblemen were advised of the misfortune of having the king as their guest, given the ruinous expense involved.) Archbishops, bishops and abbots provided not only economic, but also military service, particularly in the form of armoured cavalry troops. Henry I and Otto I made use of both religious and military means to defend and consolidate their eastern frontiers (particularly against Magyar invasions). With the decisive victory in 955 over the Magyars at the river Lech, south of Augsburg, their military fate was sealed; with the foundation of archbishoprics and the conversion of frontier areas to the western (rather than eastern, Byzantine) form of Christianity, the areas which were emerging as Poland and Bohemia became part of the broad currents of European civilisation. The 'eastern March', Austria, now relatively safe from Magyar attack, was thoroughly Germanised and assimilated to Bavaria.

In 962, following an earlier venture into Italy when he had designated himself King of Lombardy on marrying the former king's widow, Otto was anointed and crowned as Emperor by the Pope. The union of the German monarchy and the Roman empire was unique among European states and lasted, with all its attendant strengths, obligations, tensions and contradictions, until 1806. Since mediaeval German monarchs had to be crowned Emperor by the Pope in Rome, they were subject to a double diversion: they had both to intervene constantly in Italian politics, in order to assert and sustain their authority; and to maintain an often difficult and delicate balance between temporal and spiritual power, between Emperor and Pope. Both elements arguably played some part in the relative

Kingdom of
Denmark

Pomerania

Saxony

East
March

POLAND

(Upper)

Thuringia

Lorraine

Franconia

Bohemia

Moravia

(Lower)

FRANCE

Swabia

Bavaria

Bavarian
East
Mark

HUNGARY

Kingdom
of
Burgundy

Steiermark

Carinthia

Kingdom
of
Italy

Venice

Croatia

Rome

———— Boundary of the Empire (eastern boundary
not firmly fixed at this time)

– – – – State boundaries (kingdoms of Italy,
Burgundy and Germany)

– — – — Boundaries of duchies and marks

Map 2. The German Empire c. 1024–1125

weakness of the German monarchy, although historians are divided on this point. With the acquisition of Burgundy in 1033–4, the Emperor presided over three separate kingdoms. Yet kings of Germany had constantly to defend their borders and quell internal unrest at home; they could not afford to absent themselves too long in Italy without brewing up trouble for their return. Even in Italy, their campaigns were often arduous and unsuccessful – and prone to collapse in the face of disease. Otto II, for example, died in Rome in 983 from malaria at the age of twenty-eight. On the other hand, profits could be made from Italian adventures which could be usefully invested at home; and for the most part there were harmonious relationships between church and state during the Ottonian period.

There was a revival of intellectual life largely through the church: from monasteries, through episcopal churches, to cathedral schools, many of which were either founded or revived in the tenth century. The Salian dynasty, which was inaugurated with the election of Conrad II in 1024 following the death of the childless Henry II, generally continued Ottonian policies, with the foundation of bishoprics (such as Bamberg) and building of palaces (Goslar, Magdeburg, Aachen, Regensburg), and the erection of cathedrals, such as Speyer. But the apparent consolidation of the Imperial monarchy and union of church and state was soon to be shattered. With the transformations occurring in the two centuries after c. 1050, we enter the period conventionally termed the 'high middle ages'.

The mid-eleventh to the mid-twelfth century was a period of political conflict and religious strife. Kings were unable to control the nobility, and there was a series of revolts and civil wars, including the Saxon revolt of 1073–5, and the election of Duke Rudolf of Swabia as 'anti-king' in 1077. The great dynasties which were to stamp their mark on subsequent centuries of German history emerged in this period: the Welfs of Saxony, the Wittelsbachs in Bavaria, the Hohenstaufen (who took their name from the castle of Stauf, near Göppingen) who were granted the duchy of Swabia in 1079. The period of political insecurity and civil wars continued through the reign of Duke Lothar of Supplinburg, who was elected king (with no hereditary blood-right) in 1125 following the death of the last Salian king Henry V (1106–25). Political turbulence was only dealt with effectively under the new Hohenstaufen (or Staufer) dynasty, which lasted from 1138 to 1254, and particularly under its most illustrious representative, Federick I, 'Barbarossa' (after his red beard), who ruled from 1152 to 1190. Meanwhile, a simultaneous crisis between church and state had added to the problems of the Empire, under the last Salian kings Henry IV (1056–1106) and Henry V. In the mid and later eleventh century, church reforms – including clerical celibacy, the attempted abolition of simony, and freedom from secular control – had given the clergy a distinctive and privileged status. While Popes had been gaining in self-confidence, major German prelates – the former faithful allies of the Ottonians – had been developing their own political and territorial ambitions. Particularly when Hildebrand became Pope Gregory VII (1073–85), conflicts between Pope and Emperor came to a head, with the humiliating submission of Henry IV at Canossa in January 1077. But there continued to be a conflict with the papacy over lay investiture (the nomination of candidates for important positions in the church). The outcome of the so-called 'Investiture Contest' was the 1122 Concordat of Worms, which allowed Henry V to influence the election of German, but not Italian, prelates. This was more of a victory for the church than the king, however: German prelates continued to develop as independent feudal magnates alongside the great secular nobility. This enhanced worldly status was contemporaneous with a religious revival marked by new monastic orders and religious communities emphasising a contemplative life and spiritual withdrawal from the world, and the virtues of poverty and penance.

The high middle ages represent in a number of respects an important period of transition. The political upheavals initiated the effective replacement of the old stem duchies by new territorial lordships and the establishment of a multiplicity of principalities; it also involved a loss of prestige and authority by the Empire. Under Frederick I, extensive privileges were conceded to the magnates, despite the high-sounding imperial rhetoric proclaimed at court. The greatest of Frederick's 'overmighty subjects' was his cousin Henry the Lion, Duke of Saxony, on whom the duchy of Bavaria was conferred, and who also gained territories in northern and north-eastern Germany. Eventually, pressures from a number of nobles and prelates led to Frederick turning against his most powerful prince. After Henry the Lion's fall in 1180, a redistribution of territories confirmed the disintegration of the stem duchies and their replacement by smaller hereditary principalities held as fiefs by princes of the Empire. Political fragmentation continued under Barbarossa's successors, such that by 1250, when Barbarossa's grandson Frederick II died, the territorial powers of the princes had been consolidated.

Economically, the period was one of growth and expansion. There was an intensification of cultivation, with the extension of arable land made possible by use of the four-wheeled cart pulled by a horse (replacing the slower ox) and the three-course rotation of crops. People began to live in larger villages rather than scattered hamlets. There was also an increase in trade and in craft production. Increased trade meant an increased importance of money, and a heightened prominence of Jews as money-lenders (since they had no religious prohibition on usury). Jews tended to live in separate quarters, the first recorded instance of a walled ghetto being Speyer in 1084. From the twelfth century on, German merchants were to be found all across Europe. Craftsmen began to organise themselves in guilds and corporations, and there was an early growth of towns. Those in the south tended to be predominantly towns of craftsmen; those in the north, of merchants and traders. Increased production was related to an increasing population: at the end of the twelfth century Germany's population had increased to around seven or eight million, with more rapid increases in some areas (such as Saxony) than others. While in southern and western Germany population increase was accommodated by the extension of agricultural land at the expense of forests and marshes, in the east it led to a wave of colonisation. The Slav lands east of the river Elbe were colonised between around 1150 and 1300; and in the new villages founded in eastern territories, such as Silesia, colonising peasants were able to enjoy relatively good conditions and personal freedom. The eastwards migration and colonisation was to be of fundamental importance to German history in the later middle ages and subsequently.

Yet despite – or alongside – the growth and differentiation of German society the essentially conservative German aristocracy retained its dominant status and stamped its mark on German culture. The aristocracy was essentially a warrior class, not only feuding at home but also participating in international expeditions such as

her Iristan von Isänle·   her werther von Tüfen·

Plate 4. Illustrations of Minnesingers from the fourteenth-century Mannesse Manuscript.

the Crusades to the Holy Land. This martial class developed an elaborate code of honour – which has left a linguistic trace in the concept of 'chivalrous' conduct – and informed the flowering of a vernacular Middle High German literature around the end of the twelfth century. Authors such as Walther von der Vogelweide (whether or not he was personally a knight) gave vigorous and elevated expression to the ethos and experiences of the knightly class. The authors of a secular lyric poetry, known as *Minnesang*, expressed such sentiments as unrequited, and unrequitable, love for noble women beyond their social reach, perhaps illuminating the curious position of the formally unfree and dependent, yet socially elevated class of *ministeriales*. It was possible to have a career as a professional poet at court, superior in status but about as insecure as that of court jester or musician. As important as the lyric poetry of the high middle ages was narrative poetry: the first German version of the Tristan and Isolde legend dates from about 1170, while works of enduring value were produced by Gottfried von Strassburg (author of the most important *Tristan*), Hartmann von Aue and Wolfram von Eschenbach (best known for his *Parzival*). There was also the heroic epic, the most famous of which was the *Nibelungenlied*. Many of these works were, of course, to provide material and inspiration for the music-dramas of Richard Wagner in the nineteenth century.

The period around the end of the twelfth and the beginning of the thirteenth century represented a blossoming of courtly civilisation and chivalric culture which, associated with the powerful political legend of the Great Emperor Frederick Barbarossa, was to seem to nationalist Germans of the nineteenth century to have been a golden age of imperial greatness, a high point of German civilisation. But alongside it was soon to rise a more urban, bourgeois form of society in the later middle ages. A series of changes took place in the three centuries or so after 1200 which were to lay the foundations for what we know as 'modern' Europe.

GERMANY IN THE LATER MIDDLE AGES

Although towns were already becoming important in the twelfth century, their number, size and status increased dramatically in the course of the thirteenth century: there was something like a ten-fold increase, such that by the mid-thirteenth century there were around 3,000 towns, in the main very small in size but enjoying a certain degree of importance and self-government. Their origins and character varied: a few were based on Roman foundations, some were purposefully created as princely residences or centres of royal or seigneurial administration, while others grew out of the expansion of trade, production and markets. While some new towns were created in the colonial territories of the east, such as Riga, there continued to be a greater density of urbanisation in the southern and western parts of Germany. Their characteristic features can still be discerned in many places today: town walls and fortifications, a castle, churches, perhaps some other religious foundation, a splendid town hall, guild halls, solid burgher houses for the urban patriciate.

Interestingly, given the decentralised nature of German political life, no single town began to emerge as a royal capital along the lines of London or Paris (although for a long time Prague was an important Imperial centre). The political status of towns varied according to whether they were *Landesstädte*, towns subordinate to a local ruler (whether secular or ecclesiastical), or whether they were *Reichsstädte*, Imperial free cities formally subordinate to no-one

Plate 5. The government of Augsburg is handed over to the guilds, 1368.

below the Emperor. Towns could be either bases of princely power, or potentially powerful forces in their own right with which princes and Emperor would have to contend. Towns frequently organised themselves into leagues, or alliances, such as the Rhenish League of 1254 or the Swabian League of 1376. In the 'Great Town War' of 1387–8 these two leagues were defeated by a combination of princes, although earlier the Swabian League had been able to resist princely attacks. A new Swabian League – of a very different character – was formed in 1488. In the valleys and mountains of Switzerland, a confederation developed which was to throw off Habsburg overlordship and later, in 1648, to be formally and belatedly recognised as a separate state. The towns of south-western Germany for a variety of reasons did not adopt the Swiss model (of a confederation of urban republican cantons and farming cantons), nor did they become incorporated into Austria, entering a rather different pattern of development in the early sixteenth century. Other leagues were more in the nature of structures for economic co-operation. The most famous of these was the Hanseatic League (the term dates from 1358) of north German towns, led by Lübeck. Proud of their Hanse traditions, later twentieth-century Hamburg and Bremen still prefixed themselves with 'Hansestadt' and had HH and HB on their car number-plates. Within towns, society was far from egalitarian. Town government was dominated by a few prominent and wealthy families, with a distinctive burgher outlook. Interestingly, there was less interchange between town and country in Germany (excepting Switzerland) than in England: German burghers tended to be anti-noble in outlook, and did not leave the towns to become country gentry as in England. This sharp distinction of social caste or 'estate' was to last in Germany right up to the era of industrialisation in the nineteenth century.

Towns were however walled places of safety, to which people from the countryside could flee for protection in an age characterised by perpetual feuding and unpredictable violence. Historians differ as to whether late mediaeval Germany was a peculiarly violent society, or whether other European societies at this time were equally violent. Whatever the case may be, in Germany central power – the Emperor – proved too weak to keep the peace. In contrast to the more centralised kingdoms of England and France (and more

Plate 6. The Marienburg: founded in 1280, from 1309 it became the Residence of the Grand Master of the Order of Teutonic Knights, and was substantially rebuilt from 1324–1335.

like the fragmented territories of Italy and Spain), in Germany the notion developed that local princes were responsible for keeping the peace *within* princely territories, while it was permissible to wage war *between* princes – and indeed with almost anyone – within the Empire. This both reflected and confirmed the political fragmentation of the Empire. From the mid-fifteenth century, some princes of the Empire came together to form 'circles' or political alliances within particular areas.

The wave of colonisation of eastern, Slav territories was extremely important in the thirteenth century, as a result of pressures of population expansion. The religious Knights of the Teutonic Order, in a crusade against the heathen Slavs, began to establish a state in the far north-eastern territories from 1226. The state of Prussia, under its Grand Masters, extended over a region outside the Holy Roman Empire from the river Weichsel (Vistula) to the Memel. In the course of the fifteenth century, the powers of the Teutonic Knights began to decline. In 1410 the Teutonic Knights were defeated by the Poles at Tannenberg; conflicts continued, and eventual defeat in the Thirteen Years War (1453–66) forced their acceptance of feudal dependence on Poland and entailed the surrender of West Prussia, including Danzig (or Gdansk). In 1525 Albrecht von Hohenzollern, Grand

Master of the Teutonic Knights, turned Protestant, secularised the territories of the Teutonic Order, and became the first German duke of the now hereditary duchy of Prussia. Since 1417 the Hohenzollern dynasty (which originated in Swabia, where their impressive castle can still be seen) had held the march, or former frontier territory, of Brandenburg. These relatively under-developed, under-urbanised, economically poor colonial frontier territories of Brandenburg and Prussia were later to form the basis of a powerful state which was to dominate the course of nineteenth and early twentieth-century German history. On the estates of these areas, a landed aristocracy known as *Junker* (from *Jung Herr*, 'young lord', perhaps because younger sons, denied an inheritance at home, sought to make their fortunes in the eastern colonial territories) established itself; its grip on subsequent Prussian politics and society was to prove remarkably tenacious, its capacity to survive changing circumstances and fortunes quite extraordinary, until the material basis for its existence was finally abolished in the aftermath of the Second World War.

Between around 1200 and 1300, the population rose from perhaps 8 million to around 14 million. This remarkable population expansion had considerable implications for the condition of the peasantry. Those peasants who colonised the new eastern territories enjoyed considerable personal freedom. But a population decline began in the fourteenth century. This downturn was compounded by waves of Bubonic Plague, or Black Death, in 1348–50. In Germany, as in England, many villages were simply deserted, and the area of agricultural land shrank by about a quarter. (Interestingly, Jews – who had initially come to Germany to escape persecution elsewhere – were often selected as scapegoats for the plague: they were accused of poisoning the water, and pogroms were unleashed. Many Jews emigrated to eastern Europe, and Yiddish is in some respects a form of late mediaeval German.) Labour shortages began to lead to an improvement in conditions for peasants in the older, western parts of Germany, as lords attempted to retain increasingly scarce labour. But in the east, formerly relatively free peasants found their labour being increasingly exploited and their status subjugated, as lords attempted to extract more from fewer people. A so-called 'second serfdom' began to develop in these areas, later than the 'first' serfdom of the west. Population increase started again in the second half of the fifteenth century: over Europe as a whole, the population rose to over 60 million. The estimated population of Germany at the beginning of the sixteenth century is about 16 million. From the mid-fifteenth century, with increasing pressure on land and resources, there were periodic peasants' revolts, particularly in south-western Germany.

With the death of Frederick II's son Conrad in 1254, the Hohenstaufen line of German kings came to an end. Following an interregnum, in 1273 the Habsburg family became rulers of Austria, Styria and Carniola, a position they remarkably retained until 1918. From 1438, there was an almost continuous succession of Habsburg Emperors until the end of the Holy Roman Empire in 1806. There was a partial recentralisation of Imperial power under the initial Habsburg Emperors, Rudolf (1273–91) and his son Albert I (1298–1308). But the constitutional reforms which recognised the political realities within the Empire, and had a stabilising effect for around four hundred years, came with the reign of Charles IV. Detailed regulations for the conduct of elections to the monarchy by seven electoral princes were formulated in the Golden Bull of 1356, enacted at Nuremberg by Emperor Charles IV (1346–78). He laid the foundations for certain constitutional continuities lasting until 1806, as well as being notable for his Imperial court and castles in and near his native city of Prague (such as Karlstein Castle) and his foundation of Prague University in 1348. From the late fourteenth and early fifteenth century it became increasingly clear that Imperial powers were declining in comparison with princely territorial powers. By the end of the fifteenth century, there were essentially two tiers to German politics: there were the Imperial assemblies, or Diets (*Reichstage*) attended by Emperor, princes, heads of ecclesiastical territories, independent knights and representatives of imperial towns, for the overall federal discussion of issues affecting the Empire; and within local territories, there were territorial assemblies in which the prince met with representatives of (usually) the privileged classes in a co-operative form of joint rulership later termed a *Ständestaat*. These territorial diets (*Landtage*) were particularly important in gaining the co-operation of influential groups in assenting to and raising taxes. Government in towns was generally by an oligarchic town council.

By 1500, the political map of what was by now regularly termed the 'Holy Roman Empire of the German Nation' was exceedingly complex, a patchwork of dynastic and ecclesiastical territories dotted with Imperial free cities and the castles of independent Imperial knights. There were seven electoral principalities, around twenty-five major secular principalities and ninety ecclesiastical ones, over a hundred countships, a very large number of lesser lordships, as well as the towns. As Du Boulay has put it, 'late mediaeval Germany was a sea of political fragments in which some large pieces floated'. This fragmented collection was loosely held together by the wider protection of the Empire. Yet the Emperor was concerned not purely with rule over the territories within the Empire: his strength derived largely from his own dynastic possessions. Habsburg dominions stretched from the Low Countries, which they had acquired by marriage in 1479, to interests in Aragon, Castile, Italy (Naples and Sicily) and Burgundy, to which Charles V (1519–56) was heir. Their horizons and activities from the late fifteenth century were European, rather than purely Imperial; this was to prove not only a strength, but also a potential source of weakness, for Imperial power.

Later mediaeval Germany saw key shifts in cultural and intellectual life. The chivalric literature of the high middle ages was enriched, and soon overshadowed, by literary productions associated with the growth of urban life, as illustrated by the replacement of the knightly Minnesinger by the more urban 'master-singers'. (The best known of these was the sixteenth-century cobbler from Nuremberg, Hans Sachs.) The predominant German dialect shifted around the middle of the fourteenth century into what is known as Early New High German. Law began to be codified, as with the early record of Saxon customary law in the *Sachsenspiegel* of the early thirteenth century; later, Roman law was revived, constituting an important difference between German law and the English common law system. A number of universities which are still renowned centres of scholarship were founded in the fourteenth and fifteenth centuries: not only Prague, but also the universities of Vienna (1365), Heidelberg (1386), Leipzig (1409), Tübingen (1477) and Wittenberg (1502). The language of learning continued to be Latin, but a vernacular prose was developing, and a new class of professional bureaucrats, lawyers and secular scholars was growing alongside the old clerical intelligentsia of the church. German humanism tended to be anti-clerical and anti-papal in orientation, and sought to set the Bible in historical context.

The church itself retained its prominent status, politically and economically as well as intellectually and culturally. The aristocratic prince-bishops were major magnates in their own right, and ecclesiastical rule could be even more oppressive for common people than rule by a secular lord, since double penalties could be imposed (under ecclesiastical as well as secular law). But 'the church' and 'religion' cannot be understood as a simple monolithic entity, untouched by internal dissensions. Relations with the papacy were never free from tensions; and the papacy had itself been in political difficulties since the high middle ages (including 'Babylonish captivity' in Avignon in a period of French domination). The relative roles of Pope and General Councils gave rise to a controversy in which the 'conciliarists', who claimed that General Councils were superior to Popes, were ultimately defeated. It is also too simplistic to counterpose a secular humanism to a priestly scholasticism in the later middle ages. Individuals such as Gabriel Biel sought new religious initiatives, and currents of piety such as the *devotio moderna* (which focussed on the inner life and sought salvation in flight from the world) have been seen as contributing to the subsequent Reformation. There was also a range of more heretical traditions: the followers of John Hus (c. 1369–1415), known as Hussites, in Bohemia, the Waldensians in Bohemia in the fourteenth century and the Alpine valleys in the late fifteenth century, and an ill-defined loosely floating set of dissenting ideas. Popular religion was probably only minimally affected by theological and scholastic controversies. Historians are only beginning to piece together the likely religious experiences and practices of the non-literate majority of the population, and there is some debate about the degree to which they were 'Christianised' at all. But it is clear that there was a high component of magic involved in late mediaeval popular religion, in an attempt to assert control over an unpredictable and largely hostile natural and human environment. This magical element was incorporated into Christian practices by the late mediaeval church, with its emphasis on ritual and outward forms. A very lively fear of the after-life was promoted by vivid

Plate 7. A page from Eike von Repgow, *Sachsenspiegel*, including details of the granting of a castle as a fief.

murals depicting the devils and flames of hell, and sustained by the omnipresence of death, the reality of which is symbolised in the drawings and engravings of the Nuremberg artist Albrecht Dürer. Concern for the after-life ensured particular interest in the church's control over salvation, which could be achieved through the performance of good works – including the donation of money to church coffers. Life in the later middle ages, as half a millennium earlier, remained for most people nasty, brutish and short. Religion and magic provided a set of powerful, almost indistinguishable, means of interpreting and attempting to control the experiences of life. At the same time, the official representatives of the institutional church, the clergy, could be the object of considerable hostility and criticism.

It is clear that, by 1500, Germany had evolved a rather different political pattern from that of the more centralised monarchies of England and France. Historians have devoted a considerable amount of time to attempting to explain the weakness of the mediaeval German monarchy. Attention has been paid to such factors as Germany's relatively large size – posing problems for the assertion of effective central control in the provinces in an age before modern communications – and its lack of obvious geographical boundaries and clear frontiers. These factors were probably less important than aspects of the structure and distribution of power. This is not as tautological as it may sound. Patterns of regional delegation of authority (essential in a pre-industrial society) vary in their political consequences. Celibate clerics receiving fiefs which cannot be passed to heirs are supposedly more loyal to the king than secular lords with aspirations to dynastic greatness. But while in France clerics gained scattered possessions ensuring commitment to the maintenance of strong central power, in Germany prince-bishops soon gained considerable wealth and powers of their own – and in any event control of the church was slipping away from monarchs. Nor could kings simply appoint as dukes, and grant fiefs to, lords from other localities who, as strangers in the province over which they ruled, would be unable to develop local bases against the monarchy. For effective provincial administration depended more on the possession of allodial land than on fiefs held from the king. Also important are the characteristics of the different aristocracies in mediaeval European states, as well as the elective nature of German kingship, and the role of sheer bad luck for a number of monarchs at key periods of crisis. It is clear that any explanation of Germany's lack of effective political centralisation in the middle ages will have to refer to a number of factors, and not simply the traditional ones concerning involvement in Italy and the consequences of the Investiture Contest. But in the context of these debates it is also worth remembering that mediaeval Germany's lack of monarchical centralisation has posed more of a problem for nineteenth and twentieth-century historians, to whom the nation state seemed the most natural political unit, than it probably did for contemporaries, whose experiences of politics were largely personal and local. A question in some ways more interesting than Germany's lack of mediaeval centralisation is almost the obverse: why, in any case, should centralised states (later nation states) have developed as the political framework of developing capitalist and eventually industrial society? (And to what extent might they be superseded by new forms of supra-national economic federalism under late capitalism?) Put this way, Germany's political pattern can be set in a wider interpretive context, and not viewed purely as a succession of 'failures', 'distortions', and 'belatedness'. Moreover, if playing the game of determination of long-term consequences, the dynamism and vitality of late mediaeval German urban and intellectual life, with the contribution they made to subsequent patterns of western civilisation, should not be underplayed.

3

The age of confessionalism, 1500–1648

A cluster of changes occurring in the late fifteenth and early sixteenth centuries appear to render this period an important turning point in European history. The (re)discovery of America in 1492 opened up a new world, with significant effects on the economies and politics of the old world; the 'late mediaeval crisis of feudalism' initiated the formation of a propertyless wage-labouring class, the harbinger of developing capitalism; the emergence of an interacting system of increasingly centralised European states began to displace the dispersed sovereignty and more localised politics of feudalism; the invention of a technique of printing with movable type by Gutenberg radically altered the character of intellectual life; and the Reformation initiated by Martin Luther shattered the religious and cultural unity of mediaeval Christendom, with a process of territorial confessionalisation both sustained by and sustaining the concomitant processes of territorial state-building.

These major changes in European history should not blind us to certain continuities, particularly in relation to Germany. The period from the mid-fourteenth century to the mid-seventeenth century was characterised by a continued – and developing – territorial particularism within a relatively weak wider Imperial framework. German society continued to be largely based on feudal agrarian relations. While the economy of England expanded, that of Germany grew less rapidly, or stagnated. And for all the elements of 'modernity' that historians have sought in the Reformation, there was much that was essentially 'mediaeval' in sixteenth-century thought and beliefs.

THE GERMAN REFORMATION: THE EARLY YEARS

Politically, what was now regularly known as the 'Holy Roman Empire of the German Nation' was in some respects consolidated in a series of reforms. The Reichstag was now regularly summoned. It consisted of three chambers: the seven electoral princes (Mainz, Cologne, Trier, Bohemia, Saxony, the Palatinate, Brandenburg); the other princely rulers (four archbishops, forty-six bishops, eighty-three other spiritual rulers such as abbots, twenty-four secular princes, and 145 counts and lords); and approximately eighty-three imperial towns. A second organ of the Empire, the *Kammergericht*, or Imperial Court of Justice, was established as a permanent court of justice staffed by trained lawyers, separate from the Emperor's own court. A permanent Reich tax, the 'common penny' (*Gemeine Pfennig*) was introduced to support the Kammergericht. Attempts (not entirely successful) were made to abolish feuding and establish a permanent state of domestic peace (*Landfrieden*). The geographical boundaries of the Empire, although still contested, began to be clarified: in the 1499 Peace of Basel, which ended the Imperial war with the Swiss League, the latter were released from payment of Imperial taxes, speeding up the process of Swiss separation from the Empire which had begun in the thirteenth century. At the level of local territories, princes were beginning to develop more permanent courts and administrations, with a concomitant growth of officials; at the same time, their need for money lent a certain power to their estates, who agreed taxation – as well as enhancing the role of money-lenders and finance capitalists, of whom the most notable were the Augsburg Fugger family.

But despite the juridical crystallisation of certain patterns, the structure entailed considerable tensions and strains. Emperor Charles V (1519–56; died 1558) was nominally ruler over half of Europe: his inheritance stretched across Spain, Sicily, southern Italy, the Netherlands, Belgium and Burgundy, in addition to the Habsburg 'hereditary dominions' (*Erblande*) of Austria proper; and with the battle of Mohacs in 1526 Charles's younger brother Ferdinand added the dual sovereignty of Bohemia and Hungary to Habsburg possessions. But this apparent strength entailed an overstretching of political and financial resources, a constant

Austrian 'hereditary dominions' (*Erblande*) and fiefs and possessions of the Habsburgs

Spanish possessions of the Habsburgs

Netherlands and Burgundian possessions of the Habsburgs

—— Boundary of the Holy Roman Empire

Map 3. Europe at the time of the Reformation

indebtedness (particularly to the Fugger), and a failure to secure real power. Even Charles V's election as Emperor in 1519, against strong French competition, involved a combination of further indebtedness (heavy bribes were paid by Fugger loans) and an 'electoral capitulation' (*Wahlkapitulation*) confirming the role of the electoral princes and estates of the Empire as partners in power with the Emperor. Moreover, attempts to develop a central government (*Reichsregiment*) were not successful: the estates resisted Imperial attempts to make this part of the Imperial court, while the Emperor opposed the estates' attempts to make it an organ of federal government. And, alongside domestic problems, Charles V was more or less constantly engaged in struggles for European hegemony against France, as well as periodically warding off Turkish invasions in the south-east.

Shifting political relations within the Empire, and changing international relations within the emerging state system of early modern Europe, were injected with an explosive new element in the shape of that shattering of European religious and cultural unity known as the Reformation. In 1517, an obscure monk and academic theologian by the name of Martin Luther wrote a set of ninety-five theses, criticising abuses in the church, which he is said to have nailed on the door of the Castle Church in Wittenberg, an established practice to initiate public debate. This event, which sparked off a series of controversies leading ultimately to unbridgeable schism in European Christianity, conventionally marks the beginning of the Reformation.

Luther was born in Eisleben in 1483. He was the son of a relatively prosperous miner who – himself a peasant's son – had high aspirations for his own son and wanted him to become a lawyer. But when Martin Luther escaped being struck by lightning in 1505, he vowed to become a monk. In the course of his subsequent monastic and academic career (he eventually became Professor of Theology at Wittenberg University) Luther engaged in intense spiritual struggles as well as scholarly confrontation with the scriptures. Luther's theology showed affinities with earlier Augustinian piety; both Luther and Augustine were much influenced by St Paul. Antecedents of Lutheran thought have also been sought in humanism, with which Luther shared a dislike of scholasticism and 'prelatical paternalism' (although Luther broke with the humanists in his belief in the great omnipotence of God and powerlessness of human beings), and in those currents of piety and scholarship known as the *devotio moderna* and *via moderna*. Clearly, Luther was in dialogue with the currents of his age; but out of his spiritual anguish and intellectual labours he developed his own unique synthesis, which he propagated with energy and passion. Luther's views were expounded in an attempt not to split the church, but to purify it from abuses.

The particular abuse which provoked the ninety-five theses was the sale of 'indulgences'. The church held the view that salvation could be achieved by good works, including donations to the church, and the claim was even made that the church could intercede on behalf of relatives already dead and suffering for their sins. 'Indulgences' were sold to buy time off from purgatory, for oneself or others. This was a common practice: Luther's own prince, the Elector Frederick 'the Wise' of Saxony, had built up a considerable collection of holy relics in Wittenberg (supposedly including parts of the holy cradle, bits of swaddling clothes, and remains of infants slaughtered by Herod). Wittenberg thus became an important centre of pilgrimage, with special indulgences available from Rome for sale to pilgrims. The sale of indulgences in 1517 was particularly scandalous, however. The papal agent, Tetzel, who was also accountant to the important Fugger bankers, was sent to raise money by sale of indulgences. Half the proceeds were to go to Rome (arousing considerable resentment in Germany), while the other half would go to the Fuggers to pay off a loan to Prince Albert of Brandenburg. Albert was seeking to obtain a third episcopal dignity (the Archbishopric of Mainz, which held an electoral vote), but this was forbidden by canon law; the loan was to enable Albert to bribe the Pope. Luther objected; not only was it socially scandalous that the poor should be exploited in such a cause, but also the practice was theologically unsound: God simply could not be bought off in this way. In Luther's view (arising out of his formative 'tower experience') faith alone could be the source of salvation. In his ninety-five theses, initially written in Latin for academic disputation but rapidly translated and widely circulated, Luther produced a brilliant argument, employing all the arts of rhetoric and irony to make his case.

Within a few weeks, the theses were being printed and distributed not only from Wittenberg, but also Nuremberg, Leipzig, Basel and soon throughout Europe. Luther was summoned to Rome, but Elector Frederick ensured him a hearing in Germany instead. After disputes with Cardinal Cajetan in Augsburg, and Eck in Leipzig, it was clear that the controversy would not die down. In 1520, Luther wrote three great tracts: *The Address to the Christian Nobility of the German Nation; The Babylonish Captivity of the Church*; and *The Liberty of the Christian*. Pope Leo X moved to excommunicate Luther with the papal bull 'Exsurge Domine', which Luther proceeded to burn. A second bull in 1521, 'Decet Romanorum', effected Luther's excommunication. In 1521, the heads of state of the German nation were summoned to an Imperial Diet in Worms, to confer with the newly elected Emperor, Charles V. As part of the Diet's business, Luther was called to account for himself. After agonised self-questioning, Luther came to the conclusion that he stood by his views, and was unrepentant. On his return home, he was abducted by Frederick's men and taken into safe custody in the Wartburg Castle. Here Luther spent a productive year writing hymns (such as 'Ein' feste Burg ist unser Gott': if one visits the Wartburg Castle, one can readily appreciate the symbolism of the 'safe stronghold'), and translating the New Testament of the Bible into vernacular German. The importance of this latter exercise can hardly be overstated. Luther's view was that translation must be into the language of 'the mother in the home, the children in the street, the common man in the market place'; and his translation served to standardise and regularise written German, with New High German coming to dominate regional differences in dialect. Linguistic concerns were of course less important to Luther than his overriding aim: to bring the Word of God to all people, in a language which they would be able to understand.

What were the main points of Luther's theology? First, there was the crucial importance attached to the concept of 'justification by faith alone'. Salvation was not achieved by good works; rather, it was freely granted by God and experienced by humans as a sense of 'new birth'. This led to a certain emotionalism among some later Lutherans, an introverted concern with their spiritual state. Secondly, there was an emphasis on the Scriptures as the basis of authority (not the Pope, nor General Councils), and on a personal understanding of the Bible. Thus the role of the clergy was transformed: rather than being intermediaries between man and God, performing the rites and sacraments with automatic efficacy, they became preachers of the Word, spreaders of the Gospel to those who could not read it for themselves. Emphasis on individual experience of salvation and interpretation of the Scriptures led to the notions of 'every man a monk' and 'the priesthood of all believers'. In contrast to the mediaeval Catholic belief in a particularly holy life being dependent on being a member of the clergy, Lutherans believed that everyday work within this world was also doing God's will. (It also meant priests no longer had to be celibate; Luther himself happily embarked upon married life.) Lutheran theology appeared to promote a certain individualism, and a spiritual (if not secular) equality of believers. Luther's ideas were, however, far from strictly logical and consistent, and gave rise to a range of diverse interpretations, as well as opening the way for other individuals to propound their own versions of God's Word as expressed in the Bible.

The reception of Luther's ideas was influenced by a number of factors. For one thing, Emperor Charles V saw religious dissent within the Empire as but one problem among many. In addition to his interests in Spanish and Italian affairs, Charles V was much vexed by the 'Turkish menace'. The Emperor was a ruler with European-wide concerns, unable to spend a great deal of time in Germany, where lack of decisive Imperial intervention allowed disputes to proceed long enough to become entrenched. The reasons for the spread of Lutheran ideas among different groups are various. Considerable weight has been given to the role of printing in the rapid dissemination of Luther's ideas: while in 1518 only 150 books were published in Germany, in 1524 the number had risen to nearly a thousand. Luther himself was a great polemicist and populariser, averaging one tract every fortnight. Not only pamphlets, but also cartoons and illustrated broadsheets could be used to put across the message, as in the series illustrating contrasts between Christ and Anti-Christ, the Pope being identified with the latter. In an age when the majority of the population was illiterate, word of mouth – and popular preaching – were highly important; and the prevalence of large numbers of wandering traders and itinerant craftsmen played a role in spreading news and views from town to town. The social and economic unrest of a period of rising population and increased pressure on resources, as well as political tensions among knights, princes, cities and Emperor, all played a role in different patterns of reception of the Reformation. Prevalent anti-clericalism and anti-Papalism probably played a part in the popular appeal of Luther's ideas, the full theological import of which was understood by only very few. But the religious ferment precipitated by Luther led to movements in numerous towns throughout Germany demanding at least evangelical preaching and reform of the clergy, and often wider reforms of religious and social life. These movements were extensive enough in the years 1521–4 to threaten a major social and perhaps political upheaval. Even before the emergence of the concept of 'Protestantism', the ferment of a reforming movement became embroiled in a range of more secular concerns, affecting the development of both ideas and action.

THE GERMAN PEASANTS' WAR

In 1524–6, there were widespread revolts by peasants and common people in towns from the south-west to the north-east of Germany. Known as the 'Peasants' War' or 'Revolution of the Common Man', this mass uprising has been the subject of considerable historical debate. Following Friedrich Engels, Marxist historians have seen it as an early 'bourgeois revolution' (although lacking a mature bourgeoisie to carry it to success), while non-Marxist historians have debated the relative importance of economic, political and ideological factors in its causation and course.

The background lay in a series of earlier uprisings: the rebellion led by the 'Piper of Niklashausen' in 1476 (suppressed by the Bishop of Würzburg); the *Bundschuh* risings of 1493 and 1502, 1513 and 1517; the 'Poor Conrad' revolt of 1514; and a wave of peasant rebellions in 1513–17. In 1524, unrest began initially in the southern Black Forest and Lake Constance area; in the course of 1525 it spread, with risings in Upper Swabia, along the Danube, in Franconia, Thuringia and Saxony, with an isolated revolt as far afield as East Prussia. By late April 1525, around 300,000 peasants were under arms – a sizeable proportion of a total population of perhaps 16 million. Peasant armies (of between 2,000 and 15,000) were remarkably well organised, some under noble leadership (such as Götz von Berlichingen). They won initial successes in south-west Germany, partly due to overreaction, fear, and rapid capitulation on the part of some authorities, and partly due to the fact that the army of the Swabian circle of princes happened to be away in Italy, fighting with Emperor Charles V against Francis I of France. After a decisive victory for Charles V in this quite unconnected conflict, the princes returned to quell peasant unrest. Superior organisation, and the capacity for links across localities, aided the princes' suppression of peasant uprisings. In all, around 100,000 peasants were killed, and many more maimed and blinded.

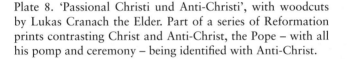

Plate 8. 'Passional Christi und Anti-Christi', with woodcuts
by Lukas Cranach the Elder. Part of a series of Reformation
prints contrasting Christ and Anti-Christ, the Pope – with all
his pomp and ceremony – being identified with Anti-Christ.

Some of the peasants' leaders were not peasants but clergy; and
some of the supporters were not peasants but artisans and plebians,
the lower ranks of the urban population. Nor was it the most down-
trodden, impoverished members of the peasantry who revolted, but
rather the more prosperous peasants who led the revolts. A combination of political and economic grievances were involved, arising
from pressure on land and resources, greater differentiation and
friction within peasant communities, lords' attempts to gain higher
rents and entry fines, and political encroachments on the autonomy
of peasant communities (the *Gemeinde*). Also important was the
religious ferment and questioning of all authority promoted by the
'Luther affair', and encapsulated in the slogan of 'godly law'. Reformation influence is for example evident in the 'Twelve Articles of

the Swabian Peasantry', adopted by the Memmingen Peasant Parliament of March 1525. The first of these Articles demanded the right of a community to elect its own pastor to preach the gospel, and to be maintained by the great tithe, before subsequent Articles entered the nitty-gritty of demands concerning labour services, leases, rents, use of resources, punishment of crimes, and so on. The twelfth Article concluded that 'all should be organised strictly according to the Scriptures', which were scoured throughout for appropriate references in support of demands.

There were differences of programme and courses of action among rebels in different areas. The Swabians were relatively moderate. In Franconia, peasants attacked the privileges of nobles and clergy, in addition to demanding abolition of feudal dues, and gained as allies the townspeople from Rothenburg-ob-der-Tauber; the besieged canons of the Cathedral Chapter of Würzburg were ultimately relieved by the princes. In Thuringia, by May 1525, Thomas Müntzer had set up an egalitarian theocracy with a radical programme; but the projected alliance of peasants, townspeople and miners was savagely suppressed and Müntzer executed. Peasant attempts in the Upper Rhine area to negotiate a peace were unsuccessful, and the peasants were slaughtered. Urban governments in Imperial free cities in southern Germany were generally able to retain order, while in the territorial towns to the north there was considerable urban unrest. In Salzburg and the Habsburg domains, the last major surge of revolt occurred under the leadership of Michael Gaismair in Tyrol, who in 1526 drafted the 'Tyrolean Constitution' for a republic based on a Christian egalitarianism.

The peasants and common townspeople participating in the uprisings had been seeking social and economic change, based on notions of 'godly law' founded on the Bible: they upheld a scripturally based vision of a realisable alternative secular order. This was neither a mediaeval utopian, millenarian movement, nor a simple rebellion against abuses of the existing system, but rather a failed social revolution. One of the consequences of its failure was a further enhancement of the powers of territorial rulers. It is clear that the Reformation played some role in the inspiration of the Peasants' War; but the latter also played a role in diverting the course of the Reformation. Luther himself initially criticised both peasants and princes, in his 'Admonition for Peace' of April 1525; but following a preaching tour south of the Harz, in the course of which he was nearly killed, Luther wrote his incensed diatribe 'Against the Robbing and Murdering Hordes of Peasants'. This effectively ended the possibility of the Lutheran Reformation appealing equally to all social classes: Luther employed the Scriptures to support his own social prejudices in favour of a worldly order upheld by obedience to secular authority. From this point on, egalitarian forms of Reformation would remain largely sectarian, in opposition to Luther's princely Reformation.

THE DEVELOPMENT OF THE GERMAN REFORMATION

A number of princes adopted the Reformation for political and economic as well as religious reasons: they were not averse to getting rid of papal jurisdiction and taxation, nor to the secularisation of church properties (although many princes gained less than is often supposed). By 1528, Lutheran rulers included Albrecht von Hohenzollern in Prussia, Landgrave Philip of Hesse, the Margrave of Brandenburg-Ansbach, Count Albrecht of Mansfeld, the Duke of Schleswig and Duke Ernest of Brunswick-Lüneburg. Given the dynastic rivalries between Hohenzollerns and Wettins, Saxony turned into a particularly important centre of the Reformation. In some places, it was nobles and estates who pressured for reform and were resisted by the princes, particularly in the Habsburg and Wittelsbach lands. Many cities rapidly adopted the Reformation, including Erfurt, Zwickau, Magdeburg, Nuremberg, Bremen, the Swiss city of Zurich, Strasbourg, Frankfurt, and in 1534, Augsburg. By the early 1530s, around two-thirds of Imperial cities had indicated their allegiance to evangelical principles. There were variations in the course of the urban Reformation according to local conditions and circumstances. In Nuremberg, for example, popular pressure from below gave added weight to the city council's inclination to accept the Reformation; but dependence on long-distance trade necessitated the goodwill of the Emperor and neighbouring Catholic princes; so Nuremberg did not go so far as to join the militant Protestant League led by Philip of Hesse. A moderate Reformation within the city walls allowed the council to appoint preachers and control doctrine, while maintaining a conciliatory attitude towards important Catholic powers outside the city. Other towns experienced a more radical Reformation. Particularly violent were events in Münster. In 1534 the Anabaptist John of Leyden became dictator in a theocracy characterised by common ownership of property, intense communal regulation of personal life, polygamy and terror. A siege ended finally in defeat for the Anabaptists, and a massacre initiated by the princes. Anabaptism later became quietist and pacifist, an inward-turning and apolitical form of religious community. In the Swiss town of Zurich, a more radical social as well as religious Reformation was influenced by Zwingli, who disagreed with Luther on a number of points, including interpretation of the words 'this is my body' in the eucharist, leading to the Swiss notion of communion as a symbolic memorial service in contrast to the more literal Lutheran conception. In Geneva, the Frenchman John Calvin (1509–64) developed an altogether more logical, rational system of theology. Calvinism constituted a 'second Reformation' to complete what was perceived as only a partially effected reformation under the first generation of reformers. While there were different theological currents within Calvinism, it has chiefly come to be seen as distinct from Lutheranism with respect to the key notion of predestination. In Calvin's view, not only could one not achieve salvation by good works (as in the Catholic view); one could also not achieve it by faith (the Lutheran view). Rather, the great omnipotent God had *predestined* every individual to be either one of the elect (the saved) or among the damned; there was nothing mere mortals could do to influence their predetermined destiny. Calvinist religious communities were characterised by extreme social discipline; and individual conduct, far from being fatalistic (as the doctrine of predestination would logically suggest) was characterised by self-discipline, the psychological consequence of perpetually seeking for signs of being one of God's elect. Theological differences and debates among Protestants of different persuasions were to multiply in subsequent generations.

The notion of 'Protestant' itself derives from the so-called 'Protestation of Speyer' of 1529, protesting against the decision to enforce the Edict of Worms outlawing supporters of Luther. (Germans still distinguish between adherents of 'Evangelical' and 'Reformed'

confessions, while the English – whose national Reformation managed to combine elements of both traditions in a pragmatic Eliz-
abethan compromise – tend to adopt the more unitary term
'Protestant', to include later sectarian variants as well as the established church.) But Luther and his early followers had no intention of causing an irreversible split in Christianity; they merely
wanted to purge the church of what they considered to be heretical
abuses of doctrine and practice. Repeated attempts were made to
settle differences or come to terms. At the 1530 Diet of Augsburg –
which Luther, still under the ban of Empire, was unable to attend –
Luther's Wittenberg colleague, Philipp Melanchthon, drafted the so-
called 'Augsburg Confession', a relatively irenical document making
many concessions to Catholics. Its omissions angered the Swiss reformers; but it was signed by the Protestant rulers present, and, for
all its ambiguities, has remained the basis of the Lutheran faith. The
1530 Diet of Augsburg was a moment at which opportunities for reconciliation still appeared open; but a series of misperceptions and
increased intransigence led to a hardening of fronts. Religious affairs
were complicated by Imperial politics, in the context of Charles V's
attempts to have his brother Ferdinand pre-elected as German king,
arousing fears on the part of such prominent Catholics as the
Bavarian Wittelsbachs that the Habsburgs were attempting to make
the Imperial crown hereditary. Partly in response to the pre-election
of Ferdinand, which after much politicking and bribery was effected in January 1531, the League of Schmalkalden was formed
in February 1531 as the military defence force of Protestants, initially comprising six princes and ten cities, subsequently joined by
most Protestant states.

Continued attempts were made to reach agreement between
Catholics and Protestants. From 1532, the Emperor was particularly
preoccupied with combating the Turks, and pursuing Habsburg interests in southern Europe. But in 1539–40 he turned his attention
again to pacification of German affairs. At the inconclusive 1541
Diet of Regensburg it became clear that the split was unbridgeable,
and the Lutheran doctrine of obedience to authority was reshaped to
mean obedience to the territorial prince or local ruler, and not to the
Emperor. Despite the support of Protestant princes in his continuing
conflict with France (after concessions in the Speyer Diet of 1544),

the Emperor determined on war against the 'heretics' in Germany, to be supported by papal troops and money. A few months after Luther's death in 1546, the Schmalkaldic War erupted, in the course of which the Emperor succeeded in capturing Wittenberg, and nearly had Luther's body disinterred from its tomb in the Castle Church. But Charles V was himself weakened by conflicts with the papacy, and in the context of splits among Catholics Charles V issued the relatively moderate Augsburg Interim of 1548. This pacified neither Catholics nor Protestants, and military and political disturbances continued, complicated by Imperial plans for a divided succession (between the Spanish and Austrian branches of the Habsburg family) and French involvement with princely opposition to the Emperor. In 1552 the Treaty of Passau registered the collapse of Imperial constitutional and religious ambitions. It accepted that transfers or seizures of ecclesiastical property and changes in religious worship would not be revoked nor demands made for restitution. Finally, in the realisation that there was effective political stalemate, and that neither Catholicism nor Protestantism was about to disappear, a pragmatic settlement of differences – an agreement to disagree – was reached in the 1555 Diet of Augsburg.

The 1555 Peace of Augsburg was intended as a means of terminating the internal political unrest by freezing the existing positions of Catholics and Lutherans. It excluded from consideration all variants of Protestantism other than Lutheranism; it failed to tackle problems connected with Zwinglians and a range of sectarians, and did not foresee the problems that would be posed by the development of Calvinism as a powerful alternative version of Protestantism. The notion was accepted that princes should have the power to determine the internal religious complexion of their territories; but that they should not engage in missionary activities to convert other territories or to protect co-religionists elsewhere. Anyone dissenting from the religious confession of a given territory would have to emigrate; only cities could incorporate religious minorities. 'Freedom' of religion thus meant freedom at the territorial, rather than individual, level: freedom for the prince to determine the religious complexion of his territory, later known as the principle of *cuius regio, eius religio*. This was an ironic outcome of a struggle which had started as a struggle for individual experience of faith, a direct individual relationship with God, and freedom of the individual conscience. Authoritarian territorial churches, far from confirming the scriptural basis of religion, rather enshrined the role of political determination of doctrine. And in breaking the cultural unity of politically fragmented late mediaeval Germany, it sealed the pattern of territorialisation of German politics.

The Peace of Augsburg left a number of problems unresolved: not only the question of Calvinism and the sects, but also the question of who determined the religious confession of cities. There were further problems concerning the 'ecclesiastical reservation', which aided the survival of Catholicism by ensuring that there would be an orthodox successor to any archbishop, bishop or abbot who personally turned Protestant. Moreover, for all the pragmatism about the settlement, in the later sixteenth century a zealous Counter-Reformation Catholicism sought to reconvert Protestants, as we shall see. In the age of confessionalism, differences between Protestants and Catholics were comparable (without stretching the comparison too far) to the ideological battle between western democracy and Soviet communism in the cold war of the late twentieth century.

It is worth pausing briefly to consider the wider long-term implications of the Reformation. In it have been sought the roots of many later developments: modern capitalism, science, individualism, secularisation and the 'demystification of the world', and assorted aspects of modern politics. Many arguments may have overstated their case: an interrelated cluster of changes were occurring, in a mutually interacting fashion, and to isolate one as a unique cause is to oversimplify. But some connections are of particular interest.

In a famous essay on *The Protestant Ethic and the Spirit of Capitalism* (originally published in 1904–5) the German sociologist Max Weber sought to point up cultural affinities between the this-worldly asceticism of Protestants and the rational ethos of sober bourgeois capitalism, with its reinvestment (rather than hedonistic enjoyment) of profits. The fine distinctions between the work ethics of Catholicism, Lutheranism and Calvinism drawn in Weber's essentially ambiguous essay – which highlighted cultural affinities rather than drawing tight causal connections – have provoked considerable subsequent controversy. Attempts to refute Weber's analysis by adducing instances of non-correlation between Protestantism and the development of capitalism fail to do justice to the subtlety of Weber's approach; for any adequate causal account, key combinations of elements were together necessary, and in other writings (such as his *General Economic History*) Weber elucidated factors other than the purely cultural. More materialist historians have seen the connections lying in the opposite direction: people engaged in early capitalist activities were more likely to find that Protestant orientations 'spoke to their condition' (to use the Quaker phrase). Detailed historical analysis of any particular situation reveals the considerable complexity of interrelationships between religious orientation and economic action. In some cases, political persecution for religious beliefs forced minority religious communities into certain sorts of economic activity. In other cases, membership of a certain social class would have predisposed or socialised individuals into adopting the cultural assumptions, style of life, and associated religious practices of that class. Simple generalisations must be regarded with a degree of flexibility, and a recognition that correlation does not always imply causation.

Connections have also been drawn between Protestantism and politics. The most prevalent generalisation in the German case is also the one perhaps least sustainable: the notion that the Lutheran doctrine of obedience to authority fostered an apolitical attitude on the part of subjects, in contrast to the Calvinist doctrine of legitimate resistance to ungodly rule. In fact, however, theology can be – and has been – interpreted in the light of circumstances to give rise to many different patterns of political attitude and activity, within relatively broad limits set by religious beliefs. More interesting are connections between patterns of religious *organisation* and politics, as well as patterns of church–state relations. It was Max Weber again who, in an essay on sects, suggested that the egalitarianism of early congregational churches and sects may have played a role in the origins of liberal democracy, particularly in seventeenth-century America. Undoubtedly of major importance, however, is the connection between confessionalisation and state-building, with interesting differences between the consequences of the English and German Reformations.

These differences lie less in the area of belief stressed in older interpretations (which emphasise the supposed quietism and passivity of German Lutheranism) than in differences in political structure and organisation. In England, a national Reformation served simultaneously to enhance the status of the national monarchy in a unitary state and to strengthen the position, economically, culturally, and politically, of the landed estates who benefited from secularised church wealth and attained powers of church patronage. In the German territories, the situation varied tremendously from one area to another. In some states, such as Württemberg, the post-Reformation church to a considerable degree managed to retain its wealth and power, in contrast to the myth of the inevitably weak and subservient territorial state church; in other areas, the church was less fortunate. Only the compilation and synthesis of a large number of local studies will help to elucidate the different factors involved. It is in any case clear that there was a close relationship between processes of confessionalisation and state-building at the territorial level in Germany. Regional studies such as that of Lippe and Lemgo by Heinz Schilling have shown variations on, and even complete reversals of, presumed contrasts between subservient Lutheran state churches and rebellious Calvinist bourgeoisies. It appears to have been less the *content* of the variant belief system than the political *form* of appropriate heterodoxy that was important in processes of self-definition and cultural-political demarcation. Schilling has suggested that the territorial monopolisation of the church in the German Reformation was both earlier than, and a precondition for, the later military and tax monopolies stressed by scholars such as Nobert Elias.

An indubitably valid generalisation that can be made about the German Reformation is that the one thing it did *not* foster was the cause of a wider German unity. Notoriously, the Empire itself was politically split, with a Catholic Emperor having to recognise religious disunity. Confessionalisation was an important factor in the development of territorial states in early modern Germany. It played a key role in the political and military conflicts of the century after 1555, which themselves fostered the growth of armies and bureaucracies. Religious differences became decreasingly important as political factors in the kaleidoscope of cross-cutting conflicts involved in the Thirty Years War, and were effectively removed as a major factor from political conflicts after 1648. Insofar as religion was a political issue in the later seventeenth and eighteenth centuries, it was generally a case of conflict *within*, rather than *between*, states. Territorial state-building had by then progressed beyond the initial stage of socioreligious legitimation.

GERMANY IN THE AGE OF COUNTER-REFORMATION

Catholics were by no means content to accept the status quo of 1555. Following the Council of Trent (1545–63) a reinvigorated Catholicism sought to win back ground it had lost. The Society of Jesus, or Jesuits (founded by the Spaniard Ignatius Loyola) pursued a vigorous campaign in Germany, building up a network of zealous proselytisers through their schools, seminaries and universities, as well as at court. The Capuchin order based in Vienna was similarly vigorous. Both Austria and Bavaria were particularly energetic centres of the Counter-Reformation, in official attempts to suppress reforming inclinations among members of the south German and Austrian nobilities. Meanwhile, Protestantism was far from united, with developing differences in what has been called the 'second Reformation'. Calvinism in particular became more important in the later sixteenth and early seventeeth centuries, starting with the conversion of the Palatinate and later including the rulers of Brandenburg and Hesse-Cassel. In Strasbourg, Martin Bucer influenced a distinctive form of Reformation, while elsewhere there continued to be differences among shades of Lutheran, Melanchthonian and other persuasions.

In all territories, of whichever religious complexion, the later sixteenth century saw religion as a vehicle for cultural demarcation from neighbouring territories, and increased state control of individual conduct. There were measures to promote public welfare, in such areas as education and care of the poor, and to instil social discipline, reduce illegitimacy rates, and regulate relations between the sexes. Church discipline and home visits by members of the clergy were obviously effective means of social control. Religious differences also promoted educational initiatives, with a second wave of university foundations. Ingolstadt, about fifty miles north of the Bavarian capital of Munich, was an important Jesuit institution. The universities of Marburg (1529), Königsberg (1544) and others were Protestant foundations; Würzburg, Salzburg and others were founded in response as Catholic universities. These institutions trained the secular bureaucrats for developing state administrations, as well as priests, theologians and other academics. While the Reformation undoubtedly also promoted the spread of primary schooling, it seems less likely than earlier supposed that it fostered the spread of mass literacy: rote learning was generally preferred at this time.

Economy and society were changing in a variety of ways in sixteenth-century Germany. There was a general expansion of the European economy. Overseas exploration, and particularly the opening up of the Americas, meant not only an influx of precious metals (particularly silver) and consequent inflation, but also a shifting of international economic relationships. There was a reorientation of European trade towards the Atlantic seaboard, with the rise of England as a significant naval power and increasing importance for the kingdoms of Spain and France. A diversification of the European economy developed, with changing relations between more developed and less developed areas, shifting locations of centre and periphery. In Germany, some towns on the Baltic and on internal overland trade routes began to decline in importance. Many towns in the later sixteenth century began to shrink within their late mediaeval walls. The declining importance of some towns was partly economic and partly political in nature. The increased price of grain meant a rising status for the agrarian nobility at the expense of urban manufacturers and traders. In the colonial territories of the east, many nobles were able to buy out peasants and even whole villages, establishing themselves as lords over large estates and subjugated peasants. The towns were also losing out to territorial princes, particularly in the western and south-western areas of Germany. After the international economic, political, cultural and intellectual significance they had enjoyed in the late middle ages, many German towns entered a period of provincialism in the later sixteenth century. There were of course notable exceptions, such as the trading city of Hamburg.

After the mid-sixteenth century, the German population expansion came to an end. The 1590s were a decade of recession, followed by a general down-turn in the European economy in the 1610s and 1620s. In late sixteenth-century Germany, social and political

Plate 9. 'The Jewish Snipper and Money-Changer'. A broadsheet criticising the supposed avarice of the Jew at a time of rampant inflation. 'Kippen' was the common practice of snipping the edges of coins, and using the shavings to make more coins. Eventually, pennies had to be weighed rather than counted; 144 full-size pennies weighed a pound.

tensions erupted in renewed peasants' revolts, as well as social unrest in the towns. In the early seventeenth century there was general expectation of war in Europe, with a preparatory raising of armies and building of protective walls and cities. Mannheim was actually constructed as a fortified princely seat in 1606. In the early seventeenth century a fall in solar energy was associated with a drop in average temperatures, reduced crop seasons and reduced agricultural production in what has been termed a 'little Ice Age' – captured well in the icy winter scenery of Brueghel's paintings. Starvation, destitution and even infanticide were not uncommon, as well as pogroms against Jews. Social tensions probably also contributed – whatever other factors were involved – to the scale and intensity of witchcraft persecutions in the sixteenth and early seventeenth centuries. Women were singled out as the scapegoat for a range of ills – theft, the failure of the harvest, illness of beasts or humans – as well as the focus of sexual fantasies and prejudices. Intellectual life combined the astronomy of Tycho Brahe and Johannes Kepler (both at the Imperial court at Prague) with belief in alchemy. For all the supposed 'modernity' of the Reformation period there was much that would seem very strange to people of the twentieth century.

THE THIRTY YEARS WAR

Historians have for some time debated the question of whether there was a 'general crisis of the seventeenth century', and, if so, how it should be characterised and explained. It is noticeable that in the mid-seventeenth century there was a wave of unrest across a number of European states, including revolts, revolutions and civil wars, such as the French Fronde and the English Revolution. Aristocratic and provincial rebellions against the increased demands made by centralising rulers were widespread. While no single explanation has been generally accepted as valid, certain common features may be noticed. Rebellions were often integrally related to processes of state-building – particularly the growth of central bureaucracies encroaching on the autonomy of local government – and with competition among European states, necessitating the maintenance of armies, and hence increased direct taxation. Increased demands on,

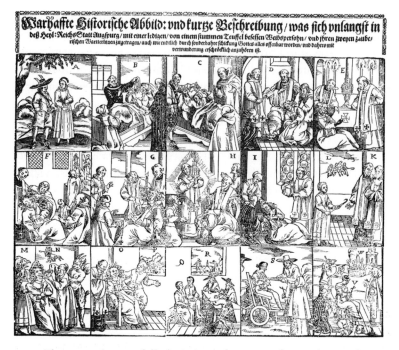

Plate 10. A very full depiction of means of exorcism and methods of dealing with a witch and her two helpers.

and extractions from, provinces and their aristocratic representatives often provoked rebellions.

In the complex circumstances of the German case, the ill-defined 'general crisis' was refracted in unique and complex ways. A combination of tensions both within the Holy Roman Empire and among the states of Europe produced a series of conflicts from 1618 to 1648 which have come to be termed the 'Thirty Years War'. These conflicts involved confessional splits within the Empire; revolts of provincial estates against their territorial ruler; resistance of territorial princes against Imperial power; and a wider set of conflicts between non-German states which were fought over German soil and enmeshed with German conflicts. These included conflicts between Spain and the Dutch, between Sweden and Poland, and between France and the Habsburgs. In thirty years of fighting, German economy and society were profoundly affected; and the settlement which finally emerged, in 1648, set patterns with long-lasting consequences for German history.

The origins of the Thirty Years War lie partly in unresolved problems left by the Peace of Augsburg (failure to recognise Calvinists, the ecclesiastical reservation) and partly in the pattern of subsequent developments. Conflicts had continued, such as the war of Cologne of 1583–8 which successfully halted the Protestantisation of ecclesiastical territory. This was particularly important in the case of Cologne, since it prevented the transformation of a Catholic into a Protestant electoral vote, which would have opened up the possibility of the election of a Protestant Emperor. Religious-political parties had formed, and although on certain issues – such as combating the Turkish threat – princes could usually transcend confessional differences, the institutions of the Empire were breaking down. After the death of Charles V, the Habsburg Emperors tended to focus more narrowly on their own domestic and dynastic concerns than on Imperial affairs, over which they had to some extent lost control in the age of confessionalism. The 1608 Imperial Diet collapsed, without either voting taxes for the Turkish war or resolving religious issues, and the Protestants walked out, forming the Protestant Union. The following year the Catholic League was formed, headed by the Jesuit-educated Maximilian of Bavaria. Henceforth the involvement of these two religious-military forces would turn local disputes into wider conflicts. This was illustrated by the War of the Jülich-Cleves Succession (1609–14) over a disputed inheritance. When the 'possessing princes' fell out, one obtained the support of the Catholic League, while the other – John Sigismund of Brandenburg – converted to Calvinism in 1613 and obtained the support of the Palatinate, the Netherlands and England.

The outbreak of the Thirty Years War proper is conventionally dated from an incident known as the 'defenestration of Prague' in May 1618 (in conscious imitation of the defenestration initiating the Hussite rebellion two centuries earlier). The Bohemian Protestant nobility had been enjoying certain religious and political freedoms since the 1609 'Letter of Majesty' of the Habsburg Emperor Rudolf II, who needed aristocratic support in his struggles with his brother, Matthias. The latter succeeded Rudolf as Emperor in 1612, but remained childless, occasioning a disputed succession. In 1617 the

Jesuit-educated, militant Catholic Archduke Ferdinand of Austria became King of Bohemia, a position he coveted since it gave him an electoral vote, and he had aspirations to become Emperor himself against Spanish claims. Under Ferdinand, energetic moves were made to reduce the political and religious privileges of the Bohemian nobility. A large protest meeting in Prague sent delegates with a petition to the palace. Discussions with Ferdinand's Deputy Governors, Martinitz and Slovata, became somewhat stormy, and, followed by their secretary, they were tipped out of the window (hence 'defenestration') by the protesting Bohemians. (A Catholic account tells us that the Virgin Mary interceded to carry Martinitz softly to the ground on her cloak, saving him 'from all harm despite his corpulent body'; the Protestant version more mundanely asserts that the fall was broken by landing in a dung heap.) The Bohemian estates then appealed to Protestants elsewhere to support their cause, inaugurating the first conflict of the war, the Bohemian Revolt. To their aid came the Elector Palatine, the Calvinist Frederick V (married to the daughter of King James I of England), whom the Bohemian estates elected as their king. Known as the 'Winter King', he lasted only a season. Ferdinand, who had been duly elected Emperor in 1619, mustered a strong Catholic coalition, including Maximilian of Bavaria as well as Spain and Poland. General Tilly, military chief of the Catholic League, inflicted a decisive defeat on the Protestants at the 1620 Battle of the White Mountain (just west of Prague) and Frederick had to flee. The Protestant Bohemian rebels had their estates confiscated, and many of them lost not only their possessions but also their lives. A substantially new nobility was installed which would be loyal to the Habsburgs, while some nobles were reconverted, and strenuous efforts were made to re-Catholicise Bohemia. (In subsequent decades, Protestantism went underground, making many secret converts among the peasantry, who would be the focus of intense Jesuit campaigns in the later seventeenth and early eighteenth centuries.)

In what was now effectively a German civil war, struggles moved northwards, through the Palatinate War, the Lower Saxon War, and north to the Baltic. Through a series of Catholic military successes, by the late 1620s the Austrian Habsburgs controlled a broad swathe of German territory, stretching almost to the shores of the Baltic, and threatened to establish a unitary state. The upstart Bohemian

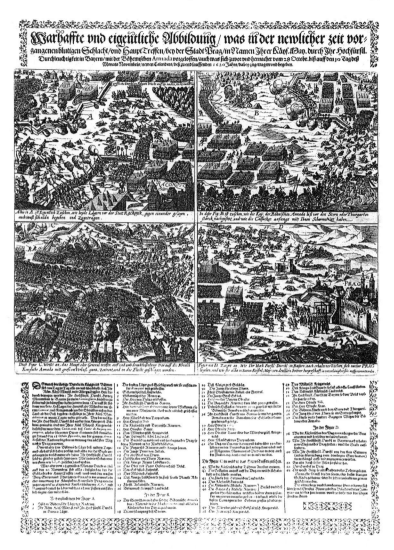

Plate 11. The Battle of the White Mountain, 1620.

General Wallenstein was elevated to the rank of prince of the Empire, being granted the duchy of Mecklenburg and a fine house in Prague as a reward for his dramatic military successes for the Catholic cause.

The increasingly powerful Emperor now sought to remould German affairs and roll back the Reformation. In the 1629 Edict of Restitution Ferdinand attempted to counter-reform a number of archbishoprics, bishoprics and cities which had converted to Protestantism, and to restitute all church properties and incomes that had been alienated since 1552. Not only did this measure radically affect the pattern of territorial power; it also constituted a transgression of the constitution, since it was issued by the Emperor without reference to the Diet or the princes, and was guaranteed to provoke anger and hostility on all manner of fronts – including among those Catholic princes who in a belated entry into the grab for spoils stood to gain less than the Emperor. By now, Ferdinand's rising powers as Emperor had aroused the suspicions even of Catholic princes, including even his most important ally, the Bavarian Duke Maximilian, whose Catholic League had in any case remained independent of Habsburg control, and who now demanded a reduction in the size of the Imperial army and the dismissal of Wallenstein. In 1630 Ferdinand did indeed dismiss Wallenstein (of whom he had also been suspicious), but did not modify the execution of the Edict of Restitution. Catholic princes continued to fear Ferdinand's ambitions. A new line-up began to develop: territorial princes against an overpowerful Emperor, rather than Catholics against Protestants.

From 1630, the conflicts became increasingly international in character. Ferdinand's attempted control of all Germany was thwarted by the intervention of the Swedish King Gustavus Adolphus. In a separate Swedish–Polish conflict, Sigismund of Poland had been forced to make peace with the Swedes in 1629, and in 1630 the Swedish army invaded Germany. The well-prepared Swedish army made relatively rapid advances into German territory at precisely the time one of the Catholics' most important Generals, Wallenstein, was out of commission. This marked a military turning point in the Protestant fortunes, coinciding with important internal political developments which were weakening princely support for the Emperor. At the same time, Cardinal Richelieu of France, involved in bitter conflicts with Habsburg Spain in a separate struggle for territorial hegemony in western Europe, was keen to support German princes – whether Protestant or Catholic – in their resistance to the Habsburg Emperor. But France was no happier about the potential prospect of a Swedish empire as neighbour. Thus what had until now been essentially a series of local German conflicts, won by the Habsburgs, became part of a wider set of conflicts involving

Sweden, France and Spain as well. With the Swedish advance, a series of agreements, often mutually contradictory, began to be made between the Swedes, certain German princes, and France, as relationships became more complicated and interests even more cross-cutting than in the earlier phase.

In 1631 the Catholic General Tilly savagely destroyed the city of Magdeburg. But the Swedish army, along with John George of Saxony, defeated Tilly near Leipzig. Gustavus Adolphus turned south, advancing through Würzburg, Frankfurt and Mainz. Meanwhile, Richelieu was strengthening French interests along the Rhine. With the powerful Swedish advance, the Protestant King Gustavus Adolphus began to look as strong and threatening to the 'liberated' German princes as had the Catholic Emperor Ferdinand. Fears grew that Germany might become instead incorporated into an expanded Swedish empire. In 1632, Ferdinand recalled Wallenstein; Tilly attempted to block the Swedish advance into Bavaria, but was fatally wounded. Wallenstein managed to force the Swedish army north, and attempted to break Saxony's alliance with Sweden. Gustavus Adolphus himself was killed at the battle of Lützen near Leipzig in November 1632; since his heir was a six-year-old daughter, his place was taken by the Swedish chancellor, Axel Oxenstierna. In the 1633 Heilbronn Convention, Protestant members of four south German circles allied with Sweden. Wallenstein meanwhile started playing games on his own initiative, and possessed the military power to realise them, such that Vienna began to plot his deposition. After conspiracies, defections and desertion, Wallenstein was murdered in 1634.

The battle of Nördlingen, of September 1634, was a catastrophe for the Swedes, and a great victory for the Spanish army under the command of Philip IV of Spain's brother, the governor of the Spanish Netherlands. The international balance of power began to shift again. The 1635 Peace of Prague saw peace between Saxony and the Emperor, and for a time suggested a revival of Ferdinand II's fortunes. Many German princes came to accept a settlement with the Emperor, and the German war as such began to peter out. Since France could no longer operate effectively through supporting German princes, France now had to intervene formally: in May 1635 France issued an official declaration of war against Spain. France,

Spain and Sweden continued fighting, despite limited settlements between individual German princes and the Emperor within the Empire. No power was now strong enough to achieve rapid and decisive results. Individual princes began to reach separate agreements with the French and the Swedes, isolating the Emperor; in effect the Empire was no longer acting as a unit with respect to foreign affairs. Brandenburg and Saxony deserted the Emperor to make separate truces with Sweden, while Bavaria made an array of agreements in a desperate effort to prevent armies from further devastating Bavarian soil. The very complexity of the situation, and the lack of clearly demarcated fronts and issues, was one reason why the wars and fighting continued to drag on for so long. In a general context of plundering, collapse of resources and creation of wastelands, a general settlement of European conflicts was finally reached in the 1648 Peace of Westphalia. Even then, the settlement took several years of wrangling, with separate discussions taking place in the Protestant and Catholic camps, meeting in Münster and Osnabrück.

THE PEACE OF WESTPHALIA AND THE EFFECTS OF THE WAR

The Peace of Westphalia represented a compromise to settle two sets of conflicts within the Empire: that between Protestants (of all persuasions) and Catholics; and that between the ambitions of the Emperor and the powers of the princes of the Empire. It also attempted to achieve a balance of power among European states, but while German affairs were largely settled, the conflict between France and Spain continued. Moreover, France and Sweden were guarantors of the Imperial Constitution, providing a basis for subsequent intervention. Nevertheless, the Peace of Westphalia was a benchmark for the Empire's public law and political life, remaining its basic constitution until the abolition of the Empire in 1806.

The Treaties of Münster and Osnabrück which constituted the Peace of Westphalia included a large number of provisions. Parts of Alsace were ceded to France, although retaining a connection with the Empire in a complex and ambiguous relationship which puzzled even Cardinal Mazarin of France, and ensured future conflicts between France and Germany. The independent duchy of Lorraine

Map 4. Germany after the Peace of Westphalia, 1648

was even less fortunate, in that its status at this time was not determined, and it continued to be fought over for some years. Sweden made considerable gains in north Germany, including western Pomerania (the eastern part went to Brandenburg); but enhanced Swedish strength in this area ensured continued conflicts with Russia and Poland. Swedish possessions remained fiefs of the Empire, but in the later seventeenth century a weaker Sweden was unable to exploit further her foothold in Germany. Brandenburg, Saxony and Mecklenberg all gained territories, Brandenburg emerging strengthened as a result of French desires to check Sweden and Austria by means of a 'third force' in north Germany. Switzerland and the Netherlands were both mentioned in the Peace, but excluded from the Empire, clarifying a previously somewhat ambiguous status; and in January 1648 Spain finally acknowledged the legal independence of the United Provinces.

With some exceptions, 'restitutions' were based on the status quo of 1618, although the position was different in the Habsburg hereditary domains: the new Catholic nobility which had been installed in Bohemia after the Battle of the White Mountain retained its position. The 'ecclesiastical reservation' was extended to Protestant bishoprics. Rights to exercise religion were based on the 'normal' year of 1624. Calvinists were now included, but not sects. Many western and southern German states accorded a limited degree of toleration to religious minorities, but religious uniformity was imposed in Austria. Austrian Habsburg possessions became more unified and consolidated as a result of the imposition of Catholicism and firm rule from Vienna. The religious boundaries created by the Peace of Westphalia lasted essentially until the population upheavals unleashed by the Second World War.

The settlement marked a step in secularisation in the sense of separation of religion and politics. It had become clear in the course of the conflicts that religious and political interests did not always neatly overlap: territorial estates and princes were sometimes more concerned to resist Imperial ambitions than to adhere to strictly confessional alignments. In future European conflicts, the balance of power would be a more important consideration than the confessional complexion of potential allies or enemies. (Mercenary soldiers hardly cared, in any case, for whose cause they were fighting, so long as they were paid; and peasants cared not at all whose army it was that ruined their crops, burnt their houses, and raped the village women.) In a wider sense, too, 1648 marked the end of the age of confessionalism. Within states, concomitant processes of centralisation and bureaucratisation of rule partially demoted the earlier importance of religious-cultural self-definition.

Territorial rulers significantly increased their powers and rights, including the right to undertake individual alliances and conduct foreign policy independently of the Empire (subject to the empty restriction that such alliances must not be directed against the Emperor). They did not quite achieve full theoretical sovereignty, but rather gained supreme power (*Landeshoheit*) within their territory, and collective power in the Diet to determine certain matters (defence, laws, taxes) without Imperial intervention. Certain medium-sized territories in particular gained in strength. Bavaria secured an electoral vote (giving a clear Catholic majority in the electoral college), as well as gaining the territory of the Upper Palatinate, indicative of

Plate 12. War depicted as a beast ravaging Germany; an exemplar of a widespread critique of war as such.

Bavaria's enhanced status and role in the later seventeenth century. Brandenburg and Saxony also emerged as more important territories. While the Thirty Years War had ensured Habsburg control of Bohemia, and a strengthened Austria was able to benefit from its wealth and resources, in the context of other enlarged and politically consolidated states the authority of the Habsburgs as German Emperors was more fragile.

What were the effects of the war on German economy and society? A powerful myth rapidly grew up of the devastation, death and destruction wrought by the war. In the absence of comprehensive and reliable data, it is not easy to put together a definitive picture. But certain points are clear. The impact of the war was very variable, in both time and place. Some territories suffered far worse effects than others, and different areas were affected at different times. Averages tell us less than analysis of 'black spots', which were roughly distributed in a swathe running from south-west to north-east. Even with these cautions, historians cannot agree on precise figures. H. S. Steinberg's estimate that there was, if any change, a slight rise in German population from 15–17 million in 1600 to 16–18 million in 1650 has been generally discredited, but there is still some debate about the extent of the decline. Geoffrey Parker suggests that the population of the Holy Roman Empire declined by around 20 per cent, from 20 million in 1618 to 16–17 million in 1648, while Rudolf Vierhaus proposes a drop from 15–16 million to 10 million. But if one considers individual areas, destruction might be on a far greater scale. Particularly badly affected areas might have lost over two-thirds of their population. Württemberg, for example, had a population of perhaps 445,000 in 1622, declining slightly to 415,000 in 1634; but in the next five years it lost more than three-quarters of its people, leaving a population of a mere 97,000 in 1639. Some areas of Germany lost between one-third and two-thirds of their population, while other areas were virtually unaffected. Explanations for population loss are also contested. The greatest killer was undoubtedly epidemics (typhoid, the plague, veneral disease), often spread by armies on the move. Certain common illnesses, such as influenza, were more likely to be fatal because of malnutrition and lowered resistance. There was also considerable internal migration and redistribution of population, with villagers, for example, periodically fleeing to towns for safety. Rural population losses have been put at about 45–50 per cent, compared with 25–30 per cent of the urban population. Not to be underestimated are the effects of the war in disrupting agricultural production. The destruction of buildings and livestock, the support of unpaid troops through foraging, the use of 'scorched earth' policies to prevent the enemy's armies living off the land, all caused immense damage to an already fragile subsistence economy.

Assessment of the overall economic impact of the war is complicated by the problem of separating the direct effects of war from the operation of longer-term trends. Some German towns – such as the old Baltic Hanseatic towns, Rostock, Stralsund and Wismar – were already declining in the later sixteenth century, as a result of the reorientation of trade towards the Atlantic; and other towns experienced rising or falling fortunes in the first half of the seventeenth century which did not correlate neatly with the progress of the war. An internal economic redistribution was taking place, with north-west Germany, and in particular Hamburg, rising at a time of decline elsewhere. Rural depopulation in the east may have been at least partly due to a pre-existing Junker policy of peasant evictions and the creation of large estates. However, against all such (very necessary) cautions, it must be remembered that towns such as Magdeburg experienced radical destruction and effectively mass murder (setting fire to churches into which women and children had been herded); and that the losses of livestock, the disruption of normal agricultural activities, the repeated flight of peasants from their land to urban safety, as well as the pillaging of soldiers, were hardly good for agricultural production. One village cobbler, Heberle, records in his diary that he had to flee from his home to Ulm on no less than thirty separate occasions; he also documents in dispiriting detail the deaths of two of his children (including a four-week-old son), his stepmother and three sisters, within the three months from 19 September to 18 December 1634. Anyone born after the 1600s would have hardly experienced life without the disruptions of war. The scale and intensity of personal tragedies, and the loss of security and stability for hundreds of thousands, should not be forgotten in the computerised averages of twentieth-century historians. And even the most revisionist of historians, seeking to refute the 'death and destruction myth', must concede that Germany's economy and population were at best stagnating – and most probably were more seriously affected – at a time when England was developing as an important trading nation and the population of England and Wales was rapidly expanding. (The total population of England and Wales trebled between 1450 and 1750, with most of this occurring from the mid-sixteenth to the mid-seventeenth centuries. Some historians suggest that it took the best part of a century after 1648 for German population to regain pre-1618 levels.) Germany was becoming an

Plate 13. A broadsheet illustrating the current craze for French fashions in the 'A-la-Mode-Kampf' of 1630.

economic backwater, a process underway already in the later sixteenth century but aided and consolidated by the deleterious effects of thirty years of warfare on German soil.

'High culture', remarkably, does not appear in retrospect to have suffered greatly: examples can readily be found of major works of art and architecture, lyric poety, novels (such as Grimmelshausen's

Dur Cromme wel. met haer gefel. noch lustich treden,
Haer Spel en Keel. klanckt tren eel. in Dorp en Steden.

Hier om een Duyt. daer om een Kluyt maer i u geen deys,
Voor Beurs en Tas. en Kan en Glas. is i avonts leys.

Plate 14. A vivid depiction of 'travellers', rootless and maimed
people with no fixed livelihood in the disrupted society of mid-
seventeenth-century Europe.

Simplicissimus), baroque theatre, music (particularly that of Schutz),
opera, ballet, as well as developments in the natural sciences, legal
and political theory. Intimations of developments which were to become more important later on were already evident: the expansion
of literacy, the production of books and newspapers, the formation of literary and scientific societies – and even the adulation of

French fashions in the 'A-la-Mode-Wesen'. It is more difficult to reconstruct changing patterns of popular culture. The evidence left by elites – those attempting to impose social control – tends to bemoan a decline in morals, an increase in drunkenness, illegitimacy, and irreligion, with the masses almost unable to 'distinguish between God and the devil', as a contemporary account suggested. Such perceptions gave rise to a number of reforming and proselytising impulses in later seventeenth-century religion. But all generations have a tendency to bewail a supposed drop in moral standards since 'the good old days'. It also seems to be the case that there were growing differences between the assumptions of the more educated classes and those of the common people. Witchcraft prosecutions began to decline, for example, in the later seventeenth century, as magistrates were no longer so sure of their ability to identify witches; but most non-educated people continued to believe in the reality and powers of witches. A process of cultural differentiation, evident in such intimate matters as thresholds of shame and embarrassment, was to become even more marked with the development of 'courtly culture' in following generations.

Whatever the necessary qualifications, the Thirty Years War marked a major watershed in German history. Its course and its conclusion confirmed and crystallised the territorial fragmentation of German politics, and marked another stage in the decentralisation of the Holy Roman Empire. Its effects on German economy and society both consolidated Germany's partial eclipse from the centre of European economic development, and laid the foundations for the rising power of princes, at the expense of estates and towns, in the subsequent century. The Germany that emerged in the age of absolutism was not that of independent aristocrats or burgher pride, but rather of small and medium-sized principalities, courtly nobilities and bureaucracies. And, for all the exceptions to which one can point, there was a widespread loss of self-confidence in German culture, and sense of a need for renewal after the generations of suffering and instability.

4

The age of absolutism, 1648–1815

The German territories emerged somewhat strengthened from the Thirty Years War, at least in respect of their political position in relation to the Empire. It was quite clear that, although they still did not formally possess full sovereignty, territorial rulers rather than the Holy Roman Emperor were the key political actors. In the period from the mid-seventeenth century to the abolition of the Holy Roman Empire under Napoleonic rule in 1806, a unique pattern of political multiplicity existed in the German lands. The Holy Roman Empire ceased to be an active political vehicle or potential basis for the development of a centralised state; on the other hand, its continued juridical functions and rather passive political protection permitted the survival of many small units, fragments which without this wider context might easily have been submerged by larger neighbours. Viewing the Empire as a whole, this was the German pattern of 'small principalities' or *Kleinstaaterei* which has led some observers to see Germany as a petty, small-scale provincial backwater compared to the increasingly powerful western European states of the later seventeenth and eighteenth centuries (notably of course England and France). Concomitant with this overall pattern of Imperial decentralisation was however a relatively high degree of centralisation of power at the territorial level. Individual rulers within the small states sought to gain more power for themselves at the expense of those below. Rulers sought to rule without reference to parliaments or estates, the representatives of the people (or at least some of the people). In the so-called 'age of absolutism' many rulers

Plate 15. The Diet of the Holy Roman Empire at Regensburg, 1653. From 1663, the Imperial Diet was no longer a body periodically summoned by the Emperor, but rather a permanent congress of ambassadors meeting in Regensburg.

attempted, with greater or lesser degrees of success, to gain greater power for themselves: to maintain standing armies, and establish loyal bureaucracies, which would be capable of raising taxes to pay for the army, and administering the territory in a profitable way. Associated with this political pattern were changes in the sociopolitical configuration within territories: independent feudal nobles became court-oriented aristocrats; self-confident burghers became dependent bureaucrats; habits of obedience and servility were stressed, for subjects rather than citizens. Again, many observers have seen these developments as having long-term implications for German political culture.

Yet all generalisations are fraught with dangers. Germany from the end of the Thirty Years War to the period of the Napoleonic Wars following the French Revolution was by no means a stagnant backwater: neither politically, nor in social and cultural developments. Of crucial importance in the longer term was the rise of Brandenburg-Prussia in this period, to become in the middle decades of the eighteenth century a powerful challenger to the dominance of Austria, and, in the nineteenth century, eventually to wrest control of the unification of 'small Germany' from an excluded Austria. Culturally, the period was one of lasting significance, with profound achievements in music, literature and philosophy, and with the growth of a literate, articulate public. Even in the renowned separation of the spheres of 'power' and 'the spirit' (*Macht* and *Geist*), the picture was by no means as simple as easy generalisations about the 'apolitical German' would have us believe. The peculiarly German variant of the Enlightenment, the *Aufklärung*, while tending to sustain rather than criticise the role of worldly rulers, at the same time was frequently embedded in the processes of secular rule with quite progressive effects, as implied in the notion of 'enlightened absolutism'.

While the impact on Germany of the French Revolution, through the Napoleonic Wars of expansion, was quite profound, it was by no means simply a catalyst propelling a sleepy Germany rapidly into the modern world of the nineteenth century. There was a dynamism in eighteenth-century Germany which must not be overlooked simply because the pattern was so very different from that of other European states, or because it is viewed, anachronistically, with the assumption that the unified nation state is the ultimate goal of

Plate 16. The Würzburg Residence, designed by Balthasar
Neumann, and mainly built in the period 1720–44.

history. The changes wrought in the late eighteenth and early nineteenth century were partly indigenous developments, deflected and
transmogrified by the impact, in a variety of ways, of the French
invasion and occupation.

ABSOLUTISM AND THE RISE OF PRUSSIA

The Peace of Westphalia in 1648 by no means ended the period of
warfare experienced by the German lands in the seventeenth century.
Wars of one sort or another continued to be fought on German soil in
the latter half of the century, and in the eighteenth. Increasingly, such
conflicts were decoupled from the Empire as such, and individual
territories made alliances or engaged in conflicts with states outside
the Empire, sometimes at odds with other territories within the Empire or with the Emperor. While religion continued to play a role
in political conflicts within territories, it was decreasingly a factor
in inter-state conflicts. Of heightened importance were wars of succession, which embroiled many German aristocratic families, with
their cross-European dynastic connections. Related to economic,
social and cultural, as well as more purely political, consequences

of the Thirty Years War and subsequent warfare were certain developing patterns of rulership within territories. In particular, some rulers made use of the argument that a more or less permanent state of warfare required a standing army, and a means of continuously financing this; and under certain circumstances they were able to achieve political changes serving to centralise their own powers.

To support a standing army, a ruler needed money: he needed an efficient means of raising taxes. If parliaments were unwilling to grant and raise the necessary taxes, they could be circumvented by developing bureaucracies with bodies of officials directly responsible to the ruler. Curiously, while such a process tended to enhance the powers of rulers by making them financially less dependent on co-rulership with estates, it also fostered the early development of more impersonal forms of government, carried by professional bureaucrats who could attempt through their expertise both to influence policy formation and also to ensure continuity across changes of regime. While the process of separating the notion of an impersonal state from the personal patrimony of the ruler was only beginning, however, the heightened importance of rulers' powers – or at least their heightened aspirations and accretions of symbolic power – tended to revolve around the development of a new court culture. The 'age of absolutism' was also the great age of the European courts.

The German territories after 1648 were of course extremely diverse in size and character. Habsburg Austria, with its large number of non-German dynastic territories in addition to its possessions and interests within the Empire, maintained a large court in Vienna. Other German states, such as Protestant Saxony, with its splendid capital in Dresden, or Catholic Bavaria, with its equally splendid capital in Munich, were also able to sustain sizeable courts. Major ecclesiastical territories, such as the larger prince-bishoprics of Mainz or Würzburg, as well as many smaller states, also sought to express and advertise a new-found sense of enhanced status. In the late seventeenth and early eighteenth century, there was considerable building of princely palaces with ornate, carefully designed gardens, often modelled on King Louis XIV's fabled palace at Versailles. Foreign artists and architects, particularly from France and Italy, were brought in to design and construct appropriate settings for the rituals and dramas of court life. Even rulers of tiny territories sought to emulate the great courts. Operas, theatres, masques, ballets, were staged; Italian and other foreign musicians and performers were brought to court; a great variety of people were employed to en-sure the organisation of activities ranging from hunting expeditions to sleigh rides. Aristocrats engaged in intrigues, seeking favour in high places; aspiring commoners attempted to ingratiate themselves and make propitious marriages for their daughters; the notion of 'courteous conduct' (*Höflichkeit*) developed, as an ideal of be-haviour appropriate at court (the *Hof*), widening the gulf in manners and life style between the select elites and the masses of the common people. In the late seventeenth and early eighteenth century it be-came fashionable to adopt French manners and phrases, the French language being viewed as superior to the German. There was in-creasing differentiation between different status groups, evident for example in the many *Kleiderordnungen*, regulations stipulating in precise detail the manner of dress appropriate to each level of the social hierarchy.

The heightened prominence of princes and courts was related to certain socioeconomic developments partially promoted by the Thirty Years War. While certain towns were already declining by the end of the sixteenth century, and others actually improved their po-sition in the first half of the seventeenth century, in general urban life in the later seventeenth century was less prosperous than a century earlier (with some notable exceptions, such as Hamburg). The centre of gravity of European trade had moved westwards, to the Atlantic seaboard, and many German towns were no longer the flourishing, self-confident centres of trade and burgher life that they had been in the earlier sixteenth century. The autonomy and self-government of towns within princely territories (although not the free cities) was more easily reduced by rulers in the later seventeenth century, while some towns were either transformed into, or newly founded as, princely residences, centres of government and administration rather than trade and industry. Similarly, in many areas the landed nobility had seen the ravages of recurrent warfare so reduce its eco-nomic circumstances that it became more dependent on the sup-port and patronage of rulers. Aristocrats were therefore more easily transformed into servants of the developing absolutist state.

The clearest case of the development of absolutism and the enhanced powers of the ruler in an increasingly bureaucratised state – and the most significant case for the subsequent course of German history – was that of Brandenburg-Prussia. Starting from rather unpromising beginnings – with its capital, Berlin, located in the infertile soil of what was known as the 'sand-box of Europe' – this state rose within a few generations to become one of the major European powers. The Hohenzollern dynasty originated in Swabia, and had by a series of haphazard processes and skilful marriage diplomacy over the centuries acquired a diverse set of territories. Its main centre by the seventeenth century was Brandenburg, which gave the rulers the title of 'Elector' of the Holy Roman Empire. The Hohenzollerns also ruled over the old colonial territory of the Teutonic Knights in East Prussia, outside the Holy Roman Empire – an important factor when it came, in 1701, to securing the title of 'king', which was impossible for rulers within the Empire. These eastern territories, however, were also somewhat problematic for rulers in that many of their Slavic subjects neither spoke German, nor shared German Christian and Roman cultural traditions. The Hohenzollerns also possessed certain culturally and economically distinct territories in the Rhenish provinces in the west. Brandenburg-Prussia thus represented not a 'unitary' state (like England) but rather a 'composite' state made up of many very different elements, with different cultural traditions, socioeconomic structures, and political institutions. The economically more prosperous western parts contrasted with the eastern colonial provinces, with their relative paucity of urban life, their impoverished nobility (known as the Prussian *Junkers*), lack of trade and industry, and distance from the main commercial and cultural centres of Europe. The subjects of this composite state professed different religious confessions, with Calvinist rulers recognising an established Lutheran church, while there were Catholic populations in the west, in addition to a number of smaller religious minorities, such as exiled French Huguenots, in the later seventeenth and eighteenth centuries (on which more below). Nor did all subjects speak German: Slavic languages, such as Polish and Lithuanian, predominated in the eastern provinces. From out of this relatively unpromising heritage, Hohenzollern rulers in the seventeenth and eighteenth centuries managed to forge a powerful centralised state, which was to dominate German affairs until its abolition in the aftermath of the Second World War.

To a certain extent, apparent disadvantages were advantages from the point of view of instituting absolutist rule. Weak towns and poor nobles were more easily picked off or co-opted, and resistance to the centralisation of power was less. The Hohenzollern dynasty was also simply lucky during this period in having an unbroken, and uncontested, succession of long-lived male rulers: the 'Great Elector' Frederick William (reigned 1640–88); the Elector Frederick III/King Frederick I (1688–1713, becoming King in 1701); the 'Soldier King' Frederick William I (reigned 1713–40); and 'Frederick the Great', King Frederick II (1740–86). Between them, these rulers built up and then exercised a formidable set of powers.

The foundations for absolutist rule were laid by Elector Frederick William (although he no doubt neither intended nor foresaw subsequent developments). In 1653, he was granted sufficient money by the Brandenburg Estates to maintain a small standing army even in peacetime, in return for recognising the enhanced rights for nobles in their own localities: confirmation of the serf (*leibeigen*) status of peasants, of the rights of nobles to appoint local church pastors, and to police and adjudicate disputes on their own landed estates. Following the War of the North of 1655–60, the foundations were laid for the bureaucracy that was to be extended and improved under the Great Elector's successors. In 1667 taxation was reorganised, such that towns were subjected to an indirect excise tax, while there was a direct 'contribution' tax for the country. This effectively separated the interests of urban burghers and rural nobility, leaving the former without political allies. It also gave the Elector an excuse not to call Diets, allowing representation of the towns to lapse. In the course of the 1670s, the self-government of towns was destroyed, and they were subordinated to a body of officials appointed by, and responsible to, the Elector. At the same time, with the foundation of the elite officer corps of the army, the Elector created a prestigious status group which would attract a previously rather independent set of nobles into central state service. The Elector's own reputation was enhanced following the Prussian victory against the redoubtable Swedes in the battle of Fehrbellin in 1675.

Frederick William's successor, Elector Frederick III (King Frederick I), considerably enhanced the symbolic aspects of power.

In 1701, Frederick crowned himself (literally, placing the crown on his own head without the help of a cleric) 'King *in* Prussia', in Königsberg, which was outside the Holy Roman Empire. The sovereign title could not of course be held in connection with any territories within the Empire; but the Emperor had to allow this coronation outside the Empire in return for Frederick's support of Habsburg policies in the War of the Spanish Succession. (It also reflected the adulation of all things French at the time, including the French exaltation of majesty under Louis XIV; other German rulers similarly attained the status of monarchs, as for example the Saxon Elector becoming King in Poland in 1697, and the ruler of Hanover becoming the British King in 1714.) Frederick I also built up court culture, with considerable building of princely palaces, largely under the guidance of the architect Andreas Schlüter (who was also responsible for a famous equestrian statue of the Great Elector). The army was nevertheless not neglected, and in fact increased rapidly in strength in the 1700s, because of the Prussian contingents fighting in the War of Spanish Succession.

Frederick I's son, the 'Soldier King' Frederick William I, despised what he considered to be the frivolity and luxury of his father's court, and turned his attention rather to building up the army and bureaucracy. A fanatic in military matters, Frederick William I sought out tall men for his prize troop of 'giant soldiers'; since contemporaries tended to laugh at this, it enabled him to build up an army almost unnoticed. In 1733, the canton system for the organisation of peasants for military training and service was finalised and made uniform, compromising between the needs of agriculture and the needs of the army, and enabling Brandenburg-Prussia to have a formidable army and a trained reserve without the expense involved in maintaining a standing army. Between a half and two-thirds of the nobility were either active or retired army officers, except in the western provinces. By the end of Frederick William's reign in 1740, perhaps 80 per cent of state revenues were spent on the army in peacetime; in the later eighteenth century, the joke was current that Prussia was not a country with an army, but rather an army with a country. At the same time, Frederick William I reorganised and built up the state administrative apparatus. The already existing General War Commissary and General Finance Directory were combined in 1723 to form the General Directory (or, to give it its magnificent full title, possible

Plate 17. Recruitment of soldiers in the early eighteenth century.

only in German, the *General-Ober-Finanz-Kriegs-und-Domänen-Direktorium*). This was refined and extended by Frederick II, who added specialised ministries and provincial chambers. The General Directory added a practical dimension to the theoretical unity of the state which had been declared in 1713, when Frederick William I pronounced his lands to be indivisible, in contrast to the Great Elector's willingness to see his lands divided among different heirs after his death. Both Frederick William I and Frederick II adopted measures to ensure the loyalty of state officials at a time when the local powers of the landed nobility were great and their reliability as servants of the crown uncertain. Frederick William I stressed the importance of rewarding merit, with commoners able to achieve noble rank by state service; he also proposed low basic salaries, with rewards for good service; and he was adamant that important nobles were under no circumstances to become officials in their own localities, where they could sustain potentially centrifugal local power bases, but rather must serve the monarch in other provinces far from home. This effectively broke the 'right of the native born' (*Jus Indignatsrecht*) which had greatly vexed the Greater Elector. Under Frederick II, Junkers continued to possess considerable powers on their own estates, and were able, for example, to thwart the king's attempts at agrarian reform; but through the office of *Landrat*, for instance, they operated as intermediaries between the crown and locality, with control of local military administration. The autonomy of urban local government was effectively abolished with the introduction of the office of *Steuerrat*.

The efficiency of this bureaucratic and military organisation should not be exaggerated. Frederick II had to rely on a second set of officials – a band of royal spies – to keep an eye on and report back on the conduct of local commissaries. He also had to devote a considerable amount of his own (not inconsiderable) energy to long and arduous journeys travelling around his far-flung domains on horseback. The length of journeys, plodding along muddy roadways, and the difficulties of communication in an age before modern media, should not be forgotten. The obstacles in the way of establishing impersonal forms of government when so much still depended on the person of the monarch must be continuously borne in mind. Even in his own lifetime, Frederick II became something of a legend, portrayed as a benevolent father-figure and popular ruler who would not hesitate to pause on his journeys to speak to peasants digging potatoes. It should perhaps be noted that the latter, the peasants, were in no position to offer any serious resistance to the claims and demands of centralised rulership, given the weak and oppressed position of peasants in the system of *Gutsherrschaft* (in which noble landlords had considerable political and legal rights over their unfree peasants) prevalent east of the river Elbe.

Thus a combination of relatively weak towns, an economically impoverished nobility, and an oppressed and servile peasantry permitted successive rulers of Brandenburg-Prussia to re-organise the administration of their diverse, territorially scattered possessions, with a progressive centralisation of power. They also – particularly under Frederick I and Frederick William I – made use of a heterodox religious movement, Pietism (on which more in a moment) to centralise ideological loyalty. Pietism was sponsored to become a form of state religion, effectively displacing the entrenched Lutheran orthodoxy which tended to sustain the local power bases of the provincial nobles on whom they were dependent for patronage.

Despite such developments, contemporaries still laughed at Frederick William I's obsession with his giant soldiers, and by 1740 Prussia was still an economically backward country, whose power

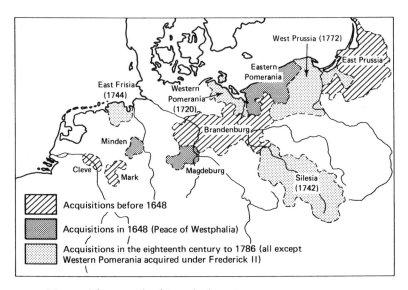

Map 5. The growth of Brandenburg-Prussia to 1786. (Danzig only became Prussian in 1793.)

could scarcely be compared with that of the established major European states, England, France or Austria. This was to change dramatically in the reign of Frederick II, who lost no time in making use of his military heritage and launching into international power politics. In 1740, Prussia invaded the Habsburg province of Silesia, and emerged from the confused War of the Austrian Succession (1740–8) in possession of this new territory. In the Seven Years War (1756–63) Frederick II was forced to defend his gain against a powerful coalition of Austria, France and Russia, directed from Vienna. His success in beating off this attack and in emerging in secure possession of Silesia established Prussia as a major European power and as at least the equal of Austria in Germany. Austrian–Prussian rivalry from this point on became a major factor in German affairs, as the era of 'dualism' opened. During the second half of Frederick II's reign Prussia was widely regarded as the leading continental state, with its formidable army, efficient administration and dynamic king. This status was apparent in Prussia's role in the first partition of Poland. Frederick II was the architect of a tripartite seizure of territory from defenceless Poland. Prussia, Austria and

Russia each acquired large tracts of Polish territory, with Frederick securing the key acquisition of Polish Prussia (later West Prussia) and thereby uniting Electoral Brandenburg with the distant Kingdom of East Prussia. This was the crucial territorial gain of Frederick II's reign, creating as it did a swathe of Hohenzollern territory stretching across central and northern Germany. Agreements within the Empire proved more difficult, particularly in connection with certain succession disputes in southern Germany. Joseph II, Emperor after 1765, had been harbouring certain designs in connection with acquiring parts of southern Germany, including a scheme for exchanging the Austrian Netherlands for the whole of Bavaria. Against this, in 1785 Frederick II constructed the League of Princes, which included the Elector of Saxony, the Archbishop of Mainz, and George III of England in his capacity as the Elector of Hanover. By the later eighteenth century, it was clear that there were now two contenders for domination of German affairs: Prussia had risen to become a powerful rival for Austria. It should be noted, however, that at this stage there was still no thought of a unified nation state: this was a concept of the future, a phenomenon of the nineteenth century.

The astonishing rise of Prussia, and the label given to this period as the 'age of absolutism', should not obliterate from view the diversity of developments in other German territories, where conditions varied tremendously. In western areas, towns were both more numerous and often more prosperous, and the peasantry lived in freer conditions under the system of *Grundherrschaft* which predominated west of the Elbe. In areas of partible inheritance, with farms being divided among a number of sons, many peasants had to ply a trade or a craft to supplement their agricultural production. While in some areas farms were large and prosperous – as is evident in the still-surviving magnificent farmhouses – in others plots of land could barely sustain a few pigs and chickens. Aristocrats ranged from important nobles to impoverished knights barely distinguishable from more affluent peasants. Political traditions varied widely, too. Some free cities, such as the former Hanse town of Hamburg, retained oligarchic traditions of urban government, in which the Senate, in conjunction with the *Bürgerschaft* and Civic Colleges, hammered out compromises in their administration of civic affairs. Small groups of notables (*Honoratioren*) generally dominated affairs

Plate 18. Nuremberg in 1774.

in urban government. The degree to which rulers in different principalities succeeded in imposing their own wills against those of
existing elites varied widely too, whether or not representative institutions fell into disuse.

A notable illustration of variety in eighteenth-century Germany is
given by the Duchy of Württemberg, in which estates were able to resist the attempts of dukes in the later seventeenth and eighteenth centuries to establish a standing army and attain financial independence.
Württemberg exceptionally succeeded in retaining a functioning parliamentary tradition right up to the formation of modern Germany
in the nineteenth century, and was often compared to England in
this respect. There were a number of reasons for the failure of
successive rulers to establish absolutist rule in Württemberg. For
one thing, the nobility had opted out of the duchy in 1514 (prefer-
ring to be independent imperial knights), thus removing a potential

aristocratic support stratum for the ruler. For another, there was an intermingling of rural and urban interests, with a relatively independent peasantry combining agricultural and artisanal occupations and having a long tradition of local autonomy evident in such phenomena as village courts. In contrast to Brandenburg-Prussia, Württemberg was a small, compact state with a single Diet or estates, in which the church and rural and urban representatives sat together. There was also a strong sense of identity in protecting the 'good old law' and also the Lutheran church tradition, particularly after the dukes converted to Catholicism in the eighteenth century. Moreover, the church had managed to retain a considerable proportion of its wealth after the Reformation, owning perhaps one-third of the Duchy. Correspondingly, the rulers had failed to benefit either financially or politically, being unable to dominate what was neither economically nor politically a dependent religious institution and clerical profession. Under these circumstances, it is scarcely surprising that more successful resistance to projects of absolutist rule could be mounted in Württemberg than in Prussia. Nevertheless, it still required the backing of foreign powers and a resolution of disputes at the Imperial level to achieve a more or less final confirmation of the rights of the estates vis-à-vis the ruler in the *Erbvergleich* of 1770.

In other territories, while estates were less successful in retaining their co-rulership functions, 'absolutist rule' yet remained far from absolute in practice. Everywhere, rulers had to contend with a range of competing interests, and work with and through different socioeconomic and professional groups (such as the clergy), in different configurations and circumstances. Often their real capacities for policy formation and implementation were actually quite restricted. The efflorescence of court culture in some instances represented virtually the only arena genuinely under the ruler's control, with policies in other spheres frequently deflected by interested parties. On the other hand, the lack of pressures in international power-political games could mean that smaller German states were able to devote relatively more attention and resources to domestic matters. There was an enormous variability among eighteenth-century German states, courts, and rulers, sometimes because of social, political and economic circumstances, sometimes because of personality

differences between rulers. The other medium-sized German territories which emerged relatively strong after the Thirty Years War,
Saxony and Bavaria, failed to achieve the phenomenal subsequent
expansion and successes of eighteenth-century Prussia. The differences in outcome between the political histories of these three states
are complex: there were similarities and differences in social structure, in patterns of economic rehabilitation after the devastations of
the war, in forms of administration, and in relations between estates
and rulers. Undoubtedly also there were key differences in the aspirations and aptitudes of the rulers, their capacities for creating and
seizing opportunities, and operating within given constraints. Moreover, the rise of Prussian military power was unique. Although many
rulers liked to have a troop of soldiers which they could proudly
display, and march up and down, and some – like the Hessian 'mercenary state', which sent many soldiers to death in the American
Revolution – indulged in mercenary military activities, the wider
protection of the Empire rendered serious military expenditure and
endeavours unnecessary for most German states.

RELIGION, CULTURE AND ENLIGHTENMENT

During the period from 1648 to 1815, long slow sea-changes were
taking place in German society and culture which were to be of
enduring importance. Not only was a military, independent, feudal
nobility being converted into a court-oriented (if still military) aristocracy; there was also the growth of a new, educated middle class,
frequently occupying positions as civil servants and minor court officials. Education and literacy were spreading, the reading public was
expanding, new modes of thinking and inquiry were being explored.
The place of Christianity in social and political life was changing:
no longer an issue over which to wage war, theology also began to
lose its intellectual pride of place; the Scriptures were historicised,
their absolute authority questioned. At the same time as the rise of
new religious currents focusing more on the inner life, there was also
the development of a practical rationalism, with changing views of
the natural world and human society. For all the platitudes about the
apolitical German, the German Enlightenment had quite pragmatic
consequences in local administration. In the later eighteenth century,

Plate 19. The altar in the monastery of Benediktbeuern, southern Bavaria.

Germany experienced an astonishing literary revival, with the rebirth of German as a literary language and vehicle of profound expression. The eighteenth century also witnessed some of Germany's greatest contributions to classical music. Whether or not one wants to assent to the notion of eighteenth-century Germany as a political backwater, it was certainly one in which important cultural currents were flowing, partly promoted and fostered by peculiarly German social and political circumstances.

The late seventeenth century saw the flowering of German baroque, particularly in the southern Catholic states, with their majestic baroque churches and monasteries symbolising the spiritual and worldly powers of the church. Italian influences were often important, as in the design of Munich's Theatinerkirche. The links with courtly culture were also evident, giving way in the course of the eighteenth century to the lighter, more secular rococo style. Lutheran orthodoxy tended rather to a subdued scholasticism in the period after the Thirty Years War, with little of the elaborate sensuous expression of Catholicism.

There were counter-currents to both Protestant and Catholic orthodoxies in the later seventeenth and eighteenth centuries. The Catholic reforming movement of Jansenism attempted to purify Catholicism from what it saw as 'superstitious' elements, although with little long-term success (much-criticised cults of images continued well into the twentieth century, particularly in rural areas). There was also something of a 'Catholic Enlightenment', partly arising in opposition to perceived excessive Jesuit influence. Within Protestantism, many individuals heeded the call of Philipp Jakob Spener for a renewal of direct religious experience, an unmediated relationship between the individual and God, expressed in an active Christian life based on personal understanding of the Scriptures. Pietists stressed the need for a completion of the Reformation, which they felt had stopped short at the level of theology with little impact on life. They emphasised the importance of personal experience of conversion and rebirth to lead a new life of active Christianity. Small groups met together in 'conventicles' to read the Bible, pray, and share their experiences of attempting to lead the godly life.

While Pietists were persecuted and expelled from some areas, such as Hamburg and Saxony, they were able to find a niche in others, largely explicable in terms of different state–church–society relations in different German territories. In Württemberg, the relatively secure established Lutheran church was able to tolerate and incorporate the Pietist impulse, which subsequently influenced generations of students in Tübingen, including such notables as Georg Wilhelm Friedrich Hegel (1770–1831) and Friedrich Schiller (1759–1805). In Prussia, as we have seen, Pietism was sponsored by the state against an entrenched and insecure Lutheran provincial orthodoxy. Through the proliferation particularly of Pietist educational institutions, starting with August Hermann Francke's renowned orphanage and schools in Halle, as well as Pietist influence at the newly founded University of Halle (1694) and later at Königsberg and elsewhere, Pietism had a major long-term impact. Its influence, although hard to evaluate precisely, was widespread and diverse. Many scholars have seen important German cultural developments, such as the focus on inner experience and individual development evident in *Empfindsamkeit* (sensibility) and the bourgeois *Bildungsroman* (novel focusing on self-development and education), as having their roots in Pietism. Others have stressed continuities between Pietism and later, secularised, cultural nationalism – as in Johann Gottfried Herder (1744–1803) – and patriotism. The by-passing of pastor and institutional church, and the meeting for discussion of one's own reading and understanding of the Bible, undoubtedly also contributed to the development of a new confidence in reason and a new meritocracy, irrespective of rank and birth, in eighteenth-century German society. Practical emphases and a belief in the promotion of talent were carried over into the expanding system of primary and secondary education particularly in Prussia, although the aim was by no means to overturn the social hierarchy. Whether Pietism contributed also to a supposed restriction of focus to the inner life at the expense of politics is a far more dubious matter. The degree to which individuals essentially concerned with religious affairs also became embroiled in secular politics varied with both circumstances and personality. Few could accuse August Hermann Francke of lack of political energy.

While some German states continued to be intolerant with respect to religious minorities, in others there was a slow development of at least limited forms of toleration, having more to do with economic and social considerations than any intellectual conviction about the moral rectitude of tolerance. Prussia, concerned with repopulation and economic regeneration after the Thirty Years War, welcomed useful religious minorities such as exiled French Huguenots after the revocation of the Edict of Nantes in 1685. Of around 300,000 who were expelled, perhaps 20,000 settled in Brandenburg-Prussia, leaving a lasting French influence in Berlin. In 1731, around 20,000 Protestants from Salzburg fled north, and other minorities, such as Mennonites, and Zinzendorf's Brüdergemeine, found homes in Prussia. Prussia was in any case a state containing a multiplicity of confessions, and its Calvinist rulers had a personal interest in religious toleration, working as they did with an established Lutheran state church.

The place of Jews was also changing in eighteenth-century Germany. Since the middle ages Jews, who had no religious prohibition on usury, had acted as commercial middle-men and providers of credit. They had been concentrated in a restricted number of ghettoes, the largest being in Frankfurt. With their distinctive styles of dress and appearance, their different religious beliefs and practices, as well as their unique and easily disliked economic role, Jews had long been a target for vicious anti-semitism. The myth had grown up of Jewish ritual murder of young boys, based on the story of the death of Simon of Trent in 1476; this myth had given rise to many 'revenge' attacks on Jews in the sixteenth century, as well as being engraved in stone on a gateway into Frankfurt as a warning to future generations. In the course of the eighteenth century, Jews began to adopt new roles, and gain a new status and slightly improved conditions in some areas of German life. The rising absolutist states found uses for Jewish capital and financial experience, particularly as rulers took a new interest in state direction and administration of economic affairs. Many Jewish families became prominent in both productive enterprises and banking. There were also individual 'court Jews', acting in all sorts of ways for their princes. One of these was Süss Oppenheimer, under Duke Karl Alexander of Württemberg, who subsequently was the subject of a rabidly anti-semitic film produced by the Nazis, *Jud Süss*. Most Jews occupied less elevated positions as small tradesmen and merchants. Their legal status varied, but in some areas was improving. In Austria, Joseph II's 1781 Edict of Toleration gave most non-Catholics the right of private exercise of religion. A series of Patents for individual provinces in 1782–3 effected a measure of Jewish emancipation, so that, for example, Jews were now allowed to settle anywhere in Vienna (and were not limited to their ghetto), although their numbers were restricted and they were not allowed to build a synagogue. Fiscal exploitation of Jews continued, although certain humiliating compulsory practices, such as the wearing of yellow armbands, were abolished. In Prussia, while Jews only achieved complete legal equality in 1811–12, they gained more limited privileges in the course of the eighteenth century. The first Jewish school was founded in Berlin in 1778, and

Jewish periodicals were founded alongside the wider expansion of newspaper and periodical production in Germany. Jews played a role in the Enlightenment, as typified by Moses Mendelssohn, who formed the subject for Lessing's play *Nathan der Weise*, itself a plea for religious toleration.

The German variant of the Enlightenment, the *Aufklärung*, arose somewhat later than the English and French Enlightenments and had its own distinctive emphases. At the end of the seventeenth and in the early eighteenth century there was a Europe-wide ferment in thought: a new cultural relativism and a new rationalism began to take precedence over revelation as the basis for authority. While there were a wide variety of answers to the great questions of the day – the problems of human suffering, the nature of good and evil, the explanation of the newly discovered variety of cultures and human beliefs, the best organisation of state and society, the possibilities of education and social engineering – Enlightenment thinkers had in common the use of critical reason as a means of questioning, analysing, exploring. English thinkers such as Francis Bacon had contributed the experimental method, while Isaac Newton explored the laws of the universe to the greater glory of God, and John Locke made important contributions to early social and political science. French philosophers such as Montesquieu, Voltaire, Diderot, d'Alembert and Rousseau all made their varied, frequently brilliant, contributions to what was a generally rather materialist, anti-clericalist, sometimes republican form of Enlightenment. In its different social and political context, the German *Aufklärung* remained more compatible with established religion and established authoritarian forms of rulership.

Although the main impact of the Enlightenment was not experienced in Germany until the middle of the eighteenth century and after, early German Enlightenment thinkers included Gottfried Wilhelm Leibniz (1646–1716), who still adhered to certain metaphysical beliefs, as well as Samuel von Pufendorf (1632–94), Christian Thomasius (1655–1728) and Christian Wolff (1679–1754). The University of Halle was curiously a centre of both Pietism and the Enlightenment, at times in acerbic competition rather than peaceful co-existence, with one or the other in ascendancy or defensive flight. The rationalism of Halle's Christian Wolff influenced generations of students, and the Enlightenment also had an impact on the development of eighteenth-century education comparable to that of Pietism.

More generally, new modes of thinking, informing oneself and discussing, spread widely in the context of an expanding reading public in the course of the eighteenth century. Books published in Latin, which were accessible only to a minority of the population, declined from about a half of all books published in the later seventeenth century to a mere 5 per cent of books published at the end of the eighteenth century. Publishers such as Nicolai attempted to have a wider, pervasive influence through the sponsored spread of Enlightenment ideas. Along with the increasing numbers of books published in German, there was a veritable explosion in the production of newspapers, magazines and periodicals of all sorts. Many were specifically directed towards, or read by, people previously excluded from literate discussion: women and younger girls now found a developing literature, as did the bourgeoisie more generally in, for example, novels about personal development. New organisations for discussion were founded: scientific societies, professional organisations, political societies, freemasons' lodges (starting with Hamburg in 1737), offered libraries and debating rooms, and promoted the circulation of news and views. A number of new universities were founded in the course of the eighteenth century, such as Göttingen in 1737. In later eighteenth-century Berlin, 'salons' became popular, frequently run by women, many of them Jewish.

Many people participating in Enlightenment thought and discussion were minor civil servants, officials in the small German states. They were concerned with practical issues of law, justice, punishment, the economy, efficient administration, and social relations in a 'well-ordered police state'. Some of them attempted to put Enlightenment ideas into practice, with policy reforms in different areas achieving greater or lesser degrees of success. In 1737, for example, Johann Jakob Moser started to publish his monumental fifty-one volumes on German law, and pursued the goal of reform with considerable vigour. The *Pietistenreskript* in Württemberg, officially according toleration to Pietists, was a result partly of the Enlightenment thinking of Bilfinger. At the same time as reforms were being instigated by secular administrations, many pastors also felt that religion should involve a practical piety, helping mankind, and far from being in opposition to the Enlightenment also sought to pursue the cause of reform.

There has been some debate about the concept of 'enlightened absolutism', which after a fall from favour has been making a re-appearance in history books. It is clear that some rulers were quite consciously influenced by Enlightenment ideas. Frederick II of Prussia, for example, was extremely interested in all things French, and had engaged in correspondence with Voltaire while still Crown Prince. On ascending the throne, Frederick II invited Voltaire to the Prussian court, and was himself known as 'the philosopher of Sans-Souci' (the latter being the name of his palace in Potsdam, near Berlin). The reforms of Maria Theresa and Joseph II of Austria must also be seen in the wider context of the Enlightenment. Often, however, the impetus for policies had less to do with the impact of philosophical ideas than with certain more immediate economic, social or military and political objectives, and while the interplay between diverse currents of Enlightenment thinking and aspects of absolutist (or would-be absolutist) rule are interesting to explore, there is no necessary connection between the two. Curiously, another generalisation that has come down about the German Enlightenment in particular is that it was essentially apolitical in implication, separating freedom in the sphere of thought and the spirit from obedience to worldly authority. This picture is actually not quite at such odds with the picture of political and social re-forming impulses which has just been sketched as might be thought. The enlightened civil servants and pastors did not question the au-thority of their princes because in many cases they did not have to; they sought to effect improvements in administration through good government under enlightened rulers. Needless to say, not all rulers rose above the level of petty despotism; but in the main, the German Enlightenment in the context of *Kleinstaaterei* could be carried by state-dependent, state-sustaining, professional classes, rather than independent critical intellectuals as in France.

Perhaps the greatest German Enlightenment thinker, Immanuel Kant (1724–1804) is the source of some of the most common gen-eralisations about the politics of the German Enlightenment. In his essay on 'What is Enlightenment?' Kant defined Enlightenment as the courage to use one's reason to think independently and critically, refusing to accept the tutelage of another's authority. Yet he was quite clear that Germans lived in an 'age of enlightenment' in which such a process was just taking place, and not an already enlightened age in which people would be mature enough to be capable of governing themselves. (In the process he had some quite derogatory comments to make about the capacity to reason of women in particular.) In the meantime, it was necessary to have strong rulers who could guarantee political stability and the ordered circumstances in which alone thinking could take place. One could not question as freely in a republic, because it would not be able to guarantee the political order of a state such as Frederick II's Prussia. Whatever the diverse subsequent interpretations of this somewhat ambiguous essay, as well as the alternative views propounded by other thinkers, the separation of power and spirit, the dualistic tradition of *Macht* and *Geist*, has been popularised as one of the enduring features of subsequent German thought (with its origins already in Lutheran theology).

There were of course other aspects to the German Enlightenment: advances in jurisprudence, in natural science, and in other subjects. Kant's epistemology, for example, has been of enduring importance: against naive empiricist views, Kant stressed that one could not 'know' reality except through human perceptions and externally imposed categories. Subsequent neo-Kantians have pointed out that such categories are not universal products of the human mind, but rather culturally relative. Kant also developed important ideas about universal morality, peace, and world citizenship. Along with Hegel, who developed a wide-ranging idealist interpretation of history, law and a great deal else, Kant ranks as one of the founders of the modern German philosophical tradition.

The latter half of the eighteenth century saw cultural currents partly parallel to, partly overlapping, partly arising from and partly in revolt against, the Enlightenment. The German literary revival of the later eighteenth century was of international and enduring cultural importance. Its greatest figure was undoubtedly Johann Wolfgang von Goethe (1749–1832), who along with contemporaries such as Schiller (1759–1805) revealed the possibilities in the previously denigrated German language for the most elevated forms of expression. Goethe's early poetry with its range over the emotions of love, responses to nature, and the fundamental questions of human existence is arguably without parallel in any language. Developing from an early period of 'Storm and Stress' (*Sturm und Drang*, a phrase taken from a play by now largely forgotten authors), through to his later classicism Goethe's career in all its manifold expressions – not only poetry, but also plays, novels, essays, an autobiography – to some extent encapsulates the development of German literature more generally at the time. While individual genius defies reduction to circumstances, it must be noted that the granting of minor posts at court, and the sponsorship of theatrical and literary production by small courts – particularly in Goethe's Weimar – undoubtedly facilitated the remarkable literary efflorescence of the later eighteenth century.

At the same time, there was the emergence of a form of 'cultural nationalism', associated particularly with the name of Johann Gottfried Herder. Reacting against the earlier predominance of French language and culture, Herder stressed the notion of a cultural community, a *Volk* (not co-terminous with the political unit, the state). He suggested that each culture must be viewed as an organic whole, valid in its own terms. This permitted a certain patriotic pride in Germanic culture. Rejecting the Enlightenment revulsion against the middle ages, there was a renewed interest in history, and particularly the history of the people. This was to lead to Romanticism, and into the nineteenth-century interest in folk tales, as with the brothers Grimm. It also was eventually to develop into the notion that the cultural nation (the *Volk*) and the political unit (the state) should indeed be co-terminous. Yet it took a considerable time before this connection was finally made, with all the consequences it ultimately brought in the more virulent forms of later German nationalism.

In another area, too, German culture in the eighteenth century produced achievements of enduring significance. Merely to mention the names of composers in eighteenth-century Germany is almost to summarise the history of that century's classical music *per se*: Johann Sebastian Bach (1685–1750); Bach's sons, particularly Carl Philipp Emanuel Bach (1714–88); Joseph Haydn (1732–1809); Wolfgang Amadeus Mozart (1756–91); and, entering a new historical period, Ludwig van Beethoven (1770–1827). While Händel settled in England (losing his umlaut in the process), and Haydn, Mozart and Beethoven were largely based in Catholic Vienna, Johann Sebastian

Bach represents the heights of north German Protestant musical expression. From 1723, he was cantor at the Thomas Church, Leipzig, where he wrote weekly cantatas for the Sunday service. It is extraordinary, given the relatively mundane nature of this task, that so many of the over two hundred cantatas that he wrote should have been of such quality. But Bach is most remarkable for the mathematical beauty and religious emotion of his great works: the Mass in B Minor, the St Matthew Passion, the Brandenburg Concertos, the Christmas and Easter Oratorios, and his sonatas for violin and cello, as well as the sheer technical virtuosity of his organ preludes and fugues. As with the genius of Goethe, the genius of Bach defies reduction, whatever may be said about the traditions on which he built and the circumstances in which he worked.

By the end of the eighteenth century, Germany was established as the *Land der Dichter und Denker* ('land of poets and philosophers') for which German culture is still renowned. New currents were developing – baroque and rococo giving way to the Empire style, Romanticism displacing Enlightenment – but the political framework remained that of a mediaeval patchwork, for all the internal reforms within states. The major impetus for political transformation came not from within, but from without: it came from the impact of the French Revolution.

THE IMPACT OF THE FRENCH REVOLUTION

As we have seen, there were reforming movements within eighteenth-century German states. In Frederick II's Prussia and Joseph II's Austria a number of projects were underway to attempt to modernise their administration and improve their economies. The relationships between absolutism and Enlightenment may have been tangential and changing; but rulers and bureaucrats were engaged in examining and implementing means of improving territorial government. In Prussia, there were measures such as the *Generalland-schulreglement* attempting to implement a uniform national system of primary schooling in 1763, the *Landratsreform* of 1766, the administrative reform of 1770, the customs and excise reform of 1766, the limited agrarian reforms of 1765–70, as well as the codification of general Prussian law which was revived in 1780 and published in its final form in 1794, firmly establishing the tradition of Prussia's being a *Rechtsstaat*. The army alone remained exempted from reforming impulses after 1763. In Austria under Joseph II there were comparable reforming impulses, particularly in connection with Joseph's attempts at reforms of the church and agrarian reform. In both Prussia and Austria, serious problems arose in the course of these measures, in that they were often imposed with little sense of a need for some measure of support; and often bureaucrats, who were more aware of social realities than their rulers, had to circumvent and even hoodwink the monarch in order to implement alternative strategies. Whatever their respective achievements in power, both Frederick II and Joseph II left ambiguous legacies in the wake of their semi-despotic, semi-bureaucratic, semi-absolutist, semi-enlightened forms of rulership. The separation between state and society was perhaps less great in some of the smaller German states, where rulers did not have to contend with large, scattered, multinational and multilingual populations (as were those of the Habsburg monarchy and, to a slightly lesser degree, Brandenburg-Prussia), but rather with more easily manageable and homogenous populations. In smaller states, reforms could in any case be less oriented towards military power and state-building, and more towards improving the living standards of the people.

There were also attempts to reform the Empire itself. Prussia's apparent disregard for certain constitutional provisions of the Empire, embodied in the Peace of Westphalia, contributed to a widespread sense that the Empire itself was in need of change; at the same time, the rise of Prussia as a challenger to Austria and potential ally of other European powers led some of the smaller and medium-sized German states to consider means of co-operating together as a form of third, counter-balancing power. There were active moves to reform the Empire in the course of the 1780s; however, these attempts had largely foundered by the start of the 1790s. The moves by the smaller states to form a 'Third Germany' (as it was later called) were frustrated by the manner in which Prussia dominated the League of Princes and simultaneously disregarded Imperial interests in favour of its own power-political designs (as in the case of Belgium); and attempts at church reform collided with Joseph II's religious reforms, as well as provoking considerable hostility in Rome. The Empire was not irretrievably moribund by the beginning of the 1790s, but it was certainly somewhat in disarray.

There was not, however, anything approaching a revolutionary situation in Germany at the start of the 1790s. It is true that there were certain social tensions (as always, but in changed forms, with harbingers of early nineteenth-century problems). The population was beginning to expand, partly perhaps as a result of agrarian reforms, partly for other reasons. Population expansion on the land was associated with increasing numbers of paupers and beggars, and periodic social unrest. There were also some intellectual grumblings of discontent, with the beginnings of a barely political liberalism evident from the 1770s. But on the whole, when the French Revolution broke out in 1789 the majority of Germans were at first content to observe it with interest – particularly in the western provinces – combined with a sense of superiority that Germany had not needed a revolution in order to achieve reforms. From 1792, with the beginning of a war between revolutionary France and the established powers of Prussia and Austria, such distanced and often sympathetic interest became increasingly difficult. As the French Revolution turned from an idealist declaration of freedom, equality and fraternity into a regime of terror and an expansionist, imperialist dictatorship, Germany was embroiled and affected in a variety of ways. Attacked, overrun, occupied, reorganised, exploited, provoked, shaken up, by 1815 Germany emerged in very different shape; and the Holy Roman Empire, which had served as its loose political framework for so many centuries, had gone. The new settlement for Europe produced by the Congress of Vienna in 1814–15, which replaced the 1648 Peace of Westphalia, was to inaugurate a very different period in Germany's history.

In 1792 French armies invaded the territories of the Holy Roman Empire. After a succession of easy French victories, by the end of 1794 all of Germany west of the Rhine was under French rule, a situation which lasted until 1814. Although a few historians (particularly East German) have scoured the archives for evidence of German Jacobins, and others (mainly westerners) have searched for early democrats or German nationalists, in the main it seems that most German subjects simply allowed themselves to be obediently incorporated into new regimes, with the somewhat untypical exception of a more or less quisling republic in Mainz under Georg Forster. The French occupation had long-lasting consequences in these areas. Administrative, judicial and legal systems were reorganised; serfdom and feudal social relations were abolished; and the bone of contention between France and Germany, over the question of whether the Rhine was 'France's frontier' or 'Germany's stream', was given considerable flesh. Disputes between France and Germany over the Saar, and Alsace and Lorraine, were to reappear and dog Franco-German relations over the next century and a half.

The small and medium-sized territories in southern and western Germany were subjected to considerable territorial reorganisation after the cession of the left bank of the Rhine was confirmed in the Treaty of Lunéville in 1801, partly on the principle that they should be compensated for losses within the Empire. In 1803, a committee of the Empire concluded the so-called *Reichsdeputations-hauptschluss*, in which a large number of previously independent small political units were abolished or subordinated to larger rulers. Thus around 350 free Imperial knights and counts lost their independence and 'unmediated' status below the Emperor, and were subordinated instead to territorial rulers. Around 112 political units were abolished, including twenty archbishoprics and prince-bishoprics, forty abbeys and convents, and all except six of the free cities. Many territorial rulers not surprisingly rather welcomed the additions to the size and status of their states, choosing to ignore Napoleon's wider aims of achieving a colonial status for their parts of Germany. With vast areas of Europe at his feet, Napoleon had himself crowned emperor in the autumn of 1804. Francis II of Austria chose at the same time to take on the title of Emperor of Austria. Under these circumstances, the smaller German states who had benefited from Napoleonic reforms chose to secede from the Holy Roman Empire and put themselves under the protection of France. In July 1806, Napoleon created the Confederation of the Rhine (*Rheinbund*), consisting of sixteen German states (including Bavaria, Württemberg, Baden and Hesse-Darmstadt) as well as the Grand Duchy of Warsaw (which lay outside the Holy Roman Empire). The Confederation adopted the Napoleonic Code and instituted a range of reforms including the abolition of serfdom. On 6 August 1806 the by now essentially meaningless Holy Roman Empire was formally abolished.

Plate 20. The battle of Jena, 1806.

Prussia had remained neutral since 1795. In September 1806, however, King Frederick William III (1797–1840) rather unwisely decided on war with France. The Prussian army, which by the later eighteenth century, after decades of non-reform, had fallen into a state of indiscipline and ill-preparedness, suffered a major military defeat against the then powerful French army in the Battle of Jena on 14 October 1806. In the 1807 Peace of Tilsit Prussia lost all territories west of the Elbe to France, as well as some eastern territories. Prussia also had to pay indemnities, and to make contributions of men and money to Napoleon's further campaigns. This defeat provided both the opportunity and the impetus for a series of reforms in Prussia.

The Prussian reforms neither amounted to a single coherent programme, nor were carried by a close-knit, homogenous group of reformers. (Indeed, two of the main reformers, often linguistically linked by a hyphen in the misleading phrase 'Stein-Hardenberg reforms', personally detested each other.) A minority of reformers exploited the situation after the Prussian defeat to effect certain previous plans for reform, while other measures were taken as a form of 'defensive modernisation' or specifically to deal with current exigencies, particularly in connection with economic and military affairs.

In 1807, serfdom was abolished. Since peasants frequently could not meet the compensation payments, their formal freedom in practice meant little. The main beneficiaries were in fact the nobles (and the legislation was in any case later modified by regulations unfavourable to the peasantry). Restrictions imposed by the notion of 'estates' as status groups defined by birth, rather than social classes, were lifted, so that nobles could now engage in middle-class occupations, while peasants and burghers could (at least in theory) buy noble lands. This transformation from a status to a class society created a potential mobility of labour, which formed a precondition for later capitalist economic development. Also important in relation to later economic growth were the abolition of the restrictive powers of the guilds, and of certain internal barriers to trade, including the urban excise tax. However, economic reforms were at this time only partial, and some measures were later reversed; noble tax exemption, for example, was abolished in 1810 but restored in 1819. Moreover, Prussian nobles retained civil jurisdiction over their former serfs until 1848, their police powers until 1872, and certain administrative powers until 1891. In the political arena, there was a certain modernisation of Prussian government, with a more streamlined system of ministries and cabinet, but as yet neither a constitution nor an all-Prussian parliament. Municipal self-government for towns was introduced, but not rural self-government. Army reforms, associated with the names of Scharnhorst, Gneisenau and Clausewitz, were carried out largely in response to the shock of French military success. In 1813 conscription was introduced, and a militia (*Landwehr*) established; and in 1814 an Army Law was passed. Again, reforms were not necessarily complete; after 1815, conscription was in practice not universal. In the sphere of education, the spread of compulsory basic schooling in the eighteenth century (which had accompanied the expansion of technically orientated secondary schools as well as aristocratic *Ritterakadamien*) was supplemented by the introduction of elite secondary schools – *Gymnasia* – across Prussia, and the establishment, under Humboldt, of a university in Berlin. The Prussian education system was to produce major achievements in the course of the nineteenth century, ranging from advances at the forefront of research through to the efficient training of one of the best-educated work-forces in industrialising Europe. Whatever the limitations, patchiness, and lack of overall coherence of the

Prussian reforms of this period, Prussia in general certainly emerged somewhat better equipped to meet the challenges of the nineteenth century.

Meanwhile, the Napoleonic Wars continued. An Austrian attempt to challenge Napoleon was defeated in 1809. But in 1812 an over-stretched and ill-equipped France was in turn defeated in Russia. In 1813 Germany's fortunes began to turn. A coalition of Austria, Prussia and Russia was able to defeat Napoleon at Leipzig. The Confederation of the Rhine was dissolved, as were the Napoleonic states in northern Germany. South German states signed treaties with Austria. The Wars of Liberation finally came to an end in April 1814. From October 1814 to June 1815 a Congress was held in Vienna, under the dominant influence of Metternich, foreign minister of Austria from 1809 to 1848 and also Austria's chancellor from 1821. The Congress of Vienna was briefly interrupted by Napoleon's escape from captivity on the island of Elba, but soon returned to its business of determining the future order of European affairs.

After twenty-two years of European warfare, the Congress of Vienna was held in festive mood, with much dancing and luxurious dinners. Its purpose however was rather serious: it had to resolve the problem of achieving a strong, stable Germany which would provide a bulwark against potential future French expansionism, while at the same time recognising that the system of a multiplicity of petty princes within a loose and ineffective imperial framework could not be restored. In the end, much of the Napoleonic reorganisation of Germany remained in place or was extended.

A German Confederation (*Deutscher Bund*) was established in place of the Holy Roman Empire. The Confederation was made up of thirty-eight states (thirty-nine after 1817): thirty-four monarchies and four free cities. The Confederation's boundaries were basically the same as those of the Holy Roman Empire. It did not correspond with the ethnic/cultural population of Germans in central Europe, since some non-German minorities (such as Italians and Czechs) were included, while some German populations were excluded. The King of England, in his capacity as ruler of Hanover (until 1837) was one of the princes participating in the Confederation. The Confederation was not itself a federal state (*Bundesstaat*), but rather a loose federation of states (*Staatenbund*). It had no common head of state, no administrative or executive organs, no common legal system, no common citizenship, and was able to make only precious few common decisions. The Federal Diet which met at Frankfurt was essentially a congress of ambassadors representing the interests of their own separate states.

These states themselves emerged as relatively strong political units, at least in comparison with their eighteenth-century predecessors. Territorially, there was considerable reorganisation. Obviously, the new states were enlarged by the absorption of smaller political units. Prussia in particular gained by its initially rather unwilling acquisition of the Rhineland and Westphalia. This was intended as a means of turning Prussia into a strong power between France and Russia. In the process, it doubled Prussia's population and gave the previously economically rather backward state the benefit of mineral riches and areas more advanced in commerce and industry. On the other hand, the disadvantage from Prussia's point of view was that it had to give up some of its land gains in the east (from the second and third partitions of Poland). But in the long term, the effective moving of Prussia westwards further shifted the balance of power between Prussia and Austria in favour of the former. Prussia became both more representative of German interests, and more important as a protector of Germany in central Europe. This was by no means necessarily a step towards a historically inevitable national unification under Prussian domination, however. The territorial states emerged from the Napoleonic period strengthened not only in sheer size, but also in a number of other respects. Rulers enjoyed full sovereignty as well as actual power. Partly as a result of, and partly in response to, the exigencies of the Napoleonic period, in many states the administrative and legal systems had been reformed and made more efficient. Where serfdom, guild privileges, and restrictions on the mobility of labour had abolished, they were not restored. In the course of the nineteenth century, many such enlarged states – such as Bavaria – built up powerful local myths and traditions, inventing and sustaining a strong regional particularism which would by no means be easily submerged in a united Germany.

The political impact of the French Revolution on Germany was profound and ultimately irreversible. There is more ambiguity about its effects in other spheres. Economically, the French continental

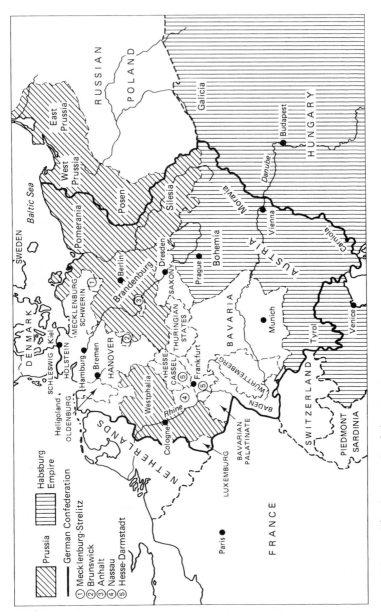

Map 6. The German Confederation in 1815.

blockade against England probably did not last long enough to be of much help to Germany's economic development. While the preconditions for later economic takeoff were established in the abolition of a variety of feudal restrictions on trade and labour mobility, the Napoleonic Wars probably on the whole retarded immediate economic development except in the Rhenish provinces directly administered by the French. Culturally, it is usually asserted that the Wars of Liberation served to turn the cultural nationalism of Herder into a new political nationalism. Yet this is probably overstated: there were only the most limited, partial stirrings of a political nationalism at this time, with local loyalties arguably very much more important. Another area where generalisation must be tempered with qualification is that of the response of Germans to revolution. German intellectuals are frequently characterised as having turned from sympathetic interest in the French Revolution to a recoiling in horror as it turned to terror. A long-standing and deep-seated fear of revolution is then supposed to have dogged German political culture throughout the next century at least. While this may roughly describe the response of a few individuals (rulers as well as intellectuals), it should by no means be held to be true of all Germans; nor can subsequent patterns of political orientation in Germany be so easily explained. The latter arose, as always, in response to a multiplicity of changing circumstances, and while political views develop within the context of existing traditions and institutional frameworks, the historical interaction of a range of factors at any given time must be examined to elucidate the relative importance of each element.

Germany in 1815 was obviously a very different place from Germany in 1648. Yet in outward appearance, it was not so very different: a still largely agricultural land, a land of villages, undulating pastures and deep forests, of mediaeval towns and castles, princely palaces, majestic churches and monasteries. All this was to change in the coming century. The French Revolution had rocked Germany politically; but in the following century, the industrial revolution was to effect even more momentous changes. With Germany's curious political heritage, the interactions between political crises and socioeconomic transformations were to have immense reverberations, still echoing in the late twentieth-century world.

5

The age of industrialisation, 1815–1918

The years from the Congress of Vienna in 1815 to the end of the First World War and the collapse of the German Empire in 1918 saw fundamental changes both in Germany and in Europe more generally. From an agrarian society, Germany was transformed into a booming centre of industrial capitalism; and competition among states in Europe became competition among imperial powers for colonies across the world. The attempted solutions to the European balance of power embodied in the Vienna settlement were relatively successful in maintaining European peace for the better part of the nineteenth century; but with the unification of a 'small' Germany, under Prussian domination, in 1871, and with Germany's rapid industrialisation and entry into competition for empire at the turn of the century, this balance was shattered. The First World War which erupted in 1914 inaugurated changes which were to have implications throughout the twentieth century, rendering Germany a very different place from what it had been in the eighteenth century.

RESTORATION GERMANY, 1815–48

The period from 1815 to the outbreak of the revolutions which swept the German states in March 1848 is conventionally labelled either the 'restoration' or the 'pre-March' (*Vormärz*) period. Both labels are to an extent misleading. Conditions after 1815 did not represent a simple restoration of pre-Napoleonic political or socioeconomic patterns; nor can the period prior to 1848 be viewed solely as a prelude to the revolutionary upheavals. Yet, even so, the period from 1815 to 1848 is in many ways a transitional one, in respect of cultural as well as political and socioeconomic developments.

Politically, the German Confederation cannot be seen simply as a step towards ultimate national unification. If anything, the territories had now increased their powers at the regional level, for a number of reasons: rulers possessed sovereignty as well as enhanced power with the rationalisation of administration, the improvements in bureaucracy and government, and the processes of centralisation of state power inaugurated in certain states in the Napoleonic period. Regional particularism, especially among the larger south German states, was to bedevil the course that national unification ultimately took. But of profound importance for this course was the strengthening of one state in particular: Prussia. With the acquisition of the Rhenish and Westphalian territories, Prussia gained not only in territorial size and population but also, crucially, in economic power and potential. Not only was Prussia now more equal to Austria in simple demographic terms; Prussia also was poised to outstrip Austria in economic development, a major factor in the century of industrialisation. Constitutionally, however, both Prussia and Austria remained relatively conservative. Prussia did not gain a united parliament, and although reforms were continued in certain provinces (with the western provinces, which were not engaged in a programme of reform, nevertheless continuing to be more progressive), centrally the programme of reforms was dropped by King Frederick William III. Major reformers had been dismissed from office by 1819–20. In Austria, the absence of a perceived need for centralisation in response to territorial or other changes, and the earlier reforms under Joseph II, added up to a programme of conservatism and inactivity in the post-Napoleonic period. Conditions in the smaller German states varied tremendously. A number of states gained constitutions at this time – Bavaria and Baden in 1818, Württemberg in 1819, Hesse-Darmstadt in 1820 – although with the exception of Württemberg, where estates and ruler jointly agreed the constitution, this was by way of an act of gracious donation on the part of rulers. Nevertheless, despite the highly restricted property franchise – and the generally less than democratic ideas of liberals, who preferred professional rule for the people to mob

Plate 21. Prince Metternich in his study.

rule by the people – it is clear that a debating chamber such as that of the lower house in Baden could provide at least a platform for practising political speech-making.

Many of the socioeconomic and legal reforms of the Napoleonic era remained in place after 1815, with variations in different territories. Legal serfdom, formerly prevalent east of the Elbe, was not restored; commutation of dues continued, although conditions were often (as in Prussia) made more difficult for peasants, while the nobility retained their status and many of their privileges. Although German society was in the process of becoming a class society, with increased mobility of labour, it was very far from being a society in which capitalist relations of production had become predominant. Moreover, despite continuities and extensions of reforms in certain areas, very soon a political reaction set in.

In the years after 1815, a number of student bodies, known as *Burschenschaften*, were founded (the first one being in Jena). A theology student by the name of Karl Sand, who belonged to such a group, in 1819 murdered the anti-liberal dramatist Kotzebue. Metternich made use of this murder as a pretext for the repressive Karlsbad Decrees of that year, which included censorship measures and increased supervision of secondary and higher education. The Vienna Final Act of 1820 incorporated these measures into the constitutional law of the Confederation. The conservative reaction inaugurated by Metternich entailed the dismissal of supposedly subversive teachers, the dissolution of *Burschenschaften*, the suppression of some newspapers, and the censorship of any publication of less than twenty *Bogen* (around 320 sides of paper) in length – a measure which provoked the writing of long-winded tracts printed in large print on very small pages, to achieve a book length of 321 pages or more to evade the censor, a nice example of the materialist determination of literary form. Despite the agrarian crises from the 'hunger years' of 1816–17 through the depression of the 1820s, political apathy appeared to prevail in the repressive circumstances of the decade or so after the Congress of Vienna.

In an inchoate manner, however, certain political tendencies were developing in the 1820s and 1830s which were subsequently to crystallise into party-political forms in the mid and later nineteenth century. Of considerable importance was the development of liberalism, which took on more political forms and colours than the liberalism of the eighteenth-century discussion groups. There were differences between the more conservative, defensive liberals in northern Germany, who wanted to restore the rights of the old estates, and the more radical, theoretical liberals of southern Germany who sought to establish new constitutions or make effective existing provisions protecting individual liberties and limiting the powers of rulers. To view German liberals as progressive, thrusting, bourgeois entrepreneurs seeking to inaugurate a new industrial capitalist society is, however, mistaken. The liberals of early nineteenth-century Germany were by and large members of the professional middle classes – primarily an educated rather than a propertied middle class, although the former did not exclude the latter – and were far from being dynamic businessmen aiming for fundamental change. Nor was liberalism necessarily co-terminous with nationalism. Attempts to trace the origins of German political nationalism in the early nineteenth century are fraught with the dangers of teleology and hindsight; but it is clear that there were quite different strands present in different combinations. There were obvious differences between the liberal desire to bring down internal trade barriers, for example,

Plate 22. The ceremonial opening of Munich University, 1826.

and the more backward-looking nationalism of the Romantics, with their glorification of an idealised mediaeval Empire, not to mention the curious glorification of all things Germanic by those indulging in what was known as *Deutschtümelei*. There was also a more diffuse form of popular radicalism evident in such phenomena as the Hambach Festival of May 1832, where perhaps 25,000 to 30,000 people gathered for music-making and political speeches. Demands for a German republic based on popular sovereignty were, however, not backed up by agreement on how to implement any particular political programme, and organisations such as that seeking to support a free press were short-lived. There were also the beginnings of a political Catholicism in this period; and, as we shall see in a moment, the sputterings of more radical movements which were to contribute to the development of socialism.

The predominant political tendency continued, however, to be a reactionary conservatism. Following the social unrest sparked off by the French July Revolution of 1830, and the popular political mobilisation evident in the Hambach Festival, the Karlsbad Decrees were revived by Metternich together with a further Six Articles in 1832, forbidding popular political meetings and associations. The notion of opposition was extended, with the inclusion of measures against what were considered to be excessive use of state Diets' powers. Further measures in 1834 sought again to achieve effective press censorship and control of university teachers and students. As it turned out, however, social and economic changes in this period were inaugurating pressures and tensions which ultimately no amount of political repression could contain.

Culturally, the period appeared also to be one of transition. There was a continued growth in the education system, following the reforms in secondary and higher education inaugurated by Humboldt in Prussia. At the lower levels of education, the German states were producing one of the most literate, appropriately educated modern work-forces in Europe (although Catholic states tended to remain behind Protestant ones). At the higher levels, German universities were producing highly qualified graduates as well as being at the forefront of many fields of research, with notable advances in the natural sciences, such as chemistry, as well as in fields such as law, theology and philology. The system of idealist philosophy developed by Friedrich Hegel was to exercise the minds of a generation and to exert continued fascination for scholars to the present day. Hegel's philosophy of history viewed history as a succession of stages in the process of 'world spirit realising itself'. It combined the Judeo-Christian conception of progress from original unity, through separation and fall, to eventual harmony and reunification at a higher level, with a more modern, secular emphasis on the empirical facts of successions of civilisations in western history. This focus on historical development was evident too in other fields of inquiry, as for example in the rise of the historical school of law as well as historical economics.

The impact of Hegel's philosophy was perhaps most important indirectly, in its transmutation through the thinking of Karl Marx (1818–83), and in the subsequent development of both empirical social science and political socialism. Marx, having briefly dallied with the ideas of Hegel's somewhat rebellious former pupils, known as the young Hegelians, crucially broke with the thinking of Hegel's critics such as Feuerbach and literally turned Hegel's idealist philosophy upside-down. While retaining the formal conceptual framework – history seen as a series of stages, in which theses produce antitheses which are resolved, through revolutionary struggles, into syntheses at a higher stage of development, which in turn produces new contradictions – Marx replaced Hegel's idealism with a new materialism. No longer did 'world spirit' provide the clue to historical dynamics; rather, people, real human beings, made their own history – although, as Marx perceptively pointed out, not in conditions of their own choosing. The social relations which developed between people in the activities of producing and reproducing served to define class relations. Historical stages were defined in terms of 'modes of production', made up of specific relations of production (class relations) and of means of production (determined largely by the level of technological development). Socioeconomic developments in any given historical stage would give rise to political struggles between classes; and revolutionary conflicts would then inaugurate the next, higher historical stage. In Marx's view, while 'Asiatic societies' were largely stagnant, western European history was dynamic: a succession of stages led from the primitive communism of tribal society, through ancient society, to feudalism, and thence to modern capitalism. In this, the penultimate stage of human history, class struggles increasingly simplified into the struggle between an ever-richer capitalist bourgeoisie, and an ever-larger, increasingly emiserated (relatively if not absolutely poorer) class-conscious proletariat. The latter, totally alienated and representing the abnegation of all humanity, would, by a revolution in its own interests, in fact inaugurate a revolution in the interests of all humanity, bringing about a communism based on plenty, in which classes would disappear, the state and ideology would wither away, and all human beings would live in peace, harmony, and self-fulfilment. This powerful vision, based partly in historical and economic analysis, partly in philosophy and political socialism, expressed in a series of extraordinarily clever tracts, essays, commentaries, and finally the major, unfinished, three volumes of *Das Kapital* (*Capital*), has exerted immeasurable influence on the course of subsequent history. It has given rise both to a wide array of diverse, often wildly conflicting interpretations, and to numerous political movements and powerful regimes – most obviously that of Soviet Russia – claiming inspiration and legitimacy, rightly or wrongly, in Marx's name. Meanwhile, in pre-March Germany, Marx was only beginning to formulate his revolutionary ideas, which had little immediate impact on German developments at the time. It was after his exile, in the tranquillity of the reading room of the British Museum in London, that his major works were formulated; even then, he only observed and commented on the course of nineteenth-century German politics from a distance. We shall return to the impact of Marxist thought in due course.

In music, Vienna was a major centre: the names of Ludwig van Beethoven (1770–1827), Franz Schubert (1797–1828), and the Strausses indicate the range of musical creativity, from the major symphonic works through the Viennese waltzes to the more intimate *Lieder* or songs. Music was both a public activity, with operas and concerts, and a private, familial occupation, with piano playing and singing as well as chamber music in small circles. On the whole, German music of the early nineteenth century represented a more secular phenomenon than the religious heights achieved in the northern Protestantism of Johann Sebastian Bach a century earlier. In the wider cultural sphere, a shift can be discerned away from the conspicuous consumption of eighteenth-century court culture towards that more sober middle-class style known as 'Biedermeier' – a term describing not only a style of furniture, but also with connotations of a slightly repressive, patriarchal, heavy middle-class atmosphere in which a certain sentimentality went along with an essentially apolitical, ascetic work ethos. In literature, the period is characterised by diversity. The classicism of the later Goethe period gave way to a sense, among certain circles, of belonging to a generation of epigones after Goethe's death in 1832. Romanticism, associated with names such as Novalis, Tieck, Hölderlin, Brentano, von Arnim, Hoffmann and the Schlegel brothers, was countered by the works of those known as members of the 'Young Germany' movement, loosely associated with Heinrich Heine.

Most profound were the subterranean changes occurring in the socioeconomic sphere. Shifts in social relations, in patterns of production, and in the political organisation of economic life combined with rapid population expansion to amount to the beginnings of a fundamental transformation of German society. The replacement

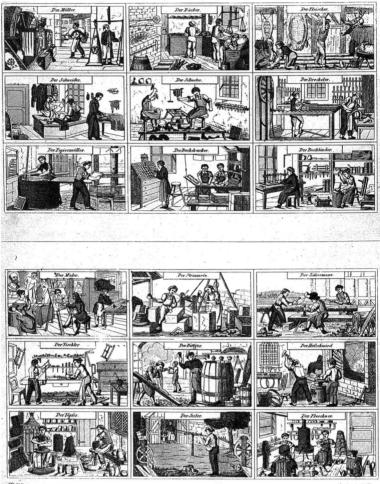

Plate 23. A variety of eighteenth- and early nineteenth-century occupations.

of a feudal, status society by a class society in the early nineteenth century provided a basis for the development of an increasingly industrial society from the 1830s. This process was slow and partial at first, but snowballed into an explosive transformation of Germany by the end of the century. Diverse processes were interrelated. Of major importance were improved communications, with programmes of road-building and hard-surfacing, the introduction of steamships on the Rhine and the building of canals to link rivers, and, fundamentally, the building of railways. The first line to be opened was that from Nuremberg to Fürth in 1835; the first line of economic importance was opened between Leipzig and Dresden in 1837. Railways both facilitated the relatively cheap and rapid transport of raw materials and products, and stimulated increased production, particularly of coal and iron. Despite public debate and controversy – which included doctors' warnings of the dangers to health of travelling at high speeds, as well as the Prussian king's publicly expressed doubts about whether being able to arrive in Potsdam a couple of hours earlier really constituted a major contribution to human happiness – the railway system continued to expand in subsequent years. Factories were established, such as the Borsig works in Berlin for the production of railway locomotives. There were also changes in production methods in such areas as textiles, with factories beginning to supplement the existing 'putting-out' system (under which workers worked in their own homes). While factory workers in industrial production remained a very tiny minority, with the largest proportion of Germans continuing to work on the land or as small-scale traders, handicraftsmen and artisans, these developments represented important harbingers of the future.

Along with the quickening of economic production went changes in the political framework of economic life. Of major importance was the development of a German Customs Union dominated by Prussia, and excluding Habsburg Austria. This started with Prussia's tariff law of 1818 which abolished differences between town and country, and transformed all of Prussia into one economic unit, with no internal tariffs. Attention was then given to the difficulties involved in transporting materials and products between the western and eastern provinces of Prussia, which were separated by other German states in between, as well as to the problem of non-Prussian enclaves. In the following years, other states were included in the Prussian system, while in 1828 Bavaria and Württemberg formed a customs union and other states, including Saxony, Hanover and Brunswick, came together in the mid-German Commercial Union, which adopted the rather negative arrangement of not charging duties on goods which were simply passing through their territories. On 1 January 1834 the German Customs Union (*Deutscher Zollverein*), comprising eighteen states with a population of 23 million, was formed. Austria preferred to remain outside this organisation, choosing her own form of customs union with Habsburg territories which lay outside the Confederation. Thus while Metternich's conservative Austria remained the predominant political force within the Confederation, increasingly Prussia gained economic predominance, and the Prussian *Thaler* became the common unit of currency within the Customs Union. Moves towards economic unification presaged the form which political unification was eventually to take.

Meanwhile, further socioeconomic changes were occurring which were to feed into more immediate political upheavals. In Europe as a whole, a population expansion had been taking place since the mid-eighteenth century. European population approximately doubled between the mid-eighteenth and the mid-nineteenth century. In Germany, much of the population growth was rural; and the food supply of a still pre-industrial economy proved insufficient to support a growing population on the land. Food riots, rural unemployment, migration to the growing towns, even emigration across the Atlantic to that land of opportunity and moving frontiers, America, were common. The growth of pauperism, and the widespread existence of acute poverty alongside the self-satisfied bourgeois society of Biedermeier Germany, gave rise to considerable social concern, expressed for example in the charitable activities of the Christian churches. The poor also at times attempted to take matters into their own hands. In 1844, for example, the Silesian weavers, who were adversely affected by the competition of the more advanced British textile industry as well as by the introduction of new production methods at home, rose in revolt. In 1846–7 a potato blight meant malnutrition and potential starvation for many, including thousands of deaths from poverty-related diseases. Social unrest coincided with the continuing unease felt by intellectuals with the repressive political conditions of Metternich's increasingly outdated conservative system. Yet the spark that finally ignited revolutionary upheavals in 1848 came not from within, but again from another revolution in France.

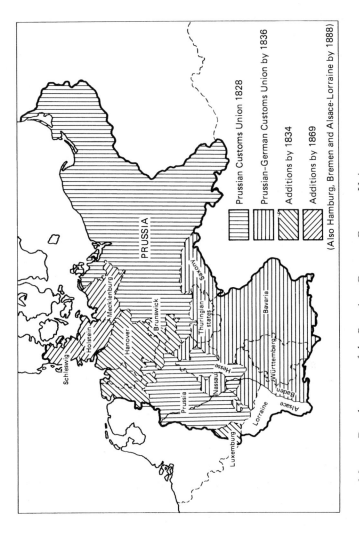

Prussian Customs Union 1828

Prussian–German Customs Union by 1836

Additions by 1834

Additions by 1869

(Also Hamburg, Bremen and Alsace-Lorraine by 1888)

Map 7. Development of the Prussian–German Customs Union

THE REVOLUTIONS OF 1848

1848 was a year of revolution across Europe. Sparked off by the news of the February Revolution in France, which toppled King Louis Philippe, there were insurrections across the German territories as a variety of groups seized the opportunity to exert pressures on frightened rulers. Involved in the German revolutions were a number of different strands: popular social unrest, often rather defensive and reactionary in nature, demanding the restoration of old forms of regulation; liberal political demands for constitutional rule, as well as for certain economic freedoms; and nationalist demands for the unification of Germany. Insofar as there was any working-class protest, it was largely limited to demands for immediate improvements in wages and working conditions: 1848 was no proletarian revolution in the Marxist sense. Because those working for unification were ultimately unsuccessful – there was no unification in 1848–9 under liberal auspices, and the unification that occurred in 1871 was of a rather different, distinctly less liberal, flavour – 1848 has often been written off as, in A. J. P. Taylor's phrase, a 'turning-point where Germany failed to turn'. Yet this is too simplistic and one-sided a view: much did emerge from the turmoils of 1848–9, and Germany was a rather different place in the 1850s from what it had been before 1848. Rather than castigating German history for what it was not – premised on some supposedly more 'normal' model of doing things – it is more helpful to attempt to clarify what did actually happen, with what causes and consequences.

As indicated above, the mid and later 1840s had seen considerable social unrest. But it was the longer-term effects of economic crisis (such as mounting indebtedness, as well as a business crisis) that were more important than immediate economic misery as preconditions for revolution. After the famine and distress of 1846–7, the economy actually improved in 1848. Moreover, it was not popular distress which formed the major basis of liberal concerns. As the events of 1848–9 proceeded, the gulf between peasant and artisan concerns on the one hand, and those of the liberals on the other, became more and more clear. Liberal goals had been slowly and variously articulated over a considerable period of time before

1848. In Prussia, liberal hopes were briefly raised with the accession of King Frederick William IV to the throne in 1840, and with moves towards a united Prussian Diet, which did indeed meet in April 1847. However, there was deadlock over the issue of constitutional reforms before granting of money, and the Diet was dismissed. In the event, Frederick William IV proved to be no liberal monarch, but rather an unbalanced, inconsistent ruler, something of an actor, who was later certified insane. Liberals in other German states were also discussing and organising for reform. There were differences between the more radical liberals, such as Hecker and Struve with their Offenburg programme, and the more moderate liberals supporting the Heppenheim programme. But these liberal pressures alone, and even in conjunction with the social distress of the 1840s, were not sufficient to cause a revolution. It was the news of the fall of the French king which stimulated popular uprisings all over Germany. In the face of widespread peasants' insurrections, artisans' riots and liberal pressures, rulers all over Germany rapidly made concessions in a panic attempt to ward off the feared threat of worse disturbances. The liberals then took advantage of the volatile situation to try to effect changes at the national level, through the subsequent electing of a national parliament to discuss constitutional reform and German unification.

The weaknesses of revolutionary forces in Germany were hence evident from the start: it took a spark from outside to ignite the revolution; there was a range of forces with different aims exerting pressure on the regimes; and the indigenous authorities capitulated almost without defence. Having withdrawn from the fray, rather than being defeated, conservative forces were able to observe the disarray and flailings of the revolutionary groups, and later to return to take control of the situation with their armed forces intact, and even strengthened by concessions to peasant demands.

In Austria, with widespread peasant insurrections and workers' revolts in various parts of the Habsburg domains, Metternich resigned on 13 March and fled to that haven for exiled reactionaries as well as revolutionaries, Great Britain. On 15 March the Austrian emperor promised a constitution and called an assembly. In the south and west German states, many rulers replaced conservatives in the administration with liberals, and made promises of reform.

Plate 24. Barricades in Berlin, 1848.

In Prussia, a comedy of errors unfolded. On hearing of the revolutionary developments in Austria, Frederick William IV made moves to call a national parliament. But in the struggles between soldiers and the Berlin crowds soldiers misunderstood the king's command to desist from shooting. Shots were fired, and fighting broke out. Uncertain how to deal with the situation, the king ordered the withdrawal of troops in an attempt to prevent civil war. Wavering, and in a romantic desire to be at one with his people, the king decided that if he could not beat the revolutionaries, he had better join them; and on 21 March he rode through Berlin draped in the revolutionary colours of black, red and gold. A liberal regime was soon installed in Berlin.

At the national level, a self-proclaimed 'pre-Parliament' had met in Frankfurt, consisting mostly of moderate liberals who outvoted a smaller group of more radical liberals, to organise the election of a national assembly. The latter, elected on the basis of a low turnout of what was in any case a rather restricted suffrage (varying in the different states), finally opened on 18 May in St Paul's church in Frankfurt. It was overwhelmingly middle-class and professional in social composition, with a preponderance of lawyers, university professors, teachers and officials, as well as some writers, journalists and clergymen. There were precisely four handicraftsmen and one solitary peasant – who was further isolated by being a Pole from Silesia. Representatives came as individuals not committed to any particular party or orientation, although perhaps between a half and two-thirds were generally liberal in inclination, while a minority (about 15 per cent) were of more extreme right-wing or left-wing views. Over time, loose groupings began to emerge, frequently named after the inns where they met for informal discussions. This august body deliberated on fundamental issues over the following months. Discussions ranged over what future constitutional form a united Germany should take; what were to be the fundamental rights of individuals; and what economic order should be adopted. Views changed not only with the principles at stake in any given argument, but also with the unfolding practicalities of politics in 1848–9. Agreement was finally hammered out or cobbled together on certain issues. Individualistic economic policies and freedom of trade were supported; a doctrine of fundamental rights was published on 28 December 1848; it was agreed that a united Germany should be a federal state with an emperor and an elected parliament and responsible ministry; and, after considerable bargaining (with the moderate liberals gaining the support of radicals for Prussia as the holder of the Imperial title, in return for supporting radical demands for a more democratic electoral system), there was an unexpected vote for almost universal manhood suffrage on 29 April 1849. But on certain major substantive issues there proved to be insurmountable problems.

It was easy enough to desire a united Germany in principle; it was infinitely harder to define the boundaries of this Germany in practice. There were three areas where the nationality issue proved problematic. The first was of course Austria, where the key issue hung on whether those parts of the Habsburg Empire which were part of the German Confederation (and previously the Holy Roman Empire) should be incorporated in a 'large Germany' (*Grossdeutschland*), or whether all Austrian territories should remain outside leaving Prussia to dominate a 'small Germany' (*Kleindeutschland*). Since the Austrian emperor was unwilling to dismember his dominions, only a radical solution could have achieved the incorporation of Austria. In the end, after heated debates, moderate proponents of the 'small-German' solution led by Heinrich von Gagern came to predominate. Secondly, there was the question of whether the Polish people in the Prussian province of Posen should be included or excluded from a national Germany. Thirdly, there was the long-running problem of the duchies of Schleswig and Holstein. A highly complex situation involving a mixture of international politics, dynastic rights and modern nationalism provided an explosive mixture in these ethnically mixed fiefs of the Danish crown. The issue in the end turned into one of power politics rather than theory: a war on Denmark, sanctioned by the Frankfurt Parliament, was in practice dependent on the military contingents of the separate German states; and when, in August 1848, the militarily most important state, Prussia, decided to pull out and sign an armistice, the Frankfurt Parliament was left looking foolish, its lack of real power clearly revealed.

The Parliament prolonged its deliberations into the spring of 1849, when it finally offered the crown of a small Germany to the King of Prussia. The latter was able, by now, to reject it with contempt. For while the Parliament had been debating, the conservatives had been regrouping and regaining power in different states; there was thus no longer any need to make concessions or capitulate to intellectuals. In the course of the summer of 1848, there had been continued radical social unrest. This was not a revolutionary movement carried by an industrial proletariat, as predicted in Marx's theory. The moderate working-class protest, such as that of the Berlin socialists led by Stephan Born, wanted trade unions, higher wages, better working conditions and regulation of factories. More important at this time were the craftsmen and artisans who felt threatened by liberal opposition to guild restrictions and support for free market forces. Artisans convoked their own national congress meeting in Frankfurt from mid-July to mid-August 1848. Nor were the members of the Frankfurt Parliament in a position to address – or redress – the grievances of peasants. In the different states of Germany, liberal or reforming regimes even themselves became increasingly frightened by mass protests and the spectre of mob rule, and were unable to control developments in the course of the summer months. Capitalising on events, conservative forces and their unvanquished armies were able, with some regrouping, to launch a counter-revolution. In the Habsburg Empire, the army suppressed uprisings in Bohemia, Hungary and northern Italy in the summer of 1848 and regained control of Vienna by the end of October 1848. In Prussia, the combination of a radical assembly and popular insurrections in the summer months stimulated the organisation of a successful conservative counter-revolution in the autumn. The liberals had in any case never possessed real military power; and they had by now lost what popular support they had ever possessed. Peasants in particular, who formed the backbone of the conscripts to the army, were bought off by conservatives who made concessions to ensure their loyalty in the troops. All over Germany in 1848–9, shaken rulers gradually regained their confidence and reasserted control, sometimes with the aid of Prussian troops restoring order elsewhere (as in Baden).

By May 1849, with liberals in disarray, the crown refused by the Prussian monarch, the members of the Frankfurt Parliament started to return home. A committed rump removed itself to Stuttgart, whence it was dispersed by troops in June 1849. Attempts in Baden and the Palatinate to enforce the new constitution approved by the Frankfurt Assembly were relatively easily suppressed by the Prussian army. The revolution appeared to be over.

It is a curious revolution to evaluate. National unification was manifestly not achieved: it foundered on the rocks of regional particularism, the unwillingness of sovereigns to subsume their sovereignty in a wider entity, and the facts of power politics. Liberals possessed both too little real power, and too little popular support, to be able to put through their programme: they also were on many issues divided amongst themselves. But it was not a revolution without consequences. Feudal social relations on the land, effectively abolished all over Germany by 1850, did not return. The organisation of economic life continued in a liberal mode, allowing rapid economic development in the 1850s. The particular system of political repression associated with Metternich did not return. The articulation of grievances, the opening of concerns with issues transcending the immediate demands of the day, aided the formation of a range of national groupings and political orientations, which were to develop into more party-political forms in the next couple of decades. Many political actors of a variety of persuasions (not least Bismarck) felt they had learnt certain lessons from 1848. Rather than being a 'turning-point where Germany failed to turn', 1848 is perhaps better characterised as a crisis constellation, from which the interacting elements emerged transformed, in new combinations facing the future under changing conditions. If a historian is determined to locate the failures of German liberalism, they are perhaps better sought in the divisions and losses of nerve of the later nineteenth and early twentieth centuries than in the particular circumstances of 1848.

THE UNIFICATION OF GERMANY

Despite the collapse of revolutionary and reforming endeavours by 1849, the return of conservative regimes was characterised by a curious combination of political reaction with frequently progressive economic policies. The 1850s saw rapid economic growth in Germany: coal, iron and textile production expanded, as did the building of railways: the length of the railway network trebled between 1850 and 1870. The percentage of the population working in factories grew from 4 per cent in 1850 to 10 per cent in 1873; and GNP per capita grew by one-third between 1855 and 1870. Although briefly interrupted after the economic crash of 1857, economic growth in Prussia stood in stark contrast to the preponderantly stagnant economy of Austria, whose industrial growth centres of Vienna, Prague and Bohemia generally were outweighed by the vast swathes of economically backward agricultural regions. Austria also had to devote a considerable proportion of the budget to military expenditure to deal with troublesome situations in Italy and the Balkans. The growing economic disparity between Prussia and Austria was an important factor in the eventual victory of Prussia over Austria in the struggle for domination of a unified Germany. Austrian attempts either to break up or join the Customs Union were foiled, and in 1865 the *Zollverein* was renewed, on Prussian terms, excluding Austria. Prussia was thus in a position to benefit from the markets of the smaller German states, which her rapidly expanding economy required. The latter were economically in no

Plate 25. Borsig's locomotive factory in Moabit, Berlin, 1855.

position to leave the Prussian-dominated Customs Union, despite their pro-Austrian political sympathies.

While a range of musical, sporting and cultural associations promoted concepts of German cultural unity through festivals, shooting contests, gymnastic events and other meetings, there was also the development of forms of political organisation transcending state boundaries. In 1859 the National Association (*Nationalverein*) was founded, providing a national forum for liberal discussions even if it was more of a pressure group than a political party. Cultural and educational associations for growing numbers of German industrial workers preceded the formation, in 1863, of Lassalle's General German Workingmen's Association (*Allgemeine Deutsche Arbeiterverein*) after initial approaches to liberal leaders had been snubbed. This organisation owed nothing to Marx and Engels, who – by now from the sidelines in London – were highly critical of Lassalle's étatist views. More in line with Marxist thinking was the Social Democratic Labour Party founded in Eisenach in 1869 under the influence of August Bebel and Wilhelm Liebknecht. Despite initial rivalry between these parties, merger in the face of increasing persecution was later achieved in 1875 at Gotha. The Gotha programme, which included many concessions to the Lassalleans, provoked heated criticism from Marx and Engels. Divisions within the socialist camp in Germany were to continue for many generations, as we shall see. Other developing political alignments in the pre-unification period included crystallisations of conservative groups, and the first beginnings of Catholic-clerical groupings in Prussia, Bavaria, and some other states. Left-wing liberals in Prussia broke away to form the German Progressive Party (*Deutsche Fortschrittspartei*) in June 1861.

More generally, in the 1850s and 1860s there was an expansion of education, the spread of faith in science and progress, and the proliferation of educational and cultural institutions such as museums, zoos, theatres and art galleries. A solid bourgeois culture was becoming rooted in an increasingly powerful economy. Yet there was an uncertainty hanging over its identity, not only in view of the unresolved question of unification, but also in respect of national identity and relations with past and future. This was evident even in the curious architectural styles of such secular temples to progress as the grandiose railway stations and pompous, quasi-mediaeval, banks and civic buildings built at this time, not to mention the extraordinary fairy-tale palaces of the unstable King Ludwig II of Bavaria. Yet at the same time, for the vast majority of ordinary German people, life appeared to go on very much as before: those peasants who were not affected by migration to the towns, or caught up in the wave of emigration to America, lived their lives in large families, in relatively compact communities usually dominated by the local church, easily unaware of or able to ignore sea-changes occurring at the national level except when exceptional events impinged upon the daily round.

What came as 'unification' in 1871 was less a result or expression of any budding German nationalism than a form of Prussian expansionism and colonisation of non-Prussian Germany, in rivalry with an excluded Austria. Austria's situation had been weakened by a number of developments in the 1850s, including the Crimean War and troubles in Italy. Increasingly, Austria turned her attention towards Germany. But the capacity of an economically backward Austria to mount a successful challenge to Prussia was by now limited. While the outcome was by no means predetermined, in the course of the 1860s the sparring matches between these rival powers came, under the guiding hand of Otto von Bismarck (who took over the nationalist card from the liberals in order to resolve a Prussian domestic crisis), to be won by Prussia.

Bismarck was the son of a Prussian Junker, educated at Göttingen and Berlin universities, and, although essentially bored by country life, proud of his Junker status. After a brief career as a bureaucrat, Bismarck became a diplomat, and as the Prussian representative at the Diet of the Confederation in Frankfurt increasingly developed a competitive approach towards Austria. After periods in St Petersburg and Paris, Bismarck was recalled to Prussia and appointed Prime Minister in the context of a serious domestic constitutional crisis. The new Prussian constitution of 1850 had included a three-class voting system based on property taxes: the wealthy few who paid the top third of property taxes in their constituency commanded one-third of the votes for an electoral college for the Prussian parliament; the next group paying the middle third of property taxes (a somewhat larger minority) controlled the next third of the votes;

while the vast majority of people who owned next to nothing and paid minimal property tax were only able to cast the last third of the votes. Since voting power was relative to the distribution of wealth on a constituency basis, minor provincial Junkers were assured of political representation despite the fact that their means could not compare with those of infinitely wealthier members of the Berlin bourgeoisie. This skewed system of representation allowed conservative Prussian Junkers to exert disproportional influence in Prussian politics, and with the failure to reform it in the light of later rapid urbanisation, it protected the power of an economically declining class until the eventual collapse of Imperial Germany in 1918. However, in the course of the 1850s, with economic growth and increasing urbanisation, it also provided the propertied liberal bourgeoisie with a growing electoral voice. From 1860, there was a conflict between crown and parliament over the issue of a proposed reform of the Prussian army under Count von Roon. All agreed that with the population expansion since the last army reforms in the early nineteenth century, some reform was needed; but the liberals disapproved of the proposed demotion of the militia (*Landwehr*) that was under middle-class control, and also wanted to restrict the length of military service to two rather than three years. Liberals themselves then split over the question of compromise, and the new Progressive party insisted on ensuring parliamentary consent to any reorganisation. The Progressives became the largest group in the Prussian parliament, increasing their seats from 110 in the December 1861 elections to 135 in May 1862, effectively producing deadlock in the conflict between crown and parliament.

Bismarck proceeded to operate without parliamentary consent on the budget; only retrospectively, in the Indemnity Bill of 1866, was consent given to the expenditures he had incurred. His policies during the period from 1863 to 1871 have given rise to a range of interpretations. He was probably less an arch-manipulator than a clever exploiter of situations as they arose. His main goal was to secure and extend the position of Prussia, in which aim he succeeded by means of three wars: that of 1864 over the Schleswig-Holstein question; the war with Austria in 1866; and the Franco-Prussian war of 1870 which culminated in the founding of the second German Empire in 1871.

The Schleswig-Holstein issue (concerning which the British politician Palmerston made the oft-quoted joke that it was so complicated that only three people had ever understood it: Prince Albert, who was dead; a German professor, who had gone mad; and Palmerston himself, who had since forgotten what it was all about) turned again, as in 1848, less on issues of principle than on power politics. While nationalist support for the resistance of the duchies to take-over by the King of Denmark could be bolstered by liberal notions of freedom, independence and self-determination, Bismarck made use of the situation both for Prussian aggrandisement and as a pretext for conflict with Austria. After a complex course of diplomatic and military developments in the spring and summer of 1864, by October 1864 (following the Danish defeat in July) a treaty gave Austria and Prussia joint administration of the duchies. Frictions over this provided the pretext for the next conflict, the Austro-Prussian War of 1866. The Confederation had effectively fallen apart, with radical Prussian proposals not being accepted, and eventual Prussian withdrawal providing the final spark to ignite a German war. Despite widespread expectations of an Austrian victory (which would have resulted in a restoration of the Confederation), Prussian economic and military superiority gave her a decisive victory over Austria at Königgrätz in July 1866. As a consequence of Austrian defeat, Austria was effectively excluded from any further involvement in German affairs.

A very new sort of political entity replaced the Confederation. The new North German Confederation was a federal state (*Bundesstaat*) rather than a federation of states (*Staatenbund*). It excluded not only Austria but also the south German states: Bavaria, Baden, Württemberg, Hesse-Darmstadt. Prussia was further enlarged by annexing Schleswig-Holstein, Hanover, Hesse-Kassel, Frankfurt and Nassau. The constitution of the North German Confederation, designed by Bismarck, allowed territorial rulers to continue to manage their own internal affairs while the head of the Confederation, the King of Prussia, was in charge of foreign affairs and army matters. A largely powerless parliament (*Reichstag*) was complemented by an upper house, the Federal Council (*Bundesrat*), effectively controlled by Prussia. This constitution was to provide a basis for that of the subsequent German Empire.

Bismarck now had considerable support within Prussia. Following the defeat of Austria the liberals had split again, with some right-wingers leaving the Progressives and, together with liberals in other north German states, forming the National Liberal Party which supported Bismarck. The conservatives had also regrouped, with the Free Conservative Party supporting Bismarck. Yet, important though the North German Confederation was, it did not quite secure Prussia's position in Germany. The south German states still resisted any extension of the scope of the Customs Union. The incorporation of the south German states into an expanding sphere of Prussian domination was achieved by means of the Franco-Prussian war of 1870. The initial crisis had to do with the question of the succession to the Spanish throne. When Spanish leaders chose a Hohenzollern prince, France objected; despite the fact that the Hohenzollern candidature was withdrawn, it suited both France and Bismarck to exacerbate the issue into a crisis, with Bismarck in particular skilfully manipulating opportunities as they arose. The result was a brief war in which the German army under the Prussian Chief of Staff, General von Moltke, and German technology (Krupp armaments) rapidly defeated the under-prepared French; and since a Republic was proclaimed in Paris in September 1870, foreign powers declined to intervene to support a revolutionary government. The war was over in 1871, and Germany annexed the French provinces of Alsace and Lorraine as well as demanding large indemnity payments.

The south German states, who in a whipping-up of nationalistic fervour had been persuaded to join the North German Confederation in the war on France, now realised that they had little option militarily and politically but to become more permanently bound to Prussia. On 18 January 1871, in a ceremony at Versailles, the German Empire was proclaimed, with the rulers of the German states offering King William I of Prussia the hereditary crown of a united Germany. Whatever nationalist mythology may subsequently have claimed, there was a great deal of grumpiness on all sides: reluctance on the part of the princes, as well as a certain sulkiness on the part of the new Emperor himself. What had been engineered, under Bismarck's guidance, was effectively the extension of Prussian power rather than the expression of nationalist enthusiasm for a united Germany.

The constitution of the second Empire made this abundantly clear. It was a federal empire, in which the constituent states retained their monarchies and considerable power over internal matters, while foreign policy and war were national areas of competence. The political structure was essentially a pyramid with three layers. The bottom layer, the parliament or *Reichstag*, was directly elected by universal manhood suffrage on a secret ballot. While it was apparently very democratic, parliamentary deputies in practice had little real power and could simply let off steam by expressing their opinions. Moreover, since there were no parliamentary salaries, anyone lacking independent means had little chance of becoming a representative in parliament. Eventually, as the German sociologist Max Weber was to point out, anyone with aspirations to wielding real power would disdain parliament in any case. While the Reichstag had veto-rights, legislation was initiated in the Federal Council, or *Bundesrat*, which constituted the middle layer and was made up of delegations from the separate states. As the largest state, Prussia possessed effective veto power in the Federal Council and was able to block any measures or constitutional amendments deemed inimicable to Prussian interests. Finally, the real concentration of power was in a few hands at the top of the pyramid: with the emperor, the chancellor, ministers, senior officials, and leading figures in the army. Nominally, the emperor – or his chancellor, depending on the interplay of personalities – possessed great power. But a power vacuum (with a weak emperor and chancellor) would in effect entail rule by the bureaucracy. Nor was the army entirely accountable. Initially, the war minister was partially answerable to the Reichstag, although the Prussian war minister was not responsible to the Reichstag on matters concerning the largest contingent of the armed forces, the Prussian army. In 1883, the Reichstag lost what minimal control it had possessed over military matters through control of the military budget, and subsequently – into the First World War and well beyond – the German army was to play a highly ambiguous, and eventually fatal, role in German politics.

Bismarck had designed this constitution to ensure his own and Prussia's powers, but in the event proved less than committed to it in principle himself. Later on, when it no longer appeared to suit his purposes, he even considered jettisoning it. Retrospectively, it can

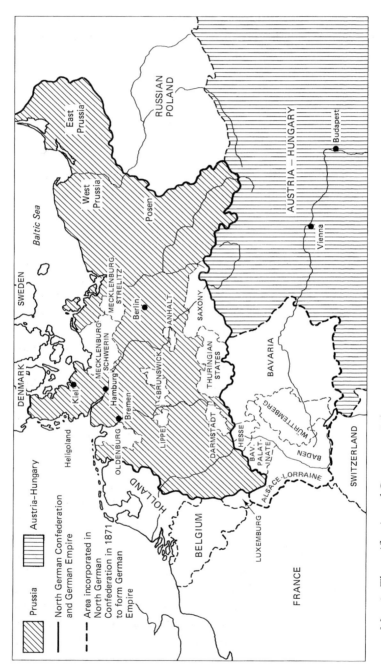

Map 8. The unification of Germany, 1867–71

also be seen that Bismarck, the moving force behind the unification of Germany, had bequeathed a highly problematic legacy for the future.

GERMANY UNDER BISMARCK

At the beginning, there was a period of enthusiastic economic activity, characterised by a great speculative boom, the founding of new companies and large enterprises, the rapid expansion of railway construction and other building projects. With a currency reform in 1871, a great deal of paper money began to circulate in addition to the money flooding into the economy as a result of France's speedy payment of reparations. The bubble of what was known as the *Gründerzeit* ('founders' years') burst in 1873, when a collapse of confidence brought an inevitable economic crash. After 1873, the early free trade policies supported by the liberals, under the influence of Rudolf von Delbrück, were repudiated in favour of an increased protectionism. Depression set in, with worsening economic conditions for many Germans. With the competition of cheap foreign grain, as well as manufactured goods, both industrialists and landowners began to clamour for import tariffs. The shift to protectionism was consolidated in 1879, with the introduction of tariffs and an increase in indirect taxes. While liberals were increasingly divided, from the 1880s onwards a conservative coalition of agrarian and industrial interests developed – although not without tensions and frictions along the way – which was to dominate Imperial Germany into the early twentieth century.

The crash of 1873 also stimulated a revival of anti-semitism in Germany. There had long been a tradition of popular hostility to Jews, and denigration of 'inferior' eastern Jews. But with assimilation in the course of the nineteenth century, certain Jews had been rising to increasingly prominent positions in German society. Jewish families were particularly visible in the field of banking: Bismarck's own banker, Bleichröder, was a Jew, while names such as Rothschild were achieving international renown. Big banks survived the crash of 1873, inaugurating an era of large financial capitalism; and Jews in particular were resented by those small enterprises and lower-middle class individuals who had suffered economic losses. In addition, anti-semitism was being given intellectual respectability by prominent academics, such as the nationalist historian Professor von Treitschke. Such views were not uniquely German – there were influential English and French racial theorists at the time – but these developments were to provide a favourable background to the more virulent forms of political anti-semitism which later developed.

The shift away from liberalism in the late 1870s was connected with the resolution of what was known as the *Kulturkampf* (roughly, 'struggle for culture' against what was seen as superstition). A combination of factors led Bismarck to wage a miscalculated campaign pitting the state against the Catholic church. In 1870 the First Vatican Council had pronounced the doctrine of papal infallibility. Dissensions among German Catholics led to an initial involvement of the state with church affairs; but extraneous political considerations soon exacerbated the situation. The Catholic Centre party, which had been formed in December 1870 to protect Catholic interests in the predominantly Protestant 'small Germany' once Austria was excluded, appeared to Bismarck to be protecting a range of opponents of the Empire. Its support of the Pope bolstered the view that the Centre party's primary loyalties did not lie with Germany. Moreover, activities of the Catholic church in Poland appeared to be strengthening Polish nationalism and inflaming an unstable situation in the eastern territories of the Empire. Claiming that external enemies were being aided by an 'enemy within', Bismarck launched a sustained and wide-ranging attack on Catholicism. Between 1871 and 1876 there were measures to bring the training and appointment of clergy, and clerical education, under greater state control, and to prohibit the activities of Jesuits in Germany. In Prussia many priests and bishops who resisted the anti-Catholic legislation were imprisoned or expelled. The Centre party ironically consolidated its support as a result of these attacks on Catholicism, doubling its popular vote in 1874. With a few exceptions (such as Eduard Lasker), liberals ignored such liberal principles as freedom of thought and supported Bismarck's anti-Catholic policies. But by the later 1870s, with the switch to more conservative protectionist economic policies, it suited Bismarck to break his ties with the liberals. With the Catholic Centre party by now numerically strong in the Reichstag, Bismarck sought a rapprochement with the Catholic leader Windthorst; and by 1879 the Kulturkampf had come to an end. It was a curious episode which achieved very little from any point of view, other than the consolidation of the Centre party, which was to be a major and relatively stable element in German politics for many decades (and, in altered and non-denominational form, to preside in the shape of the CDU over the founding decades of post-war West Germany).

The new conservatism of the 1880s was accompanied by a double-pronged strategy in relation to socialism and the working class. After the 1875 Gotha congress, the unified German Social Democratic Party had been growing in strength. It still remained small in numbers, but it was increasingly viewed as a threat by Bismarck, who considered socialists to be among the 'enemies of the Empire' (*Reichsfeinde*). In 1878, after two attempts on the emperor's life (which had nothing to do with the SPD), Bismarck succeeded in pushing an anti-socialist law through a (re-elected) Reichstag. This banned socialist meetings, organisations and associations, newspapers and periodicals. The Reichstag refused, however, to ban those of its own members who constituted the parliamentary representation of the SPD. This anti-socialist legislation (passed for three years at a time) was renewed at intervals until Bismarck's departure from politics in 1890. Since SPD deputies were still permitted to take their seats in parliament, one unintended consequence of the anti-socialist law was to turn German socialism into a very parliament-orientated phenomenon, with major concentration on winning votes and making parliamentary speeches. While thus essentially moderate in practice, German socialists sounded rather revolutionary in theory, since it was difficult to continue in the Lassallean tradition of assenting to a strong state, once the latter denied socialism its right to existence. Yet at the same time as the socialists were being politically persecuted, quite progressive social insurance legislation was being enacted. Bismarck's social insurance plans were announced in a speech by the emperor in 1881. Sickness Insurance was introduced in 1883, Accident Insurance in 1884, and Old Age and Disability Insurance in 1889. These welfare measures were not purely the result of machiavellian considerations or bread-and-circuses policies on the part of Bismarck. The depression which had started in the 1870s led to very real material distress, and growing disparities between rich and poor, which gave cause for concern to many members of German society in addition to socialists. The Christian Social Movement, for example (founded by the right-wing and rabidly anti-semitic Protestant pastor Adolf Stöcker), as well as Catholic charitable activities, provided added impetus for the measures. Thus while suppressing the political activities of the working class with one hand, Bismarck appeared to be buying them off through welfare provisions with the other. Social Democrats were themselves aware of this, and uncertain about how best to respond. Splits between those minded to accept economic improvements in a piecemeal fashion in the here and now, and those insisting on the need for radical transformation of the whole system, were to continue and become exacerbated in subsequent years.

Bismarck's foreign policy was essentially based on the development of a complex, but cautious, system of multiple alliances with other European powers. His aim was to secure Germany's European position without entering into another war. The main potential enemy – fear of whom was perhaps unduly exaggerated by Bismarck – was France. Initially Bismarck sought an alliance between the three conservative powers of Germany, Austria, and Russia (the 'Three Emperors' Alliance' of 1881, renewed for a further three years in 1884), while cultivating friendship with Britain. These arrangements were made more difficult by the rivalries and antagonisms between Austria and Russia, who had fundamental differences over south-eastern Europe. Bismarck's self-appointed role of disinterested 'honest broker' became increasingly difficult to sustain. Following the 1878 Congress of Berlin – which coincided with the shift to conservatism on the domestic front, with tariffs against the import of Russian grain an obvious irritant to Russia – Bismarck came to cultivate closer relationships with Austria, forming the Dual Alliance in 1879. Three years later this was expanded into a Triple Alliance including Italy. This did not entirely succeed in reorienting Italy's interests, while at the same time German domestic economic policies of the 1880s made England appear more of a rival. By the later 1880s, realignments were underway again, with the renewed threat of potential war with France suggesting the necessity of averting an alliance between France and Russia by once again improving relations with the latter. In 1887, Bismarck secured the Reinsurance Treaty with Russia, although the Three Emperors' Alliance between

Germany, Austria and Russia was not renewed. This in effect entailed the impossible: the reconciliation of mutually irreconcilable Russian and Austrian interests in the Balkans. In 1890, under a new emperor, the Reinsurance Treaty was not renewed. Bismarck's complex juggling act in Europe was then replaced by a more aggressive, expansionist and imperialist foreign policy which culminated eventually in the First World War. Whether the tensions and stresses involved in Bismarck's system could ever have been sustained must remain a moot point.

In March 1888, Emperor William I died at the age of ninety-one. His son, Frederick III, who succeeded him, died in June of the same year, of cancer of the throat. He was in turn succeeded by his son, William II, then aged twenty-nine. Bismarck had been facing mounting problems in the course of the 1880s, and had even considered the possibility of overthrowing the constitution he had himself designed. But instead of altering the constitution, Bismarck found that two particular features of it helped to bring about his downfall. One was the special relationship between chancellor and emperor, and the considerable powers of the latter; the second was the power of the army. The new young emperor had social ideas and political aspirations at odds with those of the ageing Bismarck. He was, for example, determined to allow the Reinsurance Treaty with Russia to lapse. He also vehemently disagreed with Bismarck's plan to engineer a constitutional crisis over a planned tightening-up of the anti-socialist legislation, which would enable Bismarck to introduce constitutional reforms, by force if necessary. The army – which was essential to the latter strategy – refused to support Bismarck's plans, and urged William II to dismiss the eminent chancellor. In 1890, at the age of seventy-five, Bismarck offered his resignation. In contrast to previous occasions, when the threat of resignation had gained Bismarck his own way, the new emperor saw the offer not as a threat but an opportunity. William II was only too pleased to have Bismarck depart his post. In the symbolic view of a widely reprinted cartoon, the ageing pilot was dropped from the German ship.

Bismarck left a highly ambiguous legacy for Germany. On the one hand, he had masterminded the unification of a Prussia-dominated, small-German, national state: a state which was to prove a powerful economic and political force in European and world affairs.

Selbst wenn der eine ebenso kräftig heizt
wie der andere bremst, kommt man doch nicht von der Stelle.
(Bismarck u. Windthorst 1884. Karikatur des „Kladderadatsch".)

Schön Wetter. — Veränderlich. — Sturm.
„Sonne bei keinen Ministern, Regirungs- oder Landtagen sehen."
(Die 3 Haare des Reichskanzlers. Aus dem „Kladderadatsch 1884.)

Papst: Ich habe noch einen Zug in petto.
Bismarck: Das wird auch der letzte sein und dann sind Sie
matt. Zeichnung aus dem „Kladderadatsch" vom Jahre 1875.)

Das Unglück beim Drachensteigenlassen.
(Wiener Karikatur auf Napoleon III. nach der Kapitulation
von Sedan. Aus Bergs „Aikesli" vom 19. September 1870.)

Der neue Peter v. Amiens und die Kreuzfahrer.
Der rücksichtslos schreitende Krebs (Bismarck) leistet den Kreuz-
zeitungsleuten Geleitschaft ...

Diesmal wirst du ein Haar darin finden.
Karikatur von Cham gegen Bismarck im Pariser Witzblatt
„Charivari" vor Ausbruch des deutsch-französischen Krieges.)

Gefahr in Sicht! Halbe Fahrgeschwindigkeit!
Anspielung auf Bismarcks Vermittlung zwischen Rußland
und England im Jahre 1878. (Aus dem Witzblatt „Punch".)

Windthorst: „Wohin soll ich fahren, nach Canossa?"
Bismarck: „Vorläufig nach Daudorf, ich werde aber an der
Ecke Wilhelmstraße aussteigen. („Kladderadatsch" 1879.)

„Es reicht immer noch nicht ganz, Gevatter."
Unsere siegestrunkenen Vettern auf der anderen Seite des Kanals
(Bismarck und Disraeli 1878. Aus dem „Schalk" vom 13. Okt.)

Entschieden ist er ein gewaltiger Redner.
Karikatur auf Bismarcks parlamentarische Tätigkeit im Nord-
deutschen Bunde. (Aus d. Wiener „Figaro" vom 5. März 1870.)

Und den politischen Eiertanz hält Bismarck
sehr von nöten, er glaubt, sie bleiben alle ganz und keines
ging zertreten. Zertreten, nein, wie ihr sie seht, dieweil er
jedes — Recht — umgeht. („Frankfurter Laterne" 20. 9. 1863.)

Die Süddeutschen werden schon noch kommen
wir sind ihnen vorderhand nur noch zu liberal." (Bismarck
im Nordd. Bund 1868. Karikatur aus dem Wiener „Figaro".)

Für eins von beiden müssen Sie entscheiden!
Odertee zur die Nomination zur Beratung d. Sozialistengesetzes.
(Karikatur des „Kladderadatsch" zur Reichstagskrisis 1881.)

ER bereitet sich vor, Memoiren zu schreiben.
Karikatur von B. Molvch. (Französische Karikatur auf Bismarcks schriftstellerische Tätigkeit nach seiner Verabschiedung.)

Der Reichskanzler legt alle seine Ämter nieder
gibt alle seine Insignien zurück und besibt sich in die wohl-
verdiente „Friedrichsruh". („Kladderadatsch" März 1890.)

Plate 26. A selection of contemporary cartoons about Bismarck.

On the other hand, the state which he had designed had authoritarian features and was riddled with political and social tensions. These were to become increasingly evident in the age of imperialism after Bismarck's fall.

SOCIETY AND POLITICS IN WILHELMINE GERMANY

Wilhelmine Germany was characterised by rapid industrialisation; by the steady rise of the SPD, symbolising increasing social confrontation; and by unstable parliamentary political alliances, with increasingly important pressure-group politics. At the head of this configuration stood Emperor William II, a man of little political aptitude, and numerous personality problems, surrounded and influenced by a small entourage of advisers. Ultimately, Wilhelmine Germany played a major role in unleashing the First World War and precipitating its own downfall. The social tensions which had dogged it were not resolved in the successor regime, the Weimar Republic, and in new forms played an important role in the eventual rise of Hitler.

Throughout the years from 1871 to the outbreak of the First World War in 1914, Germany underwent a series of changes which radically transformed its character. Demographically, there was a population increase of nearly three-quarters: Germany's population increased from 41 million in 1871 to 67.7 million in 1914, while in neighbouring France the population rose only from 36 million to 40 million. Equally striking was the rapid growth of towns and cities in Imperial Germany, swollen by a mobile, young population leaving the land in search of new opportunities in industrial centres. The metropolitan capital, Berlin, expanded rapidly, with ornate, pompous bourgeois buildings complemented by hastily thrown-up tenement blocks with dark courtyards which provided the only play areas for gangs of poverty-stricken working-class children. While some housing projects (for example, those sponsored by firms such as Siemens) provided reasonable accommodation for workers, for many the only housing was in slum conditions. Despite the rather lengthy period of economic instability and frequent crises, which lifted only in the late 1890s, Imperial Germany saw a comparatively rapid second wave of industrialisation. Germany's output of manufactured goods went up by a multiple of five at a time when Britain's output merely doubled. There was a shift from the older coal, iron and heavy engineering industries to the newer chemical and electrical concerns. Expanding use of electricity was particularly important in this period. Germany's growth contrasted with the longer, slower process of industrialisation in Britain, where there was a multiplicity of small family firms competing with one another, associated with a belief that the state should not intervene in a supposedly free market. In Germany, there was considerable state intervention, as well as an important role played by a small number of great investment banks, such as the Deutsche and Dresdner Banks. In contrast to Britain, too, there was increasing economic concentration and cartelisation. Cartels were organisations of firms producing similar products which had a common interest in fixing prices and determining conditions of production and marketing. Their number increased rapidly, from eight in 1875 to around 3,000 by the 1920s.

The different economic histories of Britain and Germany were related to different class structures. While in Britain there had been a long, slow intermingling of landed and industrial interests, in Germany there had historically been sharper status differences. In Germany, the old landowning Junker class still dominated Prussian politics through the three-class voting system (and there had been no redrawing of constituency boundaries to take account of rapid urbanisation, thus greatly favouring sparsely-populated, Junker-dominated country areas), and through Prussia Junkers dominated the Reich. Yet with the emergence of industrial society, there was an increasing disparity between the continued political power of the Junkers and their relatively declining economic status. A balance had to be found between the interests of agrarian elites and those of the various sections of industry (which themselves had by no means identical interests, since some were more in favour of protectionist policies than others). Moreover, the very rapid growth of a new industrial working class in Germany – experiencing a certain culture shock in transition from the countryside to factory life in the cities – fuelled the rapid growth of trade unions and of the SPD. In its new Erfurt programme of 1891, the SPD adopted a curious mixture of quite revolutionary principles (drafted by Karl Kautsky) and

„Mutter, Fritze is janz naß!"
„Halt'n in de Sonne, det er trocknet!"

Plate 27. A cartoon of working-class life by the Berlin artist
Heinrich Zille. The caption translates as: 'Mummy, Fritzi is
soaking wet!' – 'Well, hold him up in the sun to dry!' (The
Berlinese of the German cannot be adequately rendered in
English.)

moderate programme (drafted by the revisionist Eduard Bernstein). From 1905 onwards, it became an increasingly bureaucratic party, dogged by tensions and disputes on strategy, goals and tactics. It nevertheless became, in 1912, the largest party in the Reichstag.

There is some debate as to whether the SPD actually helped to integrate members of the working class into Wilhelmine society, giving them a social and cultural niche. The SPD organised a large number of cultural, social and sporting associations – for singing, gymnastics, cycling, rambling, chess-playing, as well as for education and self-improvement. These activities were frequently both 'bourgeois' and 'revolutionary' in import and content, as illustrated for example in the choice of both classical music and revolutionary songs. But it must also be remembered that the SPD did not correspond neatly with the whole of the German working class: while some Catholic workers switched their allegiance from the Centre party to the SPD when they moved to the cities, others remained loyal to the Centre; migrant Polish workers frequently supported Polish national organisations; and certain members of the 'Lumpen-proletariat' were neither organised nor integrated into Imperial German society, flouting its laws and conventions in lives of violence, deviant morality and petty pilfering. While the German working class had developed more rapidly, and later, than the British working class, it was less homogeneous and more varied in culture than the latter. Wilhelmine society has in fact been described as 'pillarised' (in the term of a Dutch sociologist): the separate 'pillars' consisted of a multiplicity of different sociocultural 'milieux', each of which determined the politics, unionisation, cultural activities, religious inclinations (or otherwise), rites of passage (life-cycle rituals), leisure time, and general outlook of individuals living within that particular subculture. Subtle sociological distinctions were not normally noted with precision by the elites of Imperial Germany, however, who tended simply to fear the threat of revolution from below without inquiring too closely into the real goals and capacities for action of different sections of the German proletariat.

The changing socioeconomic configurations of the period provide key clues to political developments. While the Centre party retained a steady percentage of support, it could not hope to improve its political position without loosening its specific ties with

Catholicism. It therefore remained an important, essentially stable factor in Wilhelmine politics, but not in a position to take decisive initiatives. The liberals continued divided between the more right-wing National Liberals, and the more left-of-centre Progressives. Within each of these camps there were further disagreements and divisions, not only on particular issues of the day but more generally on orientations to the political system as a whole. Support for the liberal parties was largely stagnant (with fluctuations) in the late nineteenth and early twentieth century. To an even greater extent the conservatives found their support simply disappearing with shifts in the social structure. In response, they became increasingly strident, right-wing, nationalist, and anti-semitic in an attempt to win support away from small extremist parties, of which there were quite a few particularly in the 1890s. In such a party-political context, it proved extremely difficult to achieve viable governmental coalitions or pursue consistent political policies.

In the Caprivi government of 1891–4, an attempt was made to steer a 'new course', conciliating a range of interest groups from socialists, ethnic minorities and Catholics through to industrialists. The anti-socialist laws were allowed to lapse, and social welfare legislation was extended (including regulation of working conditions and limitations on child labour and Sunday working). Courts were established for the arbitration of industrial disputes, and a finance bill proposed a progressive income tax. While this was all insufficient for socialists, it angered right-wingers. A series of commercial treaties from 1891 to 1894 was more beneficial from the point of view of some industrialists, who gained valuable markets through the reduction of tariffs: however, this was in turn disliked by conservatives representing the landowning, grain-producing interests. They set up the Agrarian League (*Bund der Landwirte*) to act as a powerful pressure group for agrarian interests. Caprivi's government foundered ultimately on the consequences of attempted reform of the army. Following a parliamentary defeat in 1892, and the subsequent passage of a compromise bill by a narrow majority in a re-elected Reichstag, Caprivi himself ultimately fell victim to a set of intrigues, in a highly charged political atmosphere in which thoughts of a coup d'état were entertained even by the emperor. In 1894 Caprivi was forced to resign.

The Hohenlohe government of 1894 to 1900 essentially represented industrial interests, and was anti-socialist in character. It also saw the restoration of the famous 'marriage of iron and rye', in which compromises were struck between agrarian and industrial elites. It was during this period that the idea of a 'negative integration of elites' developed: the Prussian finance minister Miquel used the phrase *Sammlungspolitik* in 1897 to denote the collecting up of different interest groups to achieve a consensus. In a rather negative 'solidarity of interests', agrarians and different sections of industry sought to pool their differences and combine against the perceived threat of a common enemy below. The Hohenlohe government also presided over the beginnings of more aggressive international policies. Particularly important was the foundation of the Navy League in 1898, following the appointment of Admiral von Tirpitz as Secretary of State for the Navy in 1897. Along with the Pan-German League (*Alldeutscher Verband*) founded in 1893, the Navy League was an important pressure group which received considerable financial backing from industrialists such as Krupp and Stumm. Tirpitz argued that Germany needed a rapid expansion of the navy both as a deterrent and in order to compete with that notable naval power, Great Britain. Although Germany's colonies were relatively unimportant compared with those of Britain, considerable attention was devoted to whipping up popular fervour at home in support of a German navy. The navy was to become increasingly important as a factor in domestic politics after the turn of the century.

Following a number of crises, Hohenlohe retired in 1900 and was replaced by Bülow, from 1900 to 1909. Some commercial treaties were restored while certain tariffs were increased, in an attempt to balance industrial and agrarian interests. The new tariff laws of 1902 benefited East Elbian grain producers, since they virtually precluded the import of cheap Russian grain, but in the process hurt consumers. Those who depended heavily on bread, the working class, were conciliated by the restoration of some welfare legislation. At the same time, there was a resort to 'social imperialism', in an attempt to whip up nationalistic fervour and enthusiasm for the fleet and German world power aspirations. However, after a brief improvement in the economy from 1897, a new recession began in 1903. It became increasingly difficult to reconcile the various policies, particularly in relation to the escalating expense of the navy construction programme. While budget deficits worsened, conservatives refused tax increases. Bülow experienced increasing difficulty in putting together viable parliamentary coalitions. In 1907 he dropped the Centre party and cobbled together the 'Bülow bloc' including left-liberals, which alarmed conservatives, but which in any case did not last long. In 1908 the emperor made certain intemperate remarks, upsetting foreign relations, which turned into what was known as the 'Daily Telegraph Affair'. Parliamentary parties failed to reconcile their differences and unite in criticising the emperor. Bülow had to resign when his bloc fell apart, over the issue of finance reform, in 1909.

Bülow's successor was Bethmann Hollweg, who proved totally unable to achieve a stable parliamentary base. Instead, his government had to rely on the emperor, the army and the bureaucracy. There were continued financial crises in connection with the fleet. Following the massive increase in the socialist vote (partly as a result of an electoral pact with progressive groups), the SPD in 1912 became the largest party in the Reichstag. Since the bourgeois and socialist parties refused to co-operate with each other, parliamentary deadlock ensued, enhancing even further the role of army and emperor in decision-making processes. We shall see the consequences of this for foreign policy in a moment.

Historians have engaged in spirited controversies over how best to interpret economy, society and politics in Imperial Germany. Older German historians of nationalist inclinations tended to celebrate German unification and recount tales of high politics. More recently, increased attention has been devoted to social and economic tensions. A major contribution was made in the deliberately provocative work (first published in 1973) of Hans-Ulrich Wehler, who laid particular emphasis on the 'feudal-aristocratic-military' elites' control of Prussia and hence Prussia-dominated Germany. Wehler stressed these elites' techniques of maintaining power in the face of rapid social change, ranging from simple repression, through manipulation and the splitting of opposition, to indoctrination and diversion into imperialist adventurism. The notion of 'negative integration' in the compromise between different elites and the identification of subversive common enemies (particularly socialists and

Jews) gained ground among historians. More recently, some have begun to question this essentially functionalist, top-down picture, arguing that it pays inadequate attention to those below, who were supposedly so easily suppressed and indoctrinated. More serious exploration is required to understand the varieties of working-class culture – some deferential, some subversive, some oppositional, some genuinely nationalist and patriotic – as well as to explain the divisions and failures of nerve among German liberals. Moreover, it has been pointed out that Wehler's sort of approach tends to attribute to elites a unity of purpose, and a clairvoyant consciousness of their best long-term interests irrespective of short-term differences, that they probably never possessed. There was a lot of chopping and changing of tactics, across different governments and coalitions, and it is hard to argue for continuities from Miquel's *Sammlungspolitik* of the late 1890s right through the changing governments up to the First World War. Clearly a more differentiated picture of the instabilities of Imperial Germany will have to be developed, encompassing a wide range of factors. Equally clearly, however, there were certain structural features of the sociopolitical system which played a key role in the way it was eventually to collapse.

CULTURE IN IMPERIAL GERMANY

The cultural life of Imperial Germany contained a range of diverse, often conflicting strands. On the one hand was the rather pompous, heavy 'official' culture: the culture of a recently unified society seeking to represent its aspirations towards great power status not only in the political sphere, but also symbolically, through the erection of equestrian statues of national heroes, and the construction of grandiose buildings, furnished with large, solid furniture and heavy curtains. The mixture of sentimentality and heroism of this culture was counterposed by more critical reactions to modern life from a variety of perspectives. Realist novelists elucidated the tensions and strains behind the pompous façades of bourgeois life: Theodor Fontane revealed personal strains and family crises behind social conventions in a changing society, while Thomas Mann's early novel *Buddenbrooks* chronicled the degeneration of a north German bourgeois family over the generations. Thomas Mann captured the complex changes in German social and economic life from 1835 to the late 1870s; and, while firmly anchored in the techniques of the nineteenth-century novel, *Buddenbrooks* prefigured in the figure of the last male Buddenbrook, Hanno, the repudiations of the practical world so common in the twentieth-century novel. Mann's work, spanning the period right through to the Third Reich, provided both a powerful commentary on, and a reflection of, the tensions of an artistic existence in Imperial and post-1918 Germany. Dramatists such as Hauptmann uncovered the tragic sides of human existence in materialist society. Not only imaginative writers, but also social thinkers, explored the implications for personality and family life of the bundle of changes that were occurring, in the shift from what was seen as an 'organic', traditional 'community' to a more alienating, individualistic 'society' (the distinction between *Gemeinschaft* and *Gesellschaft*). There was particular fascination with the implications of rootless life in the modern city. There were critical movements too in the visual arts. Official conceptions of acceptable art were challenged by the 'secessionist' movement, with the development in the late nineteenth and early twentieth century of new approaches such as impressionism and expressionism. Even in architecture and interior design, the more elegant *Jugendstil* style lightened the ornate pomposity of the prevailing dominant styles. Much of what later came to be known as 'Weimar culture' had its origins in pre-war Germany, particularly in changes occurring around the turn of the century.

A similar diversity characterised leisure pursuits and popular culture. On the one hand, many members of the bourgeoisie adopted certain aristocratic manners and customs, aspiring to join the reserve officer corps of the army and to achieve, if at all possible, the status mark of a duelling scar (although notions such as a 'feudalisation of the bourgeoisie' are probably overstated). On the other hand, the constraints and repressions of a stuffy bourgeois existence were literally thrown off in the youth movement. Members of the *Wandervögel* ('wandering birds') donned loose and comfortable casual clothing and set off for hiking and camping trips through the countryside, singing songs and attempting to adopt as natural a life style as possible. While critical of establishment politics (and particularly dismissive of parliamentary party politics) and of the established education system, these groups tended to be both strongly nationalistic and simultaneously anti-materialist and anti-semitic, since Jews were identified with crass money-making in modern society. The *Wandervögel* movement was in general middle-class and anti-Marxist, thus also standing in contrast to working-class and SPD forms of youth culture.

The mid-nineteenth century had been characterised by a certain positivism in outlook, a widespread faith in scientific laws and the inevitability of progress, evident for example in Darwinist evolutionary theories. Even Marxist theory was stamped by peculiarly nineteenth-century assumptions about historical laws of society and social progress. New uncertainties were evident in later nineteenth and early twentieth-century thinking. The writings of Nietzsche had a long-term and ambiguous impact, with direct influence on scholars such as Weber, and more tortuous misinterpretations by National Socialist 'theorists'. The music-dramas of Richard Wagner – still reverberating with the impulse of earlier nineteenth-century Romanticism – revived mediaeval topics (the *Meistersinger*, the *Ring*) to explore some of the profoundest tensions of nineteenth-century society. Wagner's concern with the mediaeval heritage was of course also appropriated and adapted to suit changed concerns in Nazi Germany. A new cultural pessimism, as well as a concern for the non-rational, the repressed and the unconscious, began to permeate social thought around the turn of the century. In Vienna, Sigmund Freud was working out theories of personality and techniques of psychoanalysis that were to have a profound impact on the ways in which twentieth-century Europeans and Americans think about their lives. Notions such as repression, neurosis, Freudian slip, Oedipus complex, have entered everyday language. In social and political thought, scholars such as Simmel, Tönnies and Troeltsch developed concepts and theories through which to grasp the radical changes they observed in contemporary society. The encyclopaedic works of Max Weber represented an extraordinary attempt to explore and explain the uniquely dynamic paths of western history, in comparison with patterns of society and culture in other areas of the world. And in attempting, as one commentator has put it, to bridge the gap between scientific positivism and a more historicist idealism, in elaborating generalisations which allowed space for human meanings

Plate 28. The latest in ladies' bicycling fashion, as illustrated in the popular middle-class magazine, *Die Gartenlaube*.

and motivations, Weber certainly produced a more modern form of social theory than the ambiguous writings of Marx, which failed to resolve the tensions between historical laws and human action. To encompass and account for patterns of world history, as well as to explore in detail the dynamics of his own society, Weber developed a set of social and political concepts and an explicit methodology of analysis and comparison which, for all the criticisms that have subsequently been made of it, has arguably never been surpassed in its range, erudition and richness of suggestion.

FOREIGN POLICY AND THE FIRST WORLD WAR

Undoubtedly the fact most influencing interpretations of Wilhelmine Germany is that it culminated in, and collapsed as a result of, the First World War. Debates over the causes of this war are as old as the war itself. The Versailles Treaty of 1919 laid primary responsibility on Germany in the infamous 'war guilt' clause. While the following decades witnessed a wide-ranging search for the origins of the war in pre-war diplomatic relations among the great powers, a rather different approach was already being expressed in 1928 in an essay by Eckart Kehr on the 'primacy of domestic politics' in the determination of foreign policy. This sort of approach was resurrected, in rather different ways, in the 1960s, first as a result of the reopening of the concept of Germany's war guilt in a controversial book by Fritz Fischer, and subsequently in the reinterpretations of domestic politics in Imperial Germany undertaken by scholars such as Hans-Ulrich Wehler and Volker Berghahn. Most historians would now probably agree with the verdict of James Joll, that no one factor is alone sufficient in explanation: an adequate approach must take account of both long-term and short-range factors, and encompass domestic social and political tensions, cultural orientations and preconceptions, in addition to international circumstances, shifting alliances and clashes of foreign policy interest among the great powers.

A number of elements are important when considering the general context. First, there is the shift in German foreign policy after Bismarck. There were debates among proponents of different views, ranging from notions of a strong middle European position of domination to more ambitious aspirations to world power status. In the 1890s and 1900s, the latter view gained ground. Imperialism entailed not only political but also economic considerations: a rapidly industrialising power needed markets for manufactured goods, and sources of cheap raw materials, and in this connection also needed to be able to compete with Britain. There were also cultural considerations, as in the view propounded by Weber, in his Freiburg inaugural lecture of 1895, that German culture had to be protected by a powerful nation state on the world stage. Imperialism became a cultural given, particularly in connection with the navy construction programme.

Secondly, there was the formation of alliances. The 'Triple Alliance' between Germany, Austria and Italy had already been developing in Bismarck's time (with Germany signing an alliance with Austria in 1879 and being joined by Italy in 1882). The 'Triple Entente' between France, Russia and Britain developed more slowly. Between 1891 and 1894 France and Russia developed an understanding; from 1904, Britain began to align with this (agreements with France in 1904 and Russia in 1907) after settlement of differences with France in Egypt, Morocco and the Far East, and with the increasingly apparent weakness of Tsarist Russia after defeat by Japan in 1904–5 and the revolution of 1905. These alliances were not clearly fixed, and each country tended to act in its own interests over particular issues. In 1908–9, for example, Russia failed to get French and British support in its protests against Austrian annexation of the provinces of Bosnia and Herzegovina. But the alignment of Britain, France and Russia provoked in Germany a 'fear of encirclement': a fear that Germany was surrounded by hostile forces, which made the special relationship with Austria even more important for Germany.

The development of alliances was related to a third factor of importance: an arms race. There was a general sense that war was looming, and all European states began a race to be ready for war when it came. Typical of this was German navy-building; but Russia was equally busy building railways as a rapid means of troop transport, in addition to manufacturing arms, as were other

European powers. This not only provoked a sense of inevitability about war, but also influenced strategic thinking about the timing of its outbreak, especially in Germany. A key role has, for example, been given in some accounts to an informal war council of 8 December 1912 (at which the chancellor, Bethmann Hollweg, was not present). The German emperor professed himself to be in favour of war 'the sooner the better', supported by General Moltke, while Tirpitz argued that the navy could not be ready for at least eighteen months.

It should be noted in this connection that the German chancellor, Bethmann Hollweg, was generally moderate in his desire to consolidate Germany's European position by peaceful means; but his government was without popular support, given the stalemate in the Reichstag. Great pressure was being exerted by such groups as the Pan-German League and the Central League of German Industrialists (*Centralverband deutscher Industrieller*). The chancellor's moderate position was increasingly challenged, and his arguments apparently weakened by news of a forthcoming Anglo-Russian naval agreement. Bethmann Hollweg was effectively pressurised into new strategies in south-eastern Europe as a result of his own weak position, and the paralysis of the German political system.

Finally, there is the question of how war actually broke out. A number of crises had been successfully navigated: the first Moroccan crisis of 1905, in which the French were ultimately supported by all the major European powers except Germany and Austria; and a second Moroccan crisis six years later, in which Germany and Austria again found themselves isolated. But a more problematic area proved to be that seething pot of nationalism in south-eastern Europe, the Balkans. Germany, Austria and Russia all had certain interests in this area, with Russia and Austria manipulating different nationalist movements in the crumbling Ottoman Empire while Germany was pursuing a form of economic penetration of the area, with investment in such projects as banking and railways. There had been earlier conflicts between Turkey and Austria over Bosnia-Herzegovina. In 1912–13 there was a series of Balkan wars. It was clear that the situation was unstable. Moreover, this instability coincided with the reorientation of British policy towards European and away from Imperial concerns.

The spark that finally ignited war in 1914 was an incident that could have been passed off with a few protests, and was certainly not commensurate with the scale of the hostilities it unleashed. On 28 June 1914 the Austrian heir to the throne, Archduke Franz Ferdinand, was assassinated by a young Bosnian while on an official visit to the capital of the annexed Bosnia-Herzegovina, Sarajevo. The Bosnian assassin was supported by a group of Serbian nationalists. Austria had been harbouring plans either to incorporate Serbia, or to turn it into some form of dependent satellite state. Serbian nationalists were therefore collaborating with Bosnian opponents of Austrian rule. Austria spent some time considering how to respond to this assassination; political murders were quite common in the late nineteenth and early twentieth century, and not necessarily the cause for war. Austria consulted Germany, when the emperor effectively gave the Austrians a 'blank cheque', promising German support for Austrian actions. In the light of this assurance, Austria proceeded to make use of the incident as a pretext to deliver an ultimatum to Serbia, couched in terms to which Serbia could not possibly accede. As a result, tensions were heightened. On 31 July Russian troops were mobilised. This was taken as tantamount to belligerence, necessitating an Austrian response. Germany then put into effect the so-called 'Schlieffen plan': since war on two fronts had to be avoided, France must be knocked out before fighting Russia; and in order to circumvent French defences, German troops must invade France via Belgium. But Belgian neutrality was guaranteed by Britain. Britain too spent some time considering the situation. But by 4 August decisions were made that it should be war. Thus, several weeks after the original incident, the European states chose to start the war for which they had been waiting, and in large measure chose to do so because of the policy adopted by the German Emperor and his military advisers.

The war they got, however, was not the war they had been expecting or wanting. Initially, there was considerable jubilation, with large numbers of Germans indulging in nationalist enthusiasm as they marched off to the front. Even a considerable number of socialists at least formally supported the war effort, with only a minority of the Reichstag delegation opposing the decision to vote for war credits. The emperor announced the end of civil war at home and the outbreak of 'civil peace' (*Burgfrieden*). War was consciously viewed by members of the German elites as an 'escape forwards', a 'solution to the problems of peace', a means of deflecting attention from unresolved problems at home. German soldiers marched off to war singing patriotic songs, in the happy delusion that an early victory would allow them to be home for Christmas.

In the event, the First World War was not a brief, nineteenth-century style war with a decisive battle, limited casualties, and an early end to hostilities. It was a long-drawn-out, wearisome affair characterised by mud-bespattered and shell-shocked soldiers spending days and weeks in the trenches, with advances being measured less in miles than in yards. Numbers of casualties were high, to very little effect, as in the 1916 battle of the Somme which, despite enormous loss of life, effectively ended in stalemate. The German economy was not equipped to sustain a lengthy conflict, and as food provisions and living conditions worsened there was a progressive loss of morale on the home front. From 1915, there were food riots, and major strikes from April 1917 (while in Russia in 1917 there was a successful communist revolution). Splits developed among German socialists, with the Independent Social Democratic Party (USPD) breaking away from the SPD in 1917. With setbacks in the war in 1916, and disputes over navy and submarine warfare, Tirpitz was forced to resign. In April 1917, the USA entered the war, following German U-boat (submarine) attacks on civilian vessels. In July 1917 the Bethmann Hollweg government was replaced by an effective military dictatorship under Ludendorff and Hindenburg (although there were two civilian chancellors in rapid succession). While the mass of Germans were increasingly war-weary, and while a pro-peace coalition was emerging in the Reichstag (foreshadowing the later Weimar coalition), some Germans harboured grandiose annexationist aims. In the summer of 1917 the right-wing German Fatherland Party (*Deutsche Vaterlandspartei*) was founded, supporting the army leadership. (One member of this ultra right-wing, nationalist party was Anton Drexler, subsequently leader of the German Workers' Party, DAP, which was the forerunner of the Nazi NSDAP.) Nationalist circles attempted to deflect criticism of the war into anti-semitic sentiments: it was asserted that the war was lasting so long because the Jews had not yet made enough profit from it. (Later, of course, Jews and Marxists were accused of a 'stab in the back', bringing down the German war effort from within while the army was essentially undefeated abroad.) Despite the possibility of a moderate peace at the turn of 1917–18, the Supreme Command of the Army and the annexationists continued to pursue megalomaniac plans, in the belief that domestic troubles could only be resolved, and socialism suppressed, by lucrative conquests abroad. They were somewhat boosted by the dictated peace treaty of Brest-Litovsk, imposed on post-revolutionary Russians, who were unable and unwilling to fight on, in March 1918. But by the summer of 1918 it was clear even to the most blinkered of German army leaders that the war was effectively lost.

Attempts were made to pre-empt a feared revolution in Germany by a last 'revolution from above'. The army leadership handed over to civilian command, and plans were instituted for reforms of the political structure, in line with the implications of US President Wilson's 'Fourteen Points' and in the hope of a more lenient peace treaty. Yet, as we shall see in the next chapter, within a couple of months the revolution from below had erupted; and in November 1918 the German Empire collapsed and was replaced by Germany's first parliamentary republic.

Evaluations of Imperial Germany must remain ambivalent. While older German nationalist historians celebrated Germany's unification and historic hour of imperial greatness, it is quite clear that the socioeconomic, political and cultural configuration was riddled with strains and tension. In Prussia-dominated small Germany, domestic politics lurched from one compromise to another, with no long-term resolution of major issues such as the stable incorporation of the working masses into the political system of a rapidly industrialising society still dominated by pre-industrial elites. One need not subscribe to notions of a 'belated nation' or the 'peculiarities of German history' (the *Sonderweg*), with all the teleological and evolutionary assumptions embodied in these views, to realise that no successful balance was struck between the interests of different classes in Imperial Germany. But its successor, the Weimar Republic, met with no greater success. The failure to resolve conflicting

social, political and economic interests in the context of parliamentary democracy paved the way for a more radical attempt at resolving domestic tensions: the essential abdication of the old elites, and
the handing of power to Hitler and the Nazi party in the hope that a
demagogic mass movement could both incorporate the people and
be manipulated by the elites. Tragically, this last turn in the spiral
of mounting tensions proved the most fatal.

6

Democracy and dictatorship, 1918–45

In November 1918, a parliamentary republic was proclaimed in Germany. The Weimar Republic, as it came to be known after the town in which its constitution was developed, was associated with a progressive political system, and a set of social compromises including a relatively advanced welfare state. Yet it was born out of turmoil and defeat, under near civil-war conditions; it was hampered by a harsh peace settlement, and an unstable economy; it was consistently subjected to attacks from both left and right, as large numbers of Germans rejected democracy as a form of government; and little over fourteen years after its inception, the Weimar Republic was ended when Adolf Hitler, as a constitutionally appointed chancellor, inaugurated one of the worst regimes known in human history. The disastrous demise of Weimar democracy has cast an inevitable shadow over interpretations of its course: whatever one may make of long-term interpretations of German history, it is in the Weimar Republic that the immediate causation of Hitler's rise to power has to be sought. Some accounts tend to suggest Weimar democracy was foredoomed from the start; others place far greater weight on the mistakes and decisions of individuals in the closing months in 1932–3, or on the effects of the slump after 1929. Some historians emphasise the contribution of individuals; others stress the importance of constraining, structural factors, and the limitations placed on freedom of manoeuvre and decision-making, particularly in the closing stages. Where to lay the responsibility for Hitler's rise to power, given the consequences of the Nazi regime, will continue to be hotly debated.

While the Republic's early years were characterised by instability and strife, there was a period of apparent stabilisation between 1924 and 1928. The evident weaknesses of the years from 1929 to 1933 were however not purely contingent, an 'accidental' effect of economic depression set off by the Wall Street crash, but rather were rooted in pre-existing tendencies, weaknesses, strains and attitudes. Yet this did not necessarily pre-determine the exact course of events taken in the closing years, nor the specific outcome in the appointment of Hitler as chancellor. Nor can any one factor alone explain the rise of Nazism. Simply to invoke Hitler's oratorical powers, which supposedly seduced an apolitical German people, is misguided; the story of the development and collapse of Weimar democracy is a highly complex one, with a multiplicity of factors interacting under very specific historical circumstances to produce the final outcome. In a sense, this very complexity – while making the story more difficult to grasp – is a blessing. For in response to the frequently heard question of 'whether it could ever happen again', the answer must be that it is highly unlikely that such a unique combination of a range of different factors under particular circumstances could ever occur in precisely that mixture again. Whenever, for example, extreme right-wing and racialist movements have arisen in post-war Germany, they have arisen under quite different conditions and with quite different implications.

THE WEIMAR REPUBLIC: ORIGINS AND EARLY YEARS

It was clear in the summer of 1918, even to the most ardent militarists and nationalists, that Germany had lost the war. The attempted deflection of social tensions at home into imperialist adventures abroad had failed; and defeated Germany was to face an exacerbation, rather than resolution, of the social tensions which had fed into the origins of the war. During the war previous tendencies towards the concentration of capital had increased, with large cartels monopolising prices and markets and squeezing out small businesses and small traders: the lower middle classes were more threatened than before, the large capitalists stronger. Yet at the same time the strength of the organised working class had also increased. In the desire to avoid strikes and disruption of production in the economic mobilisation for total war, industry and government had made concessions to organised labour, with improvements in working conditions and the recognition of unions as legitimate representatives of labour. There had also been a certain politicisation of sections of the population, as women and young people were brought into areas of the labour force from which they had formerly been excluded, with a war-time labour shortage. Psychologically, people's horizons and perceptions had been changed by war-time experiences in a variety of ways, whether through shell-shock and disorientation, with difficulties in adapting to and reentering civilian life, or whether through increased dependence on, and expectations of, the state, by virtue of state pensions or allowances.

There was increasing domestic unrest in Germany towards the end of the war. It was evident that things would have to change – not only because of American President Wilson's 'Fourteen Points' indicating that domestic reforms in Germany would be necessary for negotiating a modified peace treaty, but also because of pressures from below – and because of the desire of the army to evade responsibility for a 'dishonourable' peace. By the end of September it appeared opportune to army leaders to hand over power to a civilian government which could then take the opprobrium of accepting defeat; the reforms of October were not simply a 'revolution from above', in that parliamentary parties had for some time, with lesser or greater degrees of energy, been pushing for reforms. In October 1918, Prince Max von Baden became chancellor, and constitutional reforms were introduced. These included reform of the suffrage (including abolition of the Prussian three-class voting system), ministerial responsibility to parliament, and the control of the armed forces by the civilian government and not the monarchy. In effect, Emperor William II consented to what amounted to a constitutional monarchy; but the one thing he refused to do – and which might have saved the monarchy as an institution – was to abdicate in favour of one of his sons. However, these reforms – which were intended largely as a holding operation pending a return to authoritarian government – were to be overtaken by more radical developments.

At the end of October, navy leaders ordered a last – suicidal – attack on the British to redeem German honour, and on 28 October the Wilhelmshaven fleet was ordered out. Not surprisingly, a majority of sailors decided that in this hour of German defeat they would rather salvage their own lives than German honour, and they mutinied. On 3 November, demonstrations in Kiel sparked off a more general mutiny. In the first days of November all over Germany, from the north right down to Kurt Eisner's socialist government in Bavaria, there were revolutionary upheavals, and the setting up of 'councils' of soldiers, sailors and workers to replace existing local government. Berlin, too, was a centre of unrest, with shop stewards and members of the USPD debating whether there should be an armed uprising, a notion which was opposed by moderates in the SPD. By 9 November, it was clear that the emperor must abdicate. Prince Max von Baden's government resigned and William II – who had already fled Berlin – left Germany for Holland.

In this revolutionary situation, with the collapse of government under pressure of military defeat, in an industrialised state with a large, politically organised working class, conditions were surely ripe for a classic Marxist revolution. Yet, in contradiction to Marxist theory, it was in relatively backward Tsarist Russia in 1917 that a communist revolution succeeded, whereas what developed in Germany in 1918–19 was a series of fudges and compromises, satisfying neither left nor right, and embodying a set of legacies that were to prove liabilities for Germany's first attempt at democracy. These compromises were already symbolised in arrangements made in the first few days after 9 November. While apparently stabilising in the short term, they tended to paper over, rather than resolve, tensions which erupted all the more powerfully in the longer run. Furthermore, the so-called revolution of 1918 in effect amounted to little more than a political and constitutional revolution, from Empire to Republic, but it – crucially – failed to effect radical changes in the socioeconomic structure of Germany, nor did it reform key elites. Army, bureaucracy, judiciary, educational and religious establishments, retained their positions of power and influence – and used them to speak and act in the main against the new Republic.

On 9 November, Prince Max von Baden handed over power, in an act of apparent legitimacy and continuity, to SPD leader

Friedrich Ebert as 'Imperial chancellor'. Given the revolutionary tu-
mults in Berlin and rumours of more radical action, Ebert's colleague
Scheidemann proclaimed a Republic. This Republic, the exact form
of which was by no means clear as yet, faced very immediate problems and tasks: demobilising soldiers, signing an armistice, dealing
with revolts and uprisings all over Germany, rebuilding the economy and ensuring an adequate food supply, and – in the context
of all these disruptions – devising an acceptable new constitution
for post-Imperial Germany. It was by no means an easy set of tasks,
and retrospectively, historians have had little difficulty in identifying
failures of nerve or vision on the part of those in a position to affect
Germany's future.

Two very crucial compromises were reached almost immediately.
In the infamous 'Ebert–Groener pact', General Groener offered
Ebert the support of the army if Ebert would adopt a moderate
course and suppress the more radical council movements (Groener
boasting that this successfully averted the threat of Bolshevik revolution in Germany); and as time went by, Ebert came more and more
to rely on the powers of the military to suppress uprisings by force,
rather than exploring and responding to the causes of social unrest.
Secondly, in the so-called 'Stinnes–Legien agreement', the leader of
the labour unions, Carl Legien, and the industrialist Hugo Stinnes
concluded a bargain which consolidated the position of organised
labour, including the introduction of an eight-hour day, and an employers' agreement to stop supporting 'yellow unions' (or house
unions, an employer's stooge). The initial government itself was a
compromise, with a 'Council of People's Representatives' set up on
10 November consisting of three SPD and three USPD members.
While this was subsequently given some legitimacy through confirmation by Berlin council delegates, a congress of council delegates
from all over Germany in December saw the first serious splits between moderate and radical socialists. While the majority of the five
hundred delegates supported the SPD and Ebert's plans for elections
to a National Constituent Assembly which would draft a new constitution for Germany, a minority supported the more radical views
of the USPD, who criticised Ebert's 'government by procrastination'
which refused to undertake socioeconomic reform before constitutional change, or to reform the army. Ebert's defence was that there

was little point in 'nationalising bankruptcy', and that good relations with the army were essential for orderly demobilisation and reconstruction, both points which were queried at the time as well as later. In the event, the USPD finally broke with the SPD, leaving an all-SPD cabinet; and at the end of December 1918 the left-wing 'Spartacist' group, which like the USPD had increasing differences with the SPD, formed themselves into the new Communist Party of Germany, the KPD.

Unrest had by no means simply been quelled by the proclamation of a Republic. Renewed uprisings in Berlin in January 1919 were suppressed by army and Free Corps units (volunteer groups financed by industry and organised by the army), in the course of which radical leaders Rosa Luxemburg and Karl Liebknecht were murdered. This provoked bitter hostility and resentment among left-wing critics of the SPD. The split between moderate and radical socialists was to survive until the collapse of Weimar democracy, when communists viewed Social Democrats as a greater evil even than Nazis. All over Germany in the first half of 1919 it appeared as if the Social Democrats were relying on the forces of the old order to suppress initiatives in favour of the new. In Bavaria, after Kurt Eisner's assassination, a second attempt at revolution, with the proclamation of a Soviet republic in Munich in April 1919, was brutally suppressed by Free Corps units in May, with over one thousand deaths. Political violence of all shades was rife, as demobilised soldiers failed to find new roles in civilian life and sought to continue the comradeship of the trenches in paramilitary groups, while right-wingers and left-wingers attempted to effect immediate influence on an uncertain course of political events. Others simply observed, bewildered and hoping for some form of stabilisation. Meanwhile, the process of devising a new constitution was underway. Elections on 19 January 1919 – in the wake of the Spartacist uprising in Berlin – gave the SPD only 38 per cent of the vote, necessitating a coalition government. On 6 February the National Constituent Assembly opened in Weimar. On 11 February Ebert was elected President, and on 13 February a cabinet under Scheidemann was formed from the 'Weimar coalition' parties of SPD, Catholic Centre, and the liberal DDP (German Democratic Party).

Plate 29. Barricades in Berlin, March 1919.

Plate 30. The Free Corps Werdenfels, in Munich to suppress
revolutionary uprisings.

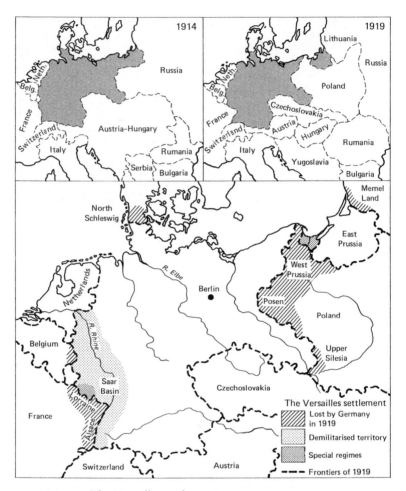

Map 9. The Versailles settlement, 1919

The Weimar Constitution, which took effect on 11 August 1919, appeared quite progressive. A President was to be elected by direct popular vote for a period of seven years, and, as a sort of 'substitute emperor' (*Ersatzkaiser*), the President had considerable powers. These included the right to appoint and dismiss chancellors, the right to dissolve parliament and call new elections, and the right to call national referenda. Ultimately the most notorious of the Weimar President's powers was embodied in Article 48 of the constitution:

Plate 31. The Kapp Putsch. Soldiers march into Berlin, March 1920.

the right to rule by emergency decree. Other provisions included a voting system of proportional representation, with universal suffrage for all adult men and women, the latter receiving the vote for the first time. The cabinet was to be responsible to parliament. A considerable degree of autonomy continued to lie with individual state governments, in what remained a relatively decentralised state.

In the early summer of 1919 the harsh terms of the Versailles peace treaty were revealed. Scheidemann's cabinet resigned and was succeeded by the Bauer cabinet, which sent a delegation to sign the Versailles Treaty on 28 June. Germany was to lose large areas of land: Alsace-Lorraine was to be returned to France, West Prussia, Upper Silesia and Posen were to go to the newly reconstructed Poland, Danzig was to become a free city under League of Nations supervision, with the 'Polish Corridor' separating East Prussia from the rest of Germany. Germany was deprived of colonies, and any union of Germany and Austria was forbidden. The army was limited to 100,000 men, and the left bank of the Rhine was to be demilitarised under Allied supervision, with Allied occupation to be phased out over a period of time. In the notorious 'war guilt clause' Germany was burdened with responsibility for the war. Reparations were as yet to be determined; when they were finally announced in the Paris conference of January 1921, they were to provoke as much indignation as the other provisions of the Versailles Treaty.

Undoubtedly it was a harsh set of peace terms, and the contrast with the settlement in the aftermath of the Second World War was, as we shall see, very marked. But even more was made of the Versailles Treaty by its critics than realities warranted. Already in August 1918 the myth of the 'stab in the back' had been propagated, asserting that domestic enemies (such as Jews and socialists) had brought down an army which was undefeated abroad but betrayed from within. This myth was inflated in the autumn of 1919 to become common currency in circles opposing the Republic. The years from 1919 to 1923 saw a series of attacks on the Republic and attempted putsches on the right, as well as continued strikes and revolutionary movements on the left, in the context of mounting economic problems. While right-wing extremists were generally treated leniently by a highly conservative judiciary, left-wingers were subjected to harsh sentences, including disproportionate use of the death penalty. In March 1920, Kapp and Lüttwitz organised a march of Free Corps units on Berlin, and Ebert's government was forced to flee to Stuttgart, since the army, under General von Seeckt, refused to fight the Free Corps soldiers. Nevertheless, at this time a general strike was sufficient to defeat the Kapp putsch. A more limited rightist coup brought to power a right-wing government, under Kahr, in Bavaria. In 1921 and again in 1923 communists unsuccessfully attempted insurrection in Saxony. There were also continued strikes, particularly in the Ruhr, in 1919 and 1920. Largely spontaneous demands for 'nationalisation' of the mines were not part of a coherent political programme, but rather for immediate economic improvements: control over improved working conditions and better wages. While the KPD and the USPD did not initiate these protests, they attempted to gain control of them; misjudging the mood of grass-roots workers, in the main they failed. More crucially, the SPD miscalculated badly, and, fearing what they now viewed as a 'Bolshevist threat' to the new Republic, overreacted and instead of responding to the causes of distress attempted to suppress the symptoms by force. While the regular army had been unwilling to fight against insurgent Free Corps units in the Kapp putsch, it was only too willing to cooperate with these against the 'Red Army' in the Ruhr and Rhine areas. Under the leadership of von Seeckt, the Army was effectively sustaining the pre-republican, Prussian tradition of being a 'state within a state'. This 'apolitical' stance, refusing to support the Republic since to do so would be 'political', later proved no barrier to markedly political actions serving to undermine the Republic. Meanwhile, splits among the left-wing parties continued. Some regrouping took place with the disbanding of the USPD in 1922 and the reabsorption of its leaders and some of its members into the SPD while most of the grass-roots joined the KPD. But the fundamental gulf between the SPD and KPD – with theoretical roots reaching back to pre-war debates, exacerbated by strategic differences, and inflamed by the bitterness arising from Liebknecht's and Luxemburg's deaths – became essentially unbridgeable.

In the Reichstag elections of June 1920, the 'Weimar coalition' parties – SPD, Centre and DDP – lost votes and there was a swing to the extremes of both right and left. (The KPD had not contested the 1919 election.) National politics were particularly complicated by mounting economic and political difficulties connected with the reparations question. When the extremely high level of reparations was finally revealed, there was consternation about how an already weak German economy could deal with repayments. Germany's economic problems were partly rooted in methods of financing the war – through loans and bonds rather than the raising of taxes – and the roots of inflation were already present before the reparations question exacerbated matters. Inflation was, however, wildly fuelled by the so-called 'policy of fulfilment' pursued by Wirth's government in 1921–2 – a policy attacked in many quarters as capitulation to the demands of the victorious powers, but in fact designed to show that Germany could not fulfil reparations payments. As one commentator has put it, Germany's currency difficulties were presented as reparations payments difficulties. Meanwhile, France under Poincaré was pursuing revisionist policies of its own, aiming to gain control of the left bank of the Rhine. Crises reached a peak under the Cuno government of November 1922–August 1923 (in which the

SPD refused to participate, opposing the inclusion of the right-wing DVP, the German People's Party). The French used the shortfall in German wood and coal deliveries as a pretext for 'supervising' production in the Ruhr area, backed up by 'protective' armed forces (including Belgian troops) which marched into the Ruhr area in January 1923 and by the summer months had reached a total of 100,000 troops –equivalent to the total permitted strength of the German Army. The Germans responded by an official policy of passive resistance, refusing to co-operate with the French occupation and also ceasing economic production – which hurt the German economy more than the French. The only apparent solution for Germany was the printing of paper money, which sent the already existing inflation spiralling totally out of control. By August 1923, bank notes were being simply stamped over to increase their value by thousands; payments were being made by the waggon-load, and money became effectively worthless. Millions of people found themselves in severe difficulties or financial ruin, particularly those on fixed incomes (such as pensions) and many of the self-employed and lower middle classes. A few large industrialists were able to make profits. The general outcome was a widespread total loss of confidence in the Republic, fear and panic, and a wave of strikes and riots. The experience of 1923 left an imprint with reverberations carrying right on well into post-war West German history.

The situation was finally brought under control by the Stresemann government of August–November 1923. A combination of currency reform, introducing the Rentenmark, and termination of passive resistance in the Ruhr, dealt with the immediate economic crises and led to a reconsideration of the reparations question. Left-wing putsch attempts (mainly communist in inspiration) in Saxony, Thuringia and Hamburg were firmly put down. Meanwhile, in the right-wing haven of Bavaria a complex set of plans were being laid by a group of nationalists, including army officers, as well as one Adolf Hitler, leader of the NSDAP (National Socialist German Workers' Party), one of many small nationalist *völkisch* parties. Inspired by Mussolini's 'March on Rome' of 1922, plans were made to effect a 'March on Berlin'. At the last minute, on 8–9 November 1923, Hitler lost the support of his more powerful and well-placed associates in the Bavarian hierarchy, and found the Nazi putsch isolated and easily suppressed, with the death of a few supporters when they were shot while marching past Munich's Feldherrnhalle. In contrast to the harsh sentences meted out to left-wingers at the time, Hitler – after a trial from which he won a great deal of beneficial national publicity – received a minimum sentence of five years, of which he in fact served only a few months, in comfortable detention in Landsberg prison, being released in time for Christmas 1924. Hitler made use of the opportunity to reflect on his long-term aims – in the process writing *Mein Kampf* – as well as on strategy and tactics. He allowed the NSDAP, which he had taken over from the previous DAP (German Workers' Party) led by Drexler, to disintegrate in his absence, so that he could impose firm leadership on his return to freedom; and he renounced the putschist approach, to adopt from 1925 the tactic of the legal, parliamentary path for anti-parliamentary ends. But the rise of this Austrian-born failed artist and ex-corporal was as yet something which no one would have predicted; for after the crises of 1923, the Weimar Republic entered a new period of apparent stabilisation.

THE PERIOD OF APPARENT STABILISATION

By 1924, it began to appear as if the early troubles of the Weimar Republic were over, and improvements appeared on a number of fronts. In November 1923, Gustav Stresemann became Foreign Minister, a position he held until his death in 1929. Interpretations of Stresemann vary. He was a member of the right-wing DVP, and only gradually became a *Vernunftrepublikaner*, a supporter of the Republic for pragmatic reasons rather than principles. His foreign policy is subject to a range of evaluations, but in general the verdict is that Stresemann was successful in regularising Germany's relations with her western neighbours, while keeping his options open in relation to Germany's eastern frontiers. The Locarno Treaty of 1925 included guarantees that Germany, France and Belgium would not alter their existing boundaries by force; there were also pacts with Poland and Czechoslovakia, but these agreements were not guaranteed. Germany regained a place in the international system, and in September 1926 became a member of the League of Nations. Stresemann hoped that the Locarno Treaty would help to defuse domestic criticism of his policies and aid his eastern strategies. In April 1926 the Berlin Treaty confirmed the new relations between Germany and Russia which had first been expressed in the Rapallo Treaty of 1922 (when Rathenau was still Foreign Minister). The Rapallo Treaty had helped to normalise already improved relations between Germany and Russia (and was not necessarily intended, as some revisionist Germans hoped, as a means to the division of Poland and a restoration of the eastern frontiers of 1914). In the 1926 Berlin Treaty Germany assured Russia of German neutrality if Russia were at war with a third power. This implied that if, for example, Russia were at war with Poland, France would not be able to come to Poland's defence via German territory.

Poland's position was thus rather weak. On the reparations front, the Dawes Plan of 1924 managed to combine German interests with American economic expansionism. Yearly payments were agreed, at a more manageable level than under previous reparations arrangements, and there was to be an initial recovery phase in which only one-fifth would be paid from Germany's own resources and four-fifths would be paid from international loans received as 'start-up' help. 'Normal' annuities would be paid by Germany from 1928/9. In July 1925, French troops began to leave the Ruhr, and the first area of the Rhineland was cleared. In January 1927 the inter-allied military commission overseeing Germany's disarmament was withdrawn. There was economic rapprochement between France and Germany, and German diplomacy mediated between the USA and France for the Kellogg–Briand pact of August 1928. As the start of normal reparations came nearer, discussions on reparations and total evacuation of the Rhineland were heightened; and in August 1929, the Young Plan was adopted (against considerable domestic right-wing opposition), setting a new total figure of reparations to be paid, with a reduced annual average in comparison with the Dawes Plan. Foreign controls would be removed, and the Rhineland was to be cleared of military occupation in June 1930, five years earlier than envisaged in the Versailles Treaty. It appeared as if, largely under Stresemann's guidance, a number of goals had been achieved: evacuation of the Ruhr, early ending of the occupation of the Rhineland, the lifting of military controls, the regularisation of Germany's relations with her neighbours, the international recognition of Germany

Plate 32. A peasant wedding in Bad Tölz, Bavaria. The culture and life-style of these peasants was very far from what has come to be known as 'Weimar culture'.

as a member of the League of Nations, a manageable set of reparations arrangements – and even a keeping open of the question of Germany's eastern frontiers, while pursuing revisionist aims by peaceful means.

In the cultural sphere, Weimar witnessed great intellectual ferment and artistic creativity: 'Weimar culture' achieved a renown reverberating far beyond its own time and place. In the natural sciences, in psychology and psychoanalysis, in social theory, new ideas were discussed and developed. In architecture, the Bauhaus school of Walter Gropius combined aesthetic and utilitarian criteria to produce styles of architecture, interior design and furniture still prevalent three-quarters of a century later. In music, the experimental work of Schönberg achieved international renown, while imported 'decadent' American jazz music caught on among certain circles and was wildly criticised by others. In prose and poetry, works by Thomas and Heinrich Mann, Erich Kästner, Rainer Maria Rilke, Stefan George, and others attained the status of classics; in drama, Bertolt Brecht – frequently in fruitful conjunction with the composer Kurt Weill – made brilliant contributions, while there were equally important movements in the field of modern art, associated with such schools as 'Der blaue Reiter', 'Die Brücke', expressionism, Dada, cubism and futurism. In a range of ways and through a variety of media, Weimar artists and intellectuals analysed, exposed, and commented on their own society, from the realistic portrayal of violence in late Weimar Berlin by Alfred Döblin to the bitter caricatures of Weimar society in the works of Georg Grosz or Käthe Kollwitz, or the posters of John Heartfield and the cartoons about Berlin low society of Heinrich Zille. The 1920s were also an era of expansion and commercialisation of popular culture, particularly with the spread of cinemas, showing silent films until the introduction of sound reels in 1929, and the expanding ownership of radios. No real political use was made of the radio until 1932, when Papen prepared the ground for the Nazis' subsequent effective hi-jacking of the medium as an instrument of propaganda. And despite obviously left-wing tendencies among much (though not all) of 'high-brow' culture, much popular culture – as in war films which did not attain the status of *All Quiet on the Western Front* – remained nationalist and what is perhaps best described in terms of the German word *kitsch*. A perceived 'decadence' in Weimar culture and life styles – including a supposed laxity of morals, symbolised in new, short, boyish hair-styles for women, the smoking of cigarettes and use of contraceptives – provoked intense and hostile criticism on the part of conservatives, particularly in the Protestant establishment, as well as from Catholic quarters. From the left, the evils of modern capitalism and the miseries of the working classes attracted bitter attacks. About the only valid generalisation that can be made about the explosive currents of creativity that have come to be known as 'Weimar culture' is that little of it served to sustain the Republic in principle: while the left attacked the social inequalities of modern industrial capitalist society, the right attacked the decadence and social-moral disintegration of modern mass democracy. An isolated – and belated – exception was Thomas Mann, who jettisoned his 'apolitical' conservatism of 1918 to speak out in defence of the Republic. But one must conclude that despite the undoubted achievements of Weimar artists and intellectuals, the impact of Weimar culture was deeply divisive and politically ambiguous.

In one further area, too, the Weimar compromise proved ambiguous, and ultimately fatally so. This was in the area of social compromise evident in the earliest days of the Republic in November 1918. At a time of weakness, in the uncertainties of the revolutionary days, employers had made concessions to representatives of organised labour. Agreements had been reached on wages, on conditions of work and the eight-hour day, and on a form of corporatism embodied in the *Zentral-Arbeits-Gemeinschaft* (Central Work Community, ZAG), with a strategy of partnership between unions and employers, and state intervention as arbitrator if necessary. In 1920 the Works Council Act laid the foundation of the German tradition of co-determination, and in the later 1920s there were discussions of economic democracy. In the period of stabilisation after 1924, there were extensions of social policy, including social housing construction and the 1927 Law on Unemployment Insurance. Yet it was not entirely a simple history of progress in industrial relations and social policy. In the crisis year of 1923 employers dropped certain agreements, including the eight-hour day; and the failure of the ZAG led to the official resignation of the main German trade union body, the ADGB, in January 1924. From 1923 onwards, unions began to lose members, funds, power and credibility. Weak and essentially defensive unions had repeatedly to rely on state intervention to coerce employers on disputed issues. Yet employers, feeling equally defensive, from 1923 onwards mounted an attack on the Weimar system which sustained this compromise, which was ultimately to prove an overwhelming attack on the Republic itself. In the Ruhr iron strike of 1928, the intention of industrialists to get rid of an interventionist social state became explicit. Moreover, even in these 'good years' of the Republic, its economic foundations were fragile. The German economy was to a considerable degree reliant on short-term loans and investment from America; if the latter's economy were to falter, Germany's would fall too.

Nor, despite the apparent stabilisation of the Weimar Republic from 1924, had many people become genuinely committed to the new political form. The election of an ageing nationalist military hero, Field-Marshal Hindenburg, as the new President to replace Friedrich Ebert after his premature death in 1925 was indicative of widespread yearnings for the old days of Imperial Germany. From 1925–6 onwards, in conjunction with General Kurt von Schleicher (de facto leader of the army from 1926), Hindenburg was positively considering plans for the development of a right-wing, authoritarian form of government excluding parliamentary and social-democratic influence. Moreover, there were continuing difficulties with party government. The system of proportional representation and a multiplicity of small parties meant that no single party was able to attain an overall majority; but the radically diverging views of the main parties led to great difficulty in forming viable coalition governments. While agreements could be reached on domestic policies between the Catholic Centre party, the liberal DVP and the conservative DNVP, they could not agree on foreign policy; but conversely, while a 'grand coalition' from the SPD through the Centre to the DVP (but excluding the DNVP) could agree on foreign policy, they could not agree on domestic issues. The only alternative was to have a minority cabinet, necessitating toleration, if not support, from either left or right. In these circumstances, with a rapid succession of cabinets and frequent interventions by the President, party politics and parliamentary government lost what little credibility they had ever been able to muster among large sections of the German people.

It is debatable whether, given the difficult circumstances of its birth, the harsh legacies of the early years, and the fragility of its social and political foundations, the Weimar Republic could have survived in the long term under favourable conditions. In the event, from 1929 onwards Weimar democracy was subjected to a series of onslaughts in a set of circumstances from which it could not hope to survive unscathed. From 1930 onwards, the question increasingly narrowed to that of what particular form the collapse of democracy would take.

THE COLLAPSE OF WEIMAR DEMOCRACY

Even before the Wall Street Crash of October 1929, there were plans afoot to dismantle parliamentary democracy in Weimar Germany. But the way in which the collapse of democracy took place was highly affected by the economic crises unleashed by world recession, which had particularly harsh reverberations in Germany. Following the relative success of the SPD in the 1928 elections, a 'grand coalition' under SPD chancellor Hermann Müller had been formed. This survived initial splits in the SPD over money for a battleship as well as wider crises over adoption of the Young Plan. But the Wall Street Crash had peculiarly serious implications, given the dependence of the German economy on short-term loans from abroad which were rapidly withdrawn. Unemployment rose rapidly, from 1.3 million in September 1929 to over 3 million by September 1930, reaching over 6 million – one in three of the working population – by the beginning of 1933. With official under-estimation of the true figure, as well as widespread short-time working, perhaps half the families in Germany were affected by the slump; and many more experienced fear of financial catastrophe, verging on panic. These circumstances had a variety of implications. They directly led to the downfall of Müller's government, which became deadlocked over the question of what to do about unemployment insurance in a situation where rising numbers out of work could no longer be supported by declining numbers in work at the levels agreed in 1927. No compromise could be reached between alternative schemes, with unions, employers, and members of the different parties all having very different positions on the matter, characterised by varying degrees of intransigence. In March 1930 the attempt to ensure that government had party-political support in parliament was abandoned: the first presidential cabinet was appointed, to rule without serious regard for democracy.

The Brüning cabinet of 1930 had already been planned for in 1929 as part of a strategy to remove power from parliament and restore it to the old elites – army, bureaucracy, and economic elites – under a presidential, authoritarian regime. After 1930 increasing use was made of Article 48 to promulgate emergency decrees, while parliamentary sittings and parliamentary legislation decreased. Brüning pursued deflationary policies, combined with a policy of fulfilling reparations payments, consciously exacerbating the deterioration of Germany's financial and employment situation with the aim of achieving a fundamental revision of the reparations question. This he did indeed achieve – at the expense of the suffering of millions of Germans – with the Hoover Moratorium ultimately leading to the end of reparations in 1932. But in the meantime fundamental

upheavals were occurring in an already highly labile domestic political situation. In the years from 1930 to 1933 two factors coincided,
which in conjunction doomed Weimar democracy: the attacks on
parliamentary government by the old elites, which in essence had
predated the economic crisis, coincided with the rise of a new mass
movement mobilising, in periods of crisis, a large proportion of the
population seduced by the appeals of a charismatic leader figure,
Adolf Hitler.

Hitler had emerged from his period of detention to refound the
NSDAP in 1925. During the later 1920s and 1930s the party sought
to widen its appeal, from its early Bavarian base, across the different regions of Germany and across a range of social groups. While
its predominant social basis remained among petty middle-class,
Protestant, rural and small-town voters, particularly in northern
and eastern Germany, it was able to gain support also among educated, upper middle-class and professional groups, as well as, to a
more limited degree, among some sections of the less well-organised
working class. (Although percentages were small, given the size of
the working class overall numbers of working-class Nazi supporters
were not inconsiderable.) In the 1928 elections, the NSDAP achieved
only 2.6 per cent of the vote, giving them twelve parliamentary seats.
The campaign against the Young Plan in 1929, in which the NSDAP
cooperated with the DNVP under the right-wing press baron
Hugenberg, gave the Nazis tremendous free publicity as well as
an aura of respectability by virtue of their association with right-
wing establishment nationalists. The electoral breakthrough for the
NSDAP came with the elections of September 1930, in which the
NSDAP became the second largest party in the Reichstag (after
the SPD) with 107 deputies. With the collapse of the parties of the
'bourgeois middle', and the rise in votes for extremist parties – the
KPD increased its mandate to seventy-seven seats – there was no
basis for a parliamentary majority in support of any viable coalition
cabinet. The SPD, however, fearful of the likely consequences of further elections, chose to 'tolerate' the Brüning presidential cabinet.
And, although the financial support of business circles was negligible as a factor in the NSDAP's success before 1930, and was not
even very important thereafter, industrialists began to perceive the
NSDAP as important in the destruction of the parliamentary system

Plate 33. A 1932 election poster for Hindenburg.

and were to become influential, particularly in 1932–3, in persuading Hindenburg that Hitler could be of some use in this project.

The political history of Germany in 1932–3 is a complex one of intrigues and miscalculations. Brüning's cabinet fell partly because of Brüning's mismanagement of Hindenburg's humiliating re-election as President (after a second ballot, in which Hitler had gained one-third of the votes). A key figure in the machinations of the summer, autumn and winter was General von Schleicher, who first engineered the short-lived government of von Papen. Von Papen raised the ban instituted by Brüning's government on the Nazi paramilitary SA and SS, and then used the violence on the streets partly as a pretext to suggest that the Prussian *Land* police were incapable of maintaining order, as a result of which the Prussian SPD-led government was deposed and a central administrator imposed on Prussia. In the elections of July 1932 the Nazis gained a staggering 230 seats, which, along with the eighty-nine seats held by the KPD, meant that there was an anti-parliamentary majority not prepared to tolerate the government of von Papen. Schleicher also played a role in unsuccessful negotiations with Hitler over the inclusion of the Nazis in a new coalition government. In August 1932, Hitler turned down Hindenburg's reluctant offer of the vice-chancellorship – a move which provoked much criticism within the NSDAP, which feared that Hitler had turned down a great chance which would not be presented again. In September, the Papen government lost a motion of no confidence by 512 votes to forty-two. On all sides, right-wing circles, industrial and agrarian elites, and army leaders, as well as President Hindenburg, were considering strategies for effectively abolishing parliamentary government, reinstalling the old elites in power, and removing the constitutional necessity for parliamentary elections. With mounting unemployment and violence on the streets, with clashes between rival paramilitary gangs of left and right, with the effective emasculation of parliament in which there was total deadlock, with bitter splits between communists and Social Democrats who could not unite in opposition to Nazism, Germany in the autumn of 1932 was verging on civil war. Yet curiously, the final blow to Weimar democracy came just as the worst of the economic crisis was beginning to pass, and as the popularity of the Nazis for the first time was in decline. In the November elections of 1932 the NSDAP lost 2 million votes and saw its parliamentary strength reduced to 196 deputies. It remained the largest party in the Reichstag, but this in itself was no reason why it should automatically lead a government, as the history of the SPD in the Weimar Republic had shown.

Briefly, Schleicher himself became chancellor in December–January 1932–3. He attempted to gain support from labour unions, as well as the radical wing of the NSDAP represented by Gregor Strasser. This simultaneously aroused the fears of industrialists

Plate 34. The Berlin rent strike of 1932. Communist and Nazi
flags hang side by side in this courtyard.

and agrarians because of Schleicher's labour-creation and taxation
schemes; nor did Strasser in the end respond favourably to Schleicher's overtures, ultimately resigning his party offices and withdrawing from the scene of political strife. It was clear that Schleicher
could as little cobble together a workable compromise among different interests as could his predecessors. He had also, perhaps unwisely, persuaded Hindenburg that the army would be unable to
keep order in the event of civil war developing. In January 1933,
von Papen initiated a series of discussions including Hitler, Hindenburg's son, and Hindenburg, in which great pressure was put on the
ageing President by industrial and agrarian interest groups (such as
the Nazi-infiltrated *Reichslandbund*) to appoint Hitler as chancellor in a new coalition cabinet. Reluctantly, at the end of January
Hindenburg, who greatly despised this upstart 'Bohemian corpo-
ral', gave in. Hitler was constitutionally appointed chancellor of
Germany on 30 January 1933.

In one sense, this represented a simple continuity with the line of presidential cabinets and authoritarian rule since 1930. In another sense, of course, it represented – because of what was to come – a fundamental break. Hitler was the leader of a party which, after the failed putsch of 1923, was openly committed to the 'path of legality' as a means to anti-parliamentary ends: the Nazis made no secret of their intention to destroy democracy. The Nazi party itself was also rather unique. Although disproportionately supported by some social groups rather than others, it did in many respects represent a broad mass movement in contrast to the narrow interest-group parties so characteristic of Weimar politics, and could at least claim to be a 'people's party' (*Volkspartei*) rising above the factional strife and class conflicts of Weimar Germany. It could promise to heal the divisions tearing society apart. With its vague, all-embracing ideology – anti-modern, anti-capitalist, anti-communist, racialist, *völkisch* – it could mean all things to all people; with its increasing sophistication in the use of mass media and the staging of political rituals (evident for example in the 1929 Nuremberg party rally) it could become a form of powerful, pagan religion; with its charismatic leader figure, Adolf Hitler, who had been discovering and improving his gifts of oratory as well as having a public image built up for him, Nazism could pose as Germany's salvation and destiny, led by the strong man for whom many Germans had long been yearning. The promise of a new, national community, which would make Germany great again and tear apart the provisions of the hated Treaty of Versailles, which would punish the 'November criminals' of 1918, which would rid Germany of the 'Jewish bacillus' that was infecting and polluting the 'Aryan' race and would outlaw the Bolsheviks and criminals who had been undermining Germany from within for so long – all this proved a powerful vision to large numbers of desperate, frightened Germans for whom Weimar democracy had meant only national humiliation, economic disaster, social conflicts and personal uncertainty. Recognising the force of such a mass movement, and recognising their own lack of a popular base, the nationalist, industrial, agrarian and military elites thought they could 'harness', 'tame' and use this movement to give their own schemes for the destruction of democracy a legitimacy which they could not on their own achieve. Hitler did not need to 'seize' power; the old elites simply opened the door and welcomed him in. Faced with such a conjunction, there was little that the weakened unions and the divided left could do to salvage a democracy which had been effectively deserted by powerful interests as well as petty bourgeois masses. The miscalculated machinations of the elites proved a sadder, more irresponsible mistake than the weaknesses and errors of those who were ultimately unable to protect and defend the inherently unstable, ill-fated Weimar Republic. In this unique combination of circumstances, Adolf Hitler came to power in Germany.

THE CONSOLIDATION OF HITLER'S POWER

It nevertheless took Hitler some time to extend his hold on power, appointed as he was to lead a cabinet in which there were only two other Nazis, Frick and Goering. Elections were called for 5 March 1933, and, despite the intimidating atmosphere following the burning of the Reichstag on 27 February, which the Nazis used as a pretext for declaring a state of emergency, the Nazis still failed to win an absolute majority at the polls. The NSDAP achieved 43.9 per cent of the vote, giving it 288 seats, while the left gained over 30 per cent of the vote (128 seats for the SPD and eighty-one for the KPD) and the Centre and Liberals together gained 18 per cent. Even together with their Nationalist coalition partners the Nazis could not immediately obtain the two-thirds majority necessary to alter the constitution by an Enabling Law to destroy democratic government. Yet, after a well stage-managed opening of the Reichstag in the Garrison Church in Potsdam on 21 March, Hitler was able to convince the Centre party and other smaller right-wing parties that they should support his plans. By preventing communists and twenty-one Social Democrats from attending the Reichstag on the evening of 23 March, Hitler ensured the passing of the Enabling Law, with only the Social Democrats courageous enough to speak and vote against the destruction of democracy in Germany. Henceforth, Hitler could pass any 'law' he wanted, without regard for parliamentary approval. In any event, the latter soon became meaningless: in the course of the early summer of 1933, all parties except the NSDAP were either outlawed (the KPD being the first to go) or

Plate 35. Propaganda for Hitler celebrating the 'Day of Potsdam' and representing Hitler as a major statesman and successor to Frederick II, sanctioned by Hindenburg.

disbanded themselves (the Centre Party formally dissolving itself on 5 July 1933). On 14 July 1933 the 'Law against the formation of new parties' effectively established a one-party state.

Moves towards 'co-ordination' (*Gleichschaltung* – literally, 'putting into the same gear') were taken in a wide range of spheres. The civil service was purged of political opponents of Nazism, as well as Jews, in the 'Law for the restoration of the professional civil service' of 7 April 1933. The powers of the different *Länder* were attacked by the Nazi seizure of local powers in March 1933, and in April ten so-called 'Reich Governors' (*Reichsstatthalter*) were appointed to assert Nazi power at the *Land* level. In May, trade unions were wound up and replaced by the 'German Labour Front' (DAF) under Robert Ley. Walter Darré took control of the 'Reich Food Estate' dealing with agriculture and the peasantry, while craftsmen and small traders were organised under an umbrella organisation, the HAGO. On 30 January 1934, one year after Hitler's appointment as chancellor, the *Reichsrat* (upper chamber of parliament) was abolished and the federal system terminated. The final major constitutional change came with the death of President Hindenburg on 2 August 1934. Hitler made use of the occasion to combine the offices of President and Chancellor in his own person as Führer, and to take personal command of the armed forces, who now swore an oath of obedience to him.

The new, personal allegiance of the army to Hitler was made easier by Hitler's decision to resolve conflicts with the SA in favour of the army. The SA, under its leader Ernst Röhm, had been developing into a rather unruly rival for both the SS and the army. Aware that he vitally needed the support of the latter for his revisionist and expansionist foreign policies, Hitler instigated the so-called 'night of the long knives' on 30 June 1934, in which leaders of the SA were murdered along with a number of other individuals with whom Hitler had fallen out (including Schleicher and Gregor Strasser). This mass murder was retroactively 'legalised' by a law passed on 3 July 1934. The SA was firmly put in its place, in relation not only to the army, but also to the SS. The latter, under Heinrich Himmler – who by 1936 had combined control of the SS and the German police, effectively concentrating control of the means of terror in the Third Reich – was able to arrest, detain, imprison, torture and murder, with no respect for law or justice. In March 1933 the first Nazi concentration camp was opened in Dachau, near Munich – to much public fanfare, with open and enthusiastic newspaper coverage. This was essentially a detention centre and forced-labour camp, in which 'anti-social elements' (including political opponents of the regime and homosexuals, as well as 'criminals' more conventionally defined) were subjected to a penal regime. While inhumane treatment, torture, malnutrition, ill-health and overwork as well as outright murder were all causes of death, these labour camps (which proclaimed on their gates the slogan that 'Arbeit macht frei', 'work liberates') were not extermination centres in the sense of those established solely or primarily for purposes of killing after 1941. Fear of arrest, and fear of informers, led to a frightened public conformity on the part of many Germans, who were forced to lead a double life, expressing their real views only in complete privacy.

At the same time as coercing the German people into conformity, measures were taken to attempt to obtain their consent to, and support for, the new national socialist community. Measures were partly ideological, partly practical. For those not excluded from the new 'people's community' (*Volksgemeinschaft*) – for those apolitical Aryans, with no Jewish blood or political antipathy – life could be made relatively comfortable in the peacetime years of Nazi Germany. An economic upswing which had started already before Hitler came to power was given further impetus by Nazi work-creation schemes (autobahn building, general construction works, and increasingly projects connected with rearmament). Nazi economic policies were geared both to autarky and to preparation for war, as well as to consumer satisfaction, objectives that were not always mutually compatible. There is some debate about the connections between Nazi economic policies and economic recovery, as well as about their effects on different groups in the population. Rearmament policies after 1936, for example, on some accounts may have actually slowed down the pace of economic recovery. Furthermore, the increased concentration of capital represented a continuation of tendencies prevalent before the Nazis came to power, further complicating analysis of causes and effects. It should be noted that certain developments were at odds with some of the pre-1933 Nazi ideology, such as the proclaimed hostility to large department stores and the emphasis on the rural virtues of 'blood and soil' – positions which were hard to combine with the industrial requirements of rearmament. One thing is however quite clear: unemployment was rapidly reduced, so that by the late 1930s there was instead a labour shortage. In contrast to the uncertainties and hardship of the Weimar years, the Nazi dictatorship was associated for many Germans with a secure income and an improved standard of living, however qualified by restrictions on personal freedom.

There was also a range of schemes designed to inculcate a sense of harmonious, regenerated national community healing the wounds of Weimar's conflicts. Programmes such as *Schönheit der Arbeit* (the beauty of labour) and *Kraft durch Freude* (strength through joy), with organised leisure activities and holiday trips for workers, and an emphasis on the notion of community even at the factory level, sought to infuse Germans with a new spirit and enthusiasm inculcated at work. Meanwhile, Goebbels' curiously entitled Ministry of Popular Enlightenment and Propaganda (created in March 1933) pumped out material designed both as light entertainment or diversion and as political indoctrination. The press and radio were co-opted, and the education system transformed into an instrument of Nazi socialisation. The burning of books by left-wing, Jewish and other 'un-German' authors on 10 May 1933, instigated by Nazi activists and presided over by Goebbels, symbolised the Nazi attempt to purge from German minds all views except their own. A range of social organisations, such as the Hitler Youth (HJ) and League of German Girls (BDM), and the Nazi women's organisations, sought to incorporate different sections of society into the new community, while the multiplicity of preexisting German organisations were outlawed, dissolved, or taken over by the Nazis. The notion of a regenerated national community under the saviour-figure of Adolf Hitler was further propagated by symbolic displays of power and unity, through the mass rituals, parades, and depiction of crowds of adoring Germans raising their arms in the *Heil* salute as Hitler passed.

The monolithic image promoted by the Nazis had a certain element of truth in it, and the notion of a charismatic Führer above all the local conflicts and frictions of everyday life represented a powerful element of cohesion. Local party bigwigs could be blamed for things people did not like, while they sighed 'if only the Führer knew . . .'. But to take the Third Reich at its face value would be mistaken. The Nazi state was by no means so streamlined, nor the population so adulatory or brainwashed, as earlier interpretations of what was called Nazi 'totalitarianism' suggested. For one thing, there remained a 'duality' of power in the Nazi state, with new party organisations duplicating, and rivalling, continuing state administrative machinery. The overlapping spheres of jurisdiction led to considerable competition and conflict in a range of areas – between

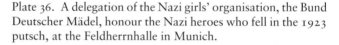

In ewiger Verbundenheit mit den Kämpfern für das Dritte Reich
ehrt die deutsche Jugend an der Feldherrnhalle in München die Gefallenen. Unser Bild zeigt die im Rahmen des Reichssporttages entsandte Abordnung des Bundes deutscher Mädel.

Plate 36. A delegation of the Nazi girls' organisation, the Bund Deutscher Mädel, honour the Nazi heroes who fell in the 1923 putsch, at the Feldherrnhalle in Munich.

rival party organisations as well as between state and party bureaucracies – with no institutionalised means of resolving disputes other than by appeal to the Führer. The only finally decisive factor was 'the Führer's wish'. On some accounts, the very notion of a charismatic Führer 'above' the fray was less an attribute of the person of Adolf Hitler himself than a consequence of the way the regime, with its plurality of competing organisations, had to function in practice. Frequently, Hitler only entered into conflicts at the last moment, in true Social Darwinist fashion allowing participants to fight it out between themselves and then backing the stronger, winning side. In many areas of policy, Hitler postponed making decisions until the last possible moment. This does not necessarily mean that he was a 'weak dictator', as some interpretations have suggested, since when it mattered to him – particularly on foreign policy – Hitler was quite determined to ensure that he got his own way. In other areas he was simply less interested in the details of policy formation. Moreover, the totalitarian notion must also be qualified with reference to the fact that certain key elites – notably industry and Army – were not 'co-ordinated' in quite the same way as more subordinate groups.

For much of the 1930s, they experienced a certain congruence of aims with the Nazis, in the areas of economic regeneration under authoritarian, anti-union auspices, and rearmament and revision of the hated Treaty of Versailles. But the congruence of aims was never complete: there were frictions and divergences of interest on a number of points, and from 1938 onwards the regime entered a more radical phase in which differences were thrown into sharper relief – complicated after 1939 because the nation was at war.

At the level of popular opinion, too, the picture is more complex than at first sight might be thought. While there was a hard core of convinced Nazis, many more joined party organisations after March 1933 out of opportunistic motives, while others remained aloof even at the cost of their professional careers or their family's livelihood. People did not swallow a 'Nazi ideology' (which was in any event not very consistent or coherent) wholesale; rather, they sympathised with certain elements – such as promotion of German national greatness and revision of the Treaty of Versailles – while criticising other elements, particularly if they were personally, materially affected by, for example, some aspect of economic policy. Many peasants, to take one illustration, had supported the Nazi emphasis on 'blood and soil' before 1933; but they soon became disenchanted with certain Nazi agrarian policies, such as the Entailed Farm Law which stipulated that medium-sized farms could only be inherited by a single heir, of German Aryan stock, and not be divided among heirs. Public opinion was fragmented: people on the whole lived on a very day-to-day level, grumbling or applauding on particular issues but failing to develop a sense of the whole. There was also a widespread lack of interest in the fate of others, once they were removed from the immediate vicinity.

This restricted focus of interest, to areas of direct concern and immediate relevance, affected even the churches, whose record in the Third Reich is ambiguous. The Protestant churches – whose members had provided a disproportionate share of the Nazi vote – soon split between the pro-Nazi 'German Christians' and the anti-Nazi 'Confessing Church', among whose number were some highly courageous opponents of Nazism such as Dietrich Bonhoeffer. Yet while the Nazis had to abandon their early plans to subvert the church for Nazism and install a Reich Bishop, the reactions of most Protestants to the regime remained mixed. Nazi attacks on

denominational schools and attempts to reorganise church structure were resisted, but many Protestants shared anti-communist
sentiments and conservative-nationalist goals with the Nazis. The
Catholic community, with its transcendent loyalty to Rome, was
initially more resilient to the attractions of Nazism, and perhaps its
'total' ideology and emphasis on community provided better protection against Nazism than did Protestant individualism. Yet in
the main Catholics no more provided an effective bastion against
Nazism than did Protestants. Reassured initially by the Concordat
concluded between the Nazi government and the Vatican in July
1933, German Catholics slowly came to resist Nazi encroachments
on their religion, such as the removal of crucifixes from classrooms
in confessional schools. But they very firmly distinguished between
'religious' matters, in which it was proper and permissible to resist Nazi policies, and 'political' affairs which were no concern
of the church. This self-limitation meant that while church leaders did in fact protest against the Nazi 'euthanasia' programme, in
which many Germans (including of course Catholics) were killed
because of mental disability or subnormality, they failed to protest
against the treatment of the Jews. While remaining to an extent
alienated from the regime, potential Catholic opposition was limited
by a restrictive legalism in their separation of 'religion' and 'politics', the sphere of the church and that of the state; the same was
also true of Protestants, who even had Luther to appeal to on this
point.

The German people were thus subjected to a mixture of coercion
and consent, as well as to changed experiences and circumstances,
changed material and social conditions, in the course of the pre-
war years, which led to a mixture of grumbling and support, approval and dissent, on different issues and at different times. But
there were some who had little freedom to be so ambivalent: there
were those who were to be excluded form the new national community, and were only too well aware of its dark side. Left-wingers
early found themselves rounded up and imprisoned, or forced to go
underground; resistance was extremely hazardous and clandestine.
Others were discriminated against because of their racial heritage or
personal practices: Jews, gypsies and homosexuals were singled out
for harsh treatment, while the Slavic peoples were denigrated. Jewish

policy in the 1930s was characterised by a series of more or less ad hoc measures: the attempted boycott of Jewish shops and businesses in April 1933, the exclusion of Jews from the civil service and certain professions, the 'Nuremberg Laws' of 1935 depriving them of citizenship rights and imposing restrictions on marriages between Jews and gentiles, the 'night of broken glass' (*Kristallnacht*) of November 1938 in which Jewish synagogues, homes and premises were attacked, burned, and looted and a number of Jews were killed. These measures were in the main initiated by Nazi activists or in response to pressures for action on the part of party radicals. Public displays of brutality commanded little general popular support among Germans. But there was much approval of the aim of 'removing' Jews from German society, and the 'aryanisation' of Jewish property (including housing) pleased the beneficiaries. The 'legalisation' of the pariah status of Jews in the Nuremberg Laws was applauded, while the destruction of property and creation of mess in the *Kristallnacht* was not. While it was quite clear that Jews were 'not wanted' (*unerwünscht*) in the new Germany of the Thousand-Year Reich, and were to be excluded from Germany's glorious future, it was by no means clear in the peacetime years that the 'final solution' to the 'Jewish question' which the Nazis had constructed would ultimately be a policy of mass murder.

There were two areas of policy in which Hitler had quite definite goals: racial policy, and foreign policy. Hitler wanted to make Germany into a 'pure' racial community; and he wanted to expand German 'living-space' (*Lebensraum*), achieving first European and then world mastery. Ultimately all else had to be subordinated to these ends. We must now turn to the radicalisation of the regime in foreign policy, war and genocide.

FOREIGN POLICY AND WAR

As early as the 1920s, in *Mein Kampf* and the (then unpublished) 'Second Book', Hitler had laid down a programme for his foreign policy. This programme consisted in revising the Treaty of Versailles, incorporating Austria and transforming Czechoslovakia and Poland into satellite states, confronting France before turning to conquer Russia, and finally achieving world domination, perhaps with Britain as some sort of junior partner which Germany would help to protect. Evidently at least the first stages of this programme commanded broad sympathy among conservative nationalist circles in Germany. Indeed, after 1930 a shift in foreign policy under Brüning's government away from Stresemann's more careful conciliation had been evident. A new, more confrontationist style went along with moves away from multilateral agreements towards a system of bilateral political and economic arrangements designed to extend Germany's influence in south-eastern and eastern Europe. When Hitler came to power in 1933, there were certain continuities with these trends, although the pace quickened and the ultimate aims were rather more ambitious. Nevertheless the compromise with the old elites which had brought Hitler to power was sustained, with some tensions and frictions, until the winter of 1937–8.

Hitler's general strategy in the 1930s was to achieve as much as possible by diplomatic means while energetically pursuing policies of rearmament. Rearmament had been secretly pursued, and different means of expanding the army canvassed, since the later 1920s. Hitler made his intentions explicit in speeches to the generals and to his cabinet within ten days of coming to power. Initially, rearmament was disguised, as with the issue of so-called 'Mefo Bills' in 1933, and in Krupp's euphemistically named 'agricultural tractor programme' which produced tanks from July 1933. By 1934 explosives, ships and aircraft were in production – all against the provisions of the Treaty of Versailles, but approved by the army. In March 1935 the existence of a German air force and of general rearmament, as well as the introduction of conscription, were finally announced to the outside world. In the meantime, Hitler had pursued individual agreements with particular countries in place of collective arrangements. He broke off German participation in the Geneva Disarmament Conference, and withdrew Germany from the League of Nations, in October 1933. In January 1934 he concluded a ten-year non-aggression pact with Poland (against the advice of the Foreign Ministry). In March 1935 the Saarland returned to Germany after a plebiscite in January. German rearmament was censured by the 'Stresa Front' of Britain, France and Italy, and by the League of Nations, in April 1935; but Britain and Germany were able to achieve a certain understanding in the Naval Agreement of

June 1935, by which Germany was to increase her navy to one-third the strength of the British navy. Although there were tensions between Italy and Germany over Austria (after an attempted coup by Austrian Nazis in 1934, in which Chancellor Dollfuss was murdered), Hitler was concerned to improve relations. He admired the Fascist leader Mussolini, and for a while trod carefully in connection with the Austrian question. In any event, the Stresa Front itself was less than solid. The preoccupation of Britain and France with the Italian invasion of Abyssinia in October 1935, as well as the mounting pressure of popular discontent in a worsening economic situation at home, presented Hitler with the opportunity and impetus for his first really risky step in foreign policy. In March 1936 German troops remilitarised the Rhineland. This, despite the relatively limited numbers of German troops, was achieved successfully, to much popular acclaim at home and little serious criticism abroad. Germany was, after all, only 'entering her own back yard'.

In 1936, Hitler announced that Germany must be ready for war within four years, and a 'Four-Year Plan' under Goering was launched. This marked a break with the previously relatively orthodox management of the economy under the former President of the Reichsbank, Hjalmar Schacht, who subsequently resigned as Minister of Economics in November 1937 because of conflicts between his ministry and Goering's Four-Year-Plan Office. Rearmament was to be vigorously pursued, but not at the expense of the living standards of consumers at home; Hitler had a perpetual eye on public opinion in general and his own popularity in particular. Shifts occurring on the foreign policy front also contributed to a loosening of ties between Hitler and his conservative nationalist allies. The Spanish Civil War, which broke out in July 1936, helped to bring Italy and Germany closer together (in their support of Franco) in the 'Rome–Berlin axis'. Ribbentrop, who for some time had been effectively running a Nazi diplomatic service in rivalry with the Foreign Ministry, and who in 1936 became Germany's Ambassador to Britain, failed to secure a British alliance with Germany. In the course of 1937, it became clear to Hitler that he would have to drop his plans for alliance with Britain, and strengthen his connections with Italy. In 1938, under Ribbentrop's influence, Japan became the third member of the 'Axis'. It also became increasingly clear that

Germany would not be able to sustain a protracted rearmaments race, and would have to go to war sooner rather than later.

In the winter of 1937–8 these developments reached the point where a split between Hitler and certain old conservatives was inevitable. A meeting in November 1937 with leaders of the army, navy, air force, as well as the Foreign Minister and the War Minister, which was reported in a memorandum by Hitler's military adjutant Colonel Hossbach, was the occasion for a lengthy harangue by Hitler on at least some of his plans for achieving German *Lebensraum*. Hitler failed to convince his audience, and was met with reservations and criticisms. But Nazi military planning in December became increasingly offensive, rather than defensive, in nature. By February 1938, Hitler had engineered a purge of the Army leadership, replacing conservatives critical of his views with others more amenable to Nazi plans. Fritsch was replaced by General von Brauchitsch; fourteen senior generals were retired, and forty-six others had to change their commands; the post of War Minister, held by Blomberg, was simply abolished, and Hitler himself became Commander-in-Chief of the Armed Forces (in addition to being Supreme Commander by virtue of his position as head of state). General Keitel became the new head of the Oberkammando der Wehrmacht (OKW) which replaced the old Wehrmacht office. In February 1938, finally, Ribbentrop replaced Neurath as Foreign Minister. The changes meant that the regime was now more specifically Nazi, less constrained by the more traditional considerations and ambitions of orthodox German nationalists.

Hitler was able to achieve two of his major foreign policy aims in the course of 1938–9 by – relatively – peaceful means. Despite Germany's reassurances in 1936 about respecting Austrian independence, which had facilitated the rapprochement with Italy, tensions continued in relation to Austria. Under considerable pressure from Goering, who took much of the initiative in the course of 1937, the Austrian issue came to a head in the spring of 1938. The Austrian chancellor Schuschnigg, who had succeeded Dollfuss, had talks with Hitler in February 1938. Schuschnigg then called a plebiscite in March 1938, formulated to predetermine the outcome; Hitler (and Goering) managed to effect a postponement and rewording of the plebiscite, and a handover of power from Schuschnigg to the Nazi

Plate 37. The Austrian town of Lienz, now part of the Greater German Reich, changes the name of one of its major squares to 'Adolf-Hitler-Platz' (as did many other places in Germany and Austria).

sympathiser Seyss-Inquart. Austrian troops were then instructed to offer no resistance when German troops marched triumphantly into Hitler's native country, greeted by welcoming crowds, and with this bloodless invasion the *Anschluss* of Austria was effected. Despite its prohibition in the Treaty of Versailles, other European powers saw little reason to protest. For Austrian Jews, the consequences were disastrous. The vicious anti-semitism of Austrian Nazis was given free rein, and Jews in a country which later purported to be 'Hitler's first victim' received worse treatment than their brethren in Germany.

Hitler did not have quite such an easy time in relation to Czechoslovakia. Unrest in connection with the sizeable ethnic German population, particularly in the Sudeten border areas, had been fomented by a right-wing party under Heinlein with support from Germany. In the course of the summer of 1938, a crisis developed – partly due to inaccurate reports of German mobilisation on the Czech border, which led to real Czech mobilisation. After a week of mounting tension, the situation was defused; but discussions were sharpened, with British Prime Minister Chamberlain playing a key role in negotiations. When, finally, at the end of the Munich Conference of September 1938 – at which Czechoslovakia was not represented – certain border areas were ceded mainly to Germany, Chamberlain made his famous return to Britain waving a piece of paper signed by Hitler and proclaiming that it meant 'peace in our time'. Chamberlain's so-called 'appeasement policy' has come in for considerable subsequent criticism as well as the defence that it helped to buy Britain time for effective rearmament. Hitler himself at the time was bitterly disappointed at his bloodless success, feeling cheated of a potentially successful war. The German people, by contrast, were relieved that the threat of war had been averted, and Hitler's domestic popularity rose accordingly. Czechoslovakia, meanwhile, had lost its effective lines of defence. When in March 1939 Hitler decided to invade what was left of Czechoslovakia, his troops were able to march into Prague with minimal opposition. Bohemia and Moravia were turned into a 'Protectorate', and Slovakia effectively became a satellite state of the German Reich. The western powers let this 'far-away country' of which they knew little, and for which they cared less, fall with no gesture of help.

On Poland, Hitler faced more serious intransigence on the part of the western powers. Memel was ceded by the Lithuanians, but the Poles refused to give way on Danzig and on 31 March the British guaranteed Polish independence. Despite this setback, Hitler had by now formed the impression that Britain was essentially weak and vacillating, and would not stand by its guarantee. On 23 August 1939 Hitler, in a surprise move, made the notorious pact with Stalin's Russia which had for so long been the ideological arch-enemy of the Nazis. The Nazi–Soviet pact was purely strategic for both Hitler and Stalin: both had an interest in carving up Poland, and while Stalin needed time for rearmament, Hitler was concerned to prevent a potential British alliance with the USSR and to be able to concentrate his attention on defeating the west without having a war on two fronts. On 1 September 1939 German troops invaded Poland. On 3 September Britain and France, honouring their pledge to Poland, declared war on Germany. The second major war of the twentieth century unleashed by Germany had begun. The German people on the whole embarked on it with foreboding, and little of

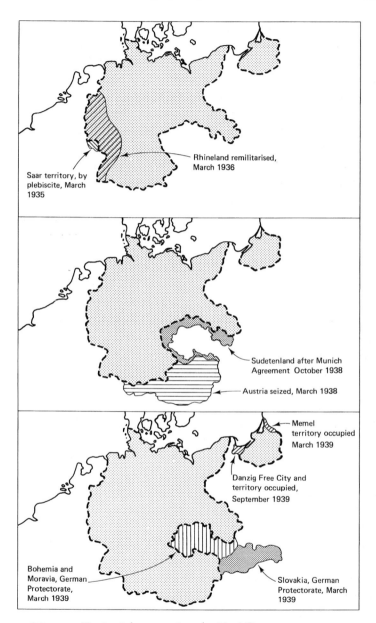

Map 10. Territorial annexations by Nazi Germany, 1935–9

the enthusiasm with which considerable numbers had greeted the outbreak of war in 1914.

The Polish campaign raised false hopes that the war would be over soon. In a lightning campaign (*Blitzkrieg*) Poland was defeated in less than three weeks. Parts of it were incorporated into an expanded Reich, and parts were transformed into the 'Generalgouvernement' under German administration. There followed during the winter months of 1939–40 the so-called phoney war or *Sitzkrieg*. In the spring of 1940 Hitler rapidly turned his attention north and west: first to Scandinavia, where the Quisling regime in Norway gave a new political concept to history, then, in May 1940, via Holland and Belgium to France, the defeat of which was followed by occupation of the northern and western parts and the installation of the compliant Vichy regime. In spring 1941 Germany attacked Yugoslavia and Greece. The unexpected early and rapid victories boosted Hitler's domestic popularity, at a time when consumer conditions were still relatively satisfactory; they also gave Hitler himself a false sense of invincibility. Goering persuaded Hitler that the German Luftwaffe was in a position to knock Britain out of the war, and a series of air-raids over Britain began. But Britain proved more resistant to invasion and defeat than the Germans had expected; and Hitler did not wait to defeat Britain and consolidate his hold in the west before turning his attention eastwards. In the summer of 1941 he decided the time had come to invade Russia, thus effecting what he had previously been concerned to avoid: war on two fronts. The Russian campaign proved disastrous. German troops were over extended and ill-equipped; and when the Russian winter came, with icy winds and deep snow, German soldiers found themselves immobilised, without adequate clothing, afflicted by frostbite and in some instances even freezing to death. The Nazi charity collections at home (the winter relief fund, WHW, including donations and one-pot meals) persuaded numerous Germans to part with boots, coats, skis; but it was too little and too late. There were also serious tactical mistakes in the military campaign, particularly in the mounting of simultaneous and overambitious offensives which could not be sustained. In 1943, at Stalingrad, the Germans finally suffered a major defeat which could not be disguised. Neither domestic morale nor Hitler's faith in his inevitable victory ever recovered.

Map 11. The partition of Poland in 1939

The invasion of Russia was the first turning point in the war. Germany had been prepared for a short, sharp war, but was not equipped to sustain a protracted conflict of the sort which now developed. The second turning point came with the transformation of what was still a European war into a world war in December 1941. There had been a separate set of conflicts in the Pacific since the early 1930s involving Japan. In December 1941 the Japanese attacked and destroyed the American fleet at Pearl Harbor, as a result of which the USA declared war on Japan. While Germany was linked with Japan as one of the axis powers, there was no compulsion for Germany to come to Japan's defence; yet Hitler took this opportunity to declare war on the USA. His megalomaniac desire

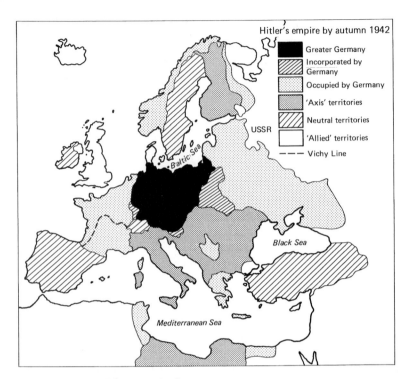

Map 12. Hitler's empire by autumn 1942

for world mastery turned a European war – which Germany at this time still had some hope of winning – into a world war, taking on the enormous military and economic might of the most advanced industrial nation in the world.

From 1942–3, the war turned against Germany, with desert campaigns in north Africa, relentless air-raids over Germany carried out by the RAF and the American air forces, and continued fighting in Italy even after the deposition of Mussolini by the Fascist Grand Council in July 1943. Germany was fighting on three fronts, and the German situation became increasingly desperate as the Russians launched an offensive in the east to coincide with the Normandy landings of the western allies on 6 June 1944. Morale on the home front plummeted, as people feared for friends and relatives at the front and suffered deteriorating conditions at home. Hitler himself became a virtual recluse, making fewer and fewer public appearances and withdrawing increasingly to his East Prussian retreat, the 'Wolf's Lair'. Wrapped up in their own troubles and concerns, the majority of German people paid little attention to a phenomenon, of which they knew more than they would later like to admit, which was taking place at precisely this time.

HOLOCAUST, RESISTANCE AND DEFEAT

Hitler's basic aims had been two-fold: to achieve *Lebensraum* for the German race; and to rid that race of what he saw as a pollutant, a bacterium, poisoning and infecting the healthy 'Aryan' stock: the Jews. Slowly, during the period after 1933, Jews had been identified, stigmatised, and excluded from the 'national community', the *Volksgemeinschaft*. Measures had been adopted to give Jews an outcaste status, and many Jews, realising they had little future in Germany, had already fled for more welcoming shores. While there had been acts of violence and discrimination against Jews, there had however been no systematic policy for totally ridding Germany of the Jewish population. In war-time, things changed. For one thing, with the conquest of territories in which there were far larger Jewish communities (particularly in the east), the 'Jewish problem' assumed new proportions. For another, more extreme circumstances suggested and promoted more radical solutions. Hitler let it be known that he wanted the expanded Reich to be 'cleansed of Jews' (*Judenrein*). Initially, schemes were actively considered for the mass deportation of Jews to a reservation in Madagascar, and Jews were even sent to southern France in preparation for shipment. In eastern Europe, there were plans for a Jewish reservation in the area around Lublin in south-eastern Poland. After the invasion of Russia in the summer of 1941, the 'final solution' became altogether more sinister.

No written Hitler-order for the extermination of the Jews has ever been found; nor, given Hitler's style of government, is such an order likely ever to have existed. But he let his wishes be known and fostered a climate in which the policy of extermination could be effected. There is some disagreement among historians as to whether the extermination programme which actually took place was the direct consequence of a pre-determined plan, or whether it developed in a more ad hoc, haphazard manner as a result of local initiatives which were later co-ordinated. Whatever the interpretation, the broad outline of facts is clear. The first mass killings of Jews were undertaken by specialist so-called *Einsatzgruppen* who arrived in Russia in the wake of the invading German troops. Jews were rounded up and taken out to forests where they dug mass graves, were lined up naked, and were then shot into the graves. This technique had serious disadvantages from the Nazi point of view: killings were relatively public and easily witnessed by passers-by, allowing the news to filter back to Germany; and those doing the shooting – which included shooting young women cuddling babies in their arms – often, despite the SS suppression of human emotions and inculcation of obedience and brutality, found themselves physically incapable of undertaking such cold-blooded murder without first imbibing copious quantities of vodka. Meanwhile, in the ghettoes in Poland, overcrowding and disease were becoming ever more serious, as more and more Jews were transported from occupied territories. From the point of view of those in charge of the Warsaw and Lodz ghettoes, some means would have to be found sooner rather than later of dealing with the increasing numbers of Jews, whether by halting the influx or disposing of those already there. The means chosen was death: immediate death by inhalation of gas, rather than shooting. Jews from the Lodz Ghetto were rounded up, from December 1941, and driven out to Chelmno (Kulmhof), about forty miles north-west of Lodz, where they were driven around in vans which had the exhaust pipes redirected to pump the exhaust fumes back inside the body of the vehicle. When the screams of those packed inside had died down, the drivers stopped and the bodies were dumped in mass graves in the forest. This too, however, proved to be a relatively 'inefficient' means of killing: it could – and did – kill tens of thousands, but could not dispose of millions.

In January 1942, a conference was called at Wannsee, in the beautiful lakeland surroundings on the west of Berlin, to co-ordinate the 'final solution' which was already taking place, under the general direction of SS-leader Heinrich Himmler. In Poland, specially designed extermination camps were opened at Belzec, Sobibor and Treblinka. Under the so-called 'Reinhard Action' (named after Reinhard Heydrich, who was assassinated in Prague in May 1942), these camps effected the liquidation of the vast majority of Polish Jews.

Plate 38. The Jewish ghetto in Radom, Poland, with a poster forbidding entry by those without police permits and warning of the danger of epidemic diseases. Jews in ghettoes were reduced into creatures readily portrayed as a serious danger to physical health, as well as, more metaphorically, a 'bacillus' or 'cancer' in the body of the nation, which needed to be 'purified' of Jewish 'contamination'.

They made use of the expertise and personnel of the now-terminated 'euthanasia' programme. The most infamous of the camps, the name of which has come to epitomise evil and suffering, was however not tucked away out of sight in eastern Poland, but was in fact within the borders of the greater German Reich: Auschwitz. Auschwitz (Oswiecim) was a major industrial centre on the main west–east railway line in Upper Silesia. The Auschwitz complex spread over several square kilometres, in and around the town, straddling both sides of the main railway line (with an extra side-line built specifically to allow trains to go directly into the extermination centre at Birkenau). Auschwitz I, an already existing prison and labour camp largely for political prisoners, was the scene of horrific 'medical' experiments under Josef Mengele; it was also the place where the use of Zyklon B gas was first tried. Auschwitz II, or Auschwitz-Birkenau, was established a few kilometres away, as a specifically designed factory for mass murder. Whole train-loads could be 'processed', the trains cleaned and readied for their empty return to the west, within three or four hours. When all the gas chambers and cremato- ria at Auschwitz-Birkenau were in full operation, it was possible to kill up to 9,000 people within twenty-four hours. Also in the town of Auschwitz was the Monowitz camp, whose inmates worked for I. G. Farben's new Buna plant at Dwory. The Auschwitz complex also supplied labour for a number of other German firms such as Krupp, Borsig and Siemens. This was no isolated, hidden concen- tration camp, but rather a vast enterprise of which large numbers of Poles and Germans were perfectly well aware. Complicity in the functioning of the Third Reich extends far beyond a small band of Nazi thugs and criminals.

The bureaucratically organised, technologically perfected and ef- ficiently executed mass murder of over 6 million Jews, as well as the almost complete annihilation of Europe's gypsy popula- tion, and the killing of numerous political opponents of Nazism or others deemed 'unworthy of life', from a whole range of cul- tural, political and national backgrounds, including communists, Social Democrats, Conservatives, Protestants, Catholics, Jehovah's Witnesses and others – this mass killing, undertaken by members of that highly cultured nation which had produced the music of Bach and the poetry of Goethe, raises questions almost impossi- ble to contemplate, let alone answer. But that does not mean that the phenomenon should be elevated to a plane of unique reprehen- sion, abstracted from real historical explanation, above causality and the focus solely of horror and shame. This reaction, which is quite understandable, nevertheless evades the real questions of re- sponsibility and guilt. Hitler created the climate and provided the impetus for mass murder – which even conflicted with other cen- tral aims of the regime, such as the need for slave labour in the war effort – but he cannot be held to be the only guilty man, as cer- tain explanations which concentrate on the takeover of Germany by a uniquely evil individual imply. Nor can responsibility be placed solely on a small band of fanatics around Hitler. Hitler did not come to power by accident; nor was his regime simply maintained by terror and coercion. Many Germans, in different capacities, facilitated the Holocaust by their actions or permitted it to continue by their inaction. By the end of 1943 at the latest, a considerable percentage of Germans – amounting to several million – knew that the Jews who were being rounded up and shipped off to the east would, directly or indirectly (via transit camps such as Theresienstadt), ultimately end up in a place not of 'resettlement' but of death. This was known, too, by governments of neutral countries and of Hitler's enemies; but powers such as Britain and the USA, for whatever range of reasons, good and bad, chose to ignore the question and concentrated rather on the military effort of defeating Germany in war.

Whatever the extent to which people 'knew' about the evils of the Nazi regime, most Germans preferred to ignore or disbelieve what did not concern them directly. Their intimations were better suppressed. There were some courageous groups and individuals in Nazi Germany who made attempts to oppose Hitler and terminate his rule. These included many clandestine left-wing opposition groups in the 1930s who continued to meet, discuss and organise, despite the flight of the SPD leadership into exile and the dispersal of KPD members to Moscow as well as the west. There were also many who had little hope of doing more than expressing their dissent in symbolic ways, like the dissident youth groups such as the 'Edelweiss Pirates' or the swing culture. For many who refused to assent or conform to the regime, there was little that simply keeping faith with like-minded souls could hope to achieve. Attempts by better-placed individuals who moved in elite circles and could hope to influence foreign opinion or alter the course of events, such as Adam von Trott, were for a variety of reasons unsuccessful. A few individuals were simply unlucky. Hitler had extraordinary good fortune in escaping assassination attempts, as when the Swabian carpenter Georg Elser single-handedly succeeded in hollowing out a pillar in the Munich Beer Hall and installing a bomb timed to go off when Hitler would be giving his speech commemorating the 1923 putsch. Unfortunately for Elser's plans, on the particular night of 9–10 November 1939, it was foggy in Munich; Hitler decided at the last minute not to fly back to Berlin as planned, but rather to leave early and take the overnight train. He thus had left the hall when the bomb exploded. Elser was arrested crossing the border to Switzerland. After detention in concentration camps throughout the war, he was finally shot in Dachau in April 1945. A group of Catholic students in Munich, known as the 'White Rose' group led by Hans and Sophie Scholl, were equally courageous in their printing and distribution of leaflets criticising the regime. Their attempts to rouse public opinion, and to connect with other resistance groups in positions to affect the regime, could do little more than keep a flame of morality burning among the prevailing self-centredness, conformity and apathy. They were caught and executed, still in their early twenties. Many others too paid with their lives.

The resistance which received most public attention in West Germany after the war was the so-called July Plot of 1944. This constituted, however, a somewhat ambiguous legacy for West German democracy. Many individuals associated with the July Plot had earlier helped the Nazi regime to power and sustained it in the 1930s. Conservative nationalists had shared many of the revisionist foreign policy goals of Hitler, and for many doubts had begun to grow only after 1938. Hopes of toppling Hitler and replacing him by a conservative regime were faced with a number of difficulties, including the oath of obedience sworn to Hitler by the army, as well as the early successes of the war which made circumstances less propitious for a coup attempt. By the summer of 1944, Germany's eventual defeat was becoming increasingly inevitable, and the accusation can be levelled against the military resistance that they simply wanted to salvage Germany from total destruction and occupation. Moreover, even taking into account differences of opinion among nationalist resistance circles about the form a post-Hitler regime should take, most of them were essentially anti-democratic in outlook. They wanted an authoritarian government by elites, and not a return to the sort of constitution embodied in the Weimar Republic; they disliked the idea of mass participation in government, and had little conception of any need for popular legitimation of a new government. In the event, their conceptions of alternative government could never be realised. The attempt by Stauffenberg to kill Hitler failed. A briefcase containing a bomb was placed by Stauffenberg under the large table in the Wolf's Lair where Hitler and others were engaged in military planning. The bomb successfully went off, and Stauffenberg, seeing the explosion after leaving the building, returned to Berlin reporting success. But the weighty

Plate 39. Although the railway lines are grassing over, and the remains of the gas chambers are falling into weed-covered rubble-holes – with passing Polish peasants going about their business much as they did when the smoke still rose from the crematoria – Auschwitz-Birkenau casts a shadow over German history which cannot be erased.

table, under which the briefcase had been pushed, shielded Hitler from the full blast of the explosion, and he survived relatively unscathed. In the wake of the July Plot the reign of terror was intensified to an extraordinary degree. Not only were the main participants in the plot arrested and killed in the most gruesome manner, but thousands more were also rounded up, imprisoned, tortured and in many cases put to death. Penalties for even the most minor 'crimes against the regime' in the winter of 1944–5 were increased, so that thousands of ordinary Germans were executed for such offences as listening to foreign radio broadcasts or making political jokes, as the many agonising detailed case-histories in Berlin's Plötzensee jail testify.

 Despite a German counter-offensive in the winter of 1944–5, by the spring of 1945 it was clear to Germany's leaders that the war was lost. Hitler's 'scorched-earth' policy exacerbated the destruction of Germany: Hitler instructed his people to fight to the last, never to surrender and to leave nothing to the victors to inherit. Hitler's view was that if the German people were not strong enough to win, then they did not deserve to survive at all. Hitler, too, went down with the country he had led to ruin. In a sort of Wagnerian *Götterdämmerung*, in his bunker under the ruins of Berlin, with the advancing Russian army ever closer, Hitler married his long-time faithful friend, Eva Braun, on 29 April 1945; and on 30 April they committed suicide. Their remains were incinerated by members of Hitler's entourage. On 2 May Berlin capitulated to the Russians, and on 7–8 May the unconditional surrender of Germany was signed. A brief provisional government under Dönitz was dissolved on 23 May, and the occupying powers assumed supreme power in Germany. Hitler's Thousand-Year Reich had ended in ruins and ashes, after twelve years which had profoundly affected the course of history. The Nazi 'national awakening' and 'revolution' had ultimately achieved only genocide and suicide; millions lay dead, the destruction was almost immeasurable; the credibility of the old German elites had been destroyed, the cycle of tensions from Imperial Germany brought to a halt; but it was far from clear, in the devastated conditions of Germany in May 1945, what form the future could possibly take.

7

The two Germanies, 1945–90

THE CREATION OF THE TWO GERMANIES

In 1945, Germany lay in ruins. The people of Germany, war-weary and concerned for an uncertain future, eked out an existence amidst the rubble and debris of the collapsed Reich. No-one – not even the occupying powers – was at this time certain what the future would hold. Yet, in the course of the next four decades, two very different Germanies emerged. In the west, the Federal Republic of Germany developed into a politically stable and economically prosperous capitalist democracy; in the east, the German Democratic Republic proved to be economically the most productive state in the communist bloc, and, until the Gorbachev era of the late 1980s, one of the Soviet Union's most reliable supporters and allies. Considering the turbulent past of these two Germanies, this double transformation, into two such different political and socioeconomic systems, is all the more remarkable.

Initially, the Allies were unsure and divided over their plans for Germany's future. War-time discussions in Teheran (1943) and Yalta (February 1945) had produced agreement that Germany should be divided into zones of occupation; and at the latter conference it was agreed that France should have her own zone, in addition to those of Britain, the USA and the USSR. Disagreements were already becoming apparent between the Soviets and the western powers on the issues of reparations and of the western frontiers of a reconstituted Poland. These differences were merely papered over at the Potsdam

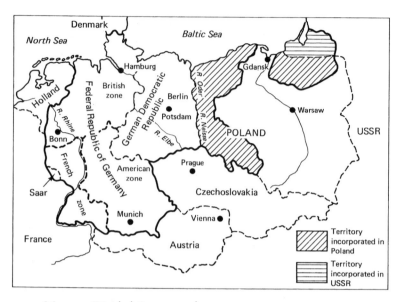

Map 13. Divided Germany after 1945

Conference of July–August 1945, when the Americans, British and Soviets agreed in principle on the general sweep of desirable policy – that Germany should be denazified, demilitarised and democratised – but failed to achieve specific, workable policy proposals that could be effected uniformly across the different zones of occupation. Since Germany, after her unconditional surrender on 8 May, was an occupied country without its own government, there could at this time be no peace treaty. Pending such a final treaty, the western frontier of Poland was for the time being accepted, for administrative purposes, as running down along the Oder and western Neisse rivers. 'Germany' was thus effectively moved westwards, with lost eastern territories becoming incorporated into Poland – which itself moved westwards, losing territory in the east – and the Soviet Union. An Allied Control Council in Berlin (which was to be under four-power control) was to coordinate policies in the different zones. Reparations were to be taken by each power separately from its own zone, except that the Soviet Union's great losses were to be recompensed by additional reparations from the western zones, part of which were however to be exchanged for foodstuffs from the largely agricultural Soviet zone. The conference was concluded with a loosely phrased 'Protocol of Proceedings'. France, although receiving a zone of occupation, was not present at the Potsdam Conference, and subsequently felt less than firmly bound by its decisions. The decisions were, however, for the most part so vague and general that a wide latitude of interpretation was possible in any case for the occupying powers.

Divergences rapidly became apparent between the different zones of occupation. The most radical changes were initially effected in the Soviet zone. The relicensing of political parties was rapidly introduced, largely to legitimise the activities of the already energetic German Communist Party (KPD). Moscow-trained German communists, under the leadership of Walter Ulbricht, had already been flown into Berlin at the end of April 1945. They quickly sought to establish control over local political affairs, and with the backing of the Soviet Military Administration (SMAD) were able to wield influence out of proportion to their numbers. Although they had initially resisted initiatives from the German Social Democrats (SPD) for closer cooperation, it became clear to the KPD by the autumn of 1945 that they were not going to achieve a mass political base on their own. After rather constrained discussions in the winter of 1945, a forced merger took place between the KPD and the SPD in the Soviet zone in April 1946, when the so-called Socialist Unity Party (SED) was created. Initially supporting the notion of a 'German road to socialism', and welcoming the co-operation of all 'anti-Fascist forces' in a popular democratic front, by 1948 the SED had been transformed into a communist-dominated, Stalinist 'Party of a New Type'. Other parties active in the Soviet zone included the Christian Democratic Union (CDU), which – as in the western zones – represented a new Christian party attempting to unite Catholics who would formerly have supported the Centre Party with bourgeois and right-wing Protestants, and the Liberal Democratic Party of Germany (LDPD). The communists themselves organised the foundation of two further parties, the Peasants' Party (DBD) and the Nationalists (NDPD), to incorporate certain potentially disaffected constituencies and to split support for the conservative parties. By 1948 all the parties in the Soviet zone were also being 'co-ordinated' and brought under the effective control of the SED.

In the meantime, radical socioeconomic changes had also been effected in the Soviet zone. One of the earliest measures was land reform: all large agrarian estates (over one hundred hectares), and those belonging to former Nazis, were expropriated, and the land was redistributed, partly to small peasants and landless labourers, partly to refugees from the east, and partly taken into state ownership. Large industries, mining and banking were nationalised, and measures were taken which were detrimental to the continued existence of small private enterprise, which was gradually squeezed out of the economy. These measures were legitimised in a variety of ways: the expropriation of Nazis and war criminals was a self-evident justification; there was also the wider argument that it was 'monopoly capitalism' as a socioeconomic system that had given rise to Nazism, and that denazification thus required the transformation of capitalism itself; and there was also a plebiscite in Saxony which produced a majority in support of certain nationalisation measures, which were then instituted in other areas as well. At the same time, the Soviet Union was extracting huge reparations from its zone. At first, machinery and stock was simply removed to the Soviet Union; when this proved inefficient, certain enterprises within the Soviet zone were taken into Soviet ownership as Soviet Joint Stock Companies (SAGs), and their profits appropriated. By 1949, the Soviet zone had undergone what amounted to a major transformation in political, economic and social life: under communist control, the historically significant Junker class and the large capitalists had completely lost their material bases of existence; a radical restructuring of industry and agriculture was underway; and the communist-dominated SED, backed by the Soviet Military Administration, had achieved a predominance in political life, effectively sabotaging any attempt at introducing genuine democracy in post-Nazi East Germany.

While denazification in the Soviet zone was fairly radical, in terms of both structural transformation and turnover of personnel, denazification in the western zones was a case of cumbersome bureaucracy, relative inefficiency, and unintended consequences. From an early, punitive concept of 'collective guilt' there rapidly developed a more discriminatory set of policies, although it was never entirely clear whether the basic aim was to cleanse Germany of Nazis, or to cleanse Nazis of the taint of Nazism; and if the latter, whether denazification was to be punitive or re-educational. In the event, categorisation of Germans into five groups, ranging from 'major offenders' through to 'exonerated', on the basis of answers to a lengthy questionnaire, developed into something of a bureaucratic nightmare. It also led Germans to try to excuse and cover up their pasts, rather than genuinely confront their degrees of complicity in the Third Reich. Despite many grumblings, including the complaint that the 'big fish' got away while the 'lesser fry' were unfairly punished, by and large former Nazis were slowly reincorporated into West German life, with the exception of major war criminals, some of whom were dealt with at the Nuremberg trials (in which all the victorious Allies co-operated) and some of whom faced trial at a later date. While generally political apathy and concern for material survival prevailed, the major political parties of the post-war period were founded or refounded. The Social Democratic Party (SPD) rapidly reformed itself, and under the leadership of Kurt Schumacher strongly opposed the activities of the communists. Members of the old Catholic Centre Party joined with Protestants in the new Christian Democratic Union (CDU), a party which was common to both the Soviet and western zones, and which had a sister party, the Christian Social Union (CSU), in Bavaria. A range of liberal parties were founded in different regions, which eventually merged to become the Free Democratic Party (FDP) nationally. In addition, there was a multiplicity of small parties, representing specific regions, issues or constituencies (such as refugees from lost eastern territories). The main political battle was however between the CDU and the SPD, with the latter initially appearing the stronger.

While no radical measures of socioeconomic transformation were undertaken in the western zones of occupied Germany, the Allies did in effect block proposed measures of socialisation and held western Germany to a capitalist market economy. Attempts were also made to split up some of Germany's economic concentration, with pressures for decartelisation. France was the most ruthless in extracting reparations from its zone. Britain relatively early – April 1946 at the latest – realised that it was going to have to import foodstuffs into its predominantly industrial zone to avert the very real threat of mass starvation. The USA very soon came to share Britain's new view of the importance of the reconstruction, rather than destruction, of

Germany's economy. There was not only the problem of feeding and in many cases rehousing the indigenous population: western Germany was flooded by refugees and expellees from the lost eastern territories, who had fled from the Red Army in the closing months of the war or delayed long enough to be forcibly expropriated by new post-war administrations. Many, after a long and weary trek (which the very old, very young, and weaker members might not survive), landed up in western zones of Germany expecting to find some sort of shelter and livelihood. The overcrowding and shortages caused by their presence exacerbated already difficult post-war conditions. For many Germans, the dictated introduction of 'democracy' was, as after the First World War, associated with national defeat, political humiliation, and social and economic dislocation – perhaps on an even greater scale than after 1918. That democracy was to be more successful on the second attempt had to do with a number of circumstances to be considered below.

Whatever the controversies over responsibility for the Cold War, it seems clear that it was not from the Soviet side that the eventual division of Germany was initiated. Stalin appeared for a long time – even up until 1952 – to be keeping his options open with respect to Germany, whatever his position on other states in Europe. Rather, it was the changes in western policy which largely precipitated the establishment of two German Republics in 1949. There had from the start been disagreements over what to do with post-Nazi Germany, not only between the western powers and the USSR, but also between and even within each of the western governments. However, after early confusions in policy formation – with vestiges of the discarded and draconian 'Morgenthau Plan' for the deindustrialisation of Germany still informing the initial American policy document JCS 1067 – a major shift can be clearly discerned in western policies towards occupied Germany from 1946–7. This shift from earlier punitive views to a generous notion of reconstruction was both symbolised and given material expression in the Marshall Plan, announced in June 1947, for the reconstruction of post-war Europe. This plan envisaged the economic and political reconstruction of Europe in directions that would benefit America's new international role, with its 'open door' policies and search for markets, as well as its 'Truman doctrine' of stemming the rising tide of communism and perceived Soviet expansionism in Europe. Offered on terms that were designed to elicit refusal on the part of non-market economies under Soviet influence, the Marshall Plan represented a major step in dissociating western Germany from the Soviet zone, and incorporating it in a wider network of western European economic and political organisations in the emerging Cold War.

In January 1947 the British and American zones had fused to become a 'Bizone', which, developed its own quasi-government, the Economic Council. The Soviet zone in response set up the German Economic Commission, similarly a proto-governmental organisation. The French, who had been pursuing a rather independent line over a number of issues, were eventually brought into co-operation with the British and Americans. The administration of the economic aid in western Germany required a currency reform, since the old Reichsmark was virtually without value in what was essentially a black-market economy where cigarettes and chocolate were effective units of currency in addition to basic barter and exchange of goods and services. The currency reform of June 1948, introducing the Deutschmark, was offered on terms that the Soviets would not accept. As well as introducing their own separate currency, the Soviets made use of this pretext to attempt to cut off the western Allies from access to Berlin, sited in the heart of the Soviet zone, by closing all land and water access to that city. The western Allies fought the Berlin blockade by means of an air-lift, flying in essential supplies right through the autumn, winter and spring of 1948–9. In one stroke, the former bastion of Prussian nationalism and Nazi militarism had become a symbol of western freedom and democracy, to be protected at all costs. The air-lift symbolised the dramatic transformation of western policies towards their part of Germany: western Germany, no longer a defeated nation of despicable Nazis, was to become a democratic ally in the fight against 'totalitarianism' and communism in the developing Cold War. From the summer of 1948, constitutional deliberations were held to work out a constitution for a new state in the western part of Germany. After an assembly of delegates from the different regions (*Länder*) had approved the new constitution (with the exception of the separatistically inclined Bavarians), the Federal Republic of Germany was formally founded in May 1949, four years after the collapse of

Hitler's Third Reich. Whatever its suppressed and hidden problems, the West German state was destined to become a partner in the developing network of western political and economic alliances in the changed post-war world. In large measure as a direct response, the German Democratic Republic was formally founded in the Soviet zone a few months later, in October 1949.

FROM ESTABLISHMENT TO CONSOLIDATION

Initially, the constitutions of the two Germanies resembled each other quite closely. Both had Presidents as formal heads of state, in addition to political leaders of government (Chancellor in the west, Prime Minister in the east); both had lower chambers of parliament theoretically representing the people as a result of national elections, and upper chambers representing the regions (*Länder*). Neither constitution prescribed a particular form of social and economic system. The constitution of the Federal Republic was, indeed, so tentative as to call itself not a constitution but a 'Basic Law' (*Grundgesetz*), and committed itself explicitly to eventual reunification of the two states; the constitution of the German Democratic Republic was consciously formulated in terms which would make reunification possible. There were however fundamental differences of principle between the political systems of the two states, which were to become more explicit as time went by. West German representative democracy was based on free general elections for a wide range of permitted parties once every four years. The East German constitution was based on the Marxist-Leninist principle of democratic centralism, in which the different permitted political parties and mass organisations represented in parliament had a certain number of seats pre-allotted to them, and in which the SED had effective control. Subsequent developments were to increase the differences between the two constitutions, as we shall see further below.

Although very real, the division of Germany was not conceived as irreversible. The existence of two Germanies only became consolidated in a series of stages: the failure of reunification initiatives in 1951; the incorporation into a range of economic, political and military alliances in east and west respectively in the course of the

1950s, and the regaining of full sovereignty in 1955; the building of the Berlin Wall in August 1961, when division was literally sealed in concrete, with the closing off of the last means of escape from east to west; the Ostpolitik of the early 1970s, which culminated in mutual recognition in 1972 and entry as full members of the United Nations in 1973; and the development of relations between the two German states in the later 1970s and 1980s, which were distinctively different from relations between any other two separate and sovereign states. The question of German division was then reopened in a startling manner with the East German revolution of autumn 1989 and the opening of the Berlin Wall.

After elections held in August 1949, the CDU emerged as the largest party in the new West German parliament (*Bundestag*). The first West German Chancellor was Konrad Adenauer, a wily Catholic and former mayor of Cologne in the Weimar Republic, who had kept an acceptably low profile during the Third Reich. He was voted Chancellor only by a majority of one vote, after considerable preliminary arm-twisting to achieve the support of FDP deputies, whose nominee, Theodor Heuss, was to become the first President of the Federal Republic. From an initial reliance on coalitions, Adenauer triumphantly led the CDU to outright victory with a majority of the popular vote in 1957. Adenauer only finally retired, after fourteen years in power, at the grand old age of eighty-seven in 1963. Adenauer's rather high-handed chancellorship (which gave the name to a new political concept, 'Chancellor-democracy') essentially set the path for West Germany's post-war development. Adenauer determinedly presided over the western integration of a partial, divided state, as well as over the less controversial, more universally acclaimed 'economic miracle' associated with his Economics Minister Ludwig Erhard. Adenauer's firm commitment to western integration – whatever his formal mouthing of sentiments about reunification – was in line with American policies for the post-war economic, political and military integration of western Europe as a bulwark against communism. In October 1949, the Federal Republic became a member of the Organisation for European Economic Co-operation (OEEC); in April 1951 West Germany entered the European Coal and Steel Community (ECSC) and in May became a full member of the Council of Europe; and in 1957, in the

Treaty of Rome, West Germany became a founder member of the European Economic Community (EEC). In 1955 the Occupation Statute lapsed and West Germany gained full sovereignty, becoming a full member of the North Atlantic Treaty Organisation (NATO), which had been founded in 1949. Despite considerable domestic opposition, constitutional amendments were introduced to permit the Federal Republic to have an army and conscription for military service in 1956. While West Germany was thus in the process of being readmitted to the community of nations, it simultaneously experienced a remarkable economic recovery. From the ruins of a defeated and devastated nation grew a materialistic society witnessing astonishing rates of growth and productivity, and conveniently suppressing the past by focussing on the task of building a prosperous future. Former Nazis were relatively easily integrated into the new conservative Germany of the 1950s, with its transitional ideology of anti-communism and its material successes giving a pragmatic legitimacy to the new democracy.

In East Germany, political and socioeconomic transformations continued. In 1952 the *Länder* were abolished, and replaced by smaller regions (*Bezirke*) which were more easily controlled from the centre. In 1958 the upper chamber of parliament, which represented the *Länder*, was somewhat belatedly abolished. The SED itself underwent a series of purges, such that the position of its party leader, Walter Ulbricht, emerged considerably strengthened. Following a poorly prepared introduction of new economic policies, when concessions for some groups were announced at the same time as increased work norms for others, there was a popular expression of discontent with the regime, involving a widespread strike on 17 June 1953. This uprising, which originated in economic protest but which rapidly expressed wider political dissatisfaction, started to fizzle out even before a display of force by Soviet tanks put a definitive end to what was an essentially leaderless expression of protest, rather than a potential revolution. The uprising precipitated a purge of many members of the SED – frequently former Social Democrats – and ironically confirmed Ulbricht's position in power – which had been seriously under question in Moscow. It also, paradoxically, put an end to real hopes of reunification of the two Germanics, and confirmed the unwillingness of the west to risk an international crisis by interfering with East German affairs, in effect seeming content to abandon East Germans to their fate. (Serious research has not upheld official East German attempts to blame the uprising on western 'agents provocateurs'; and the western powers did little more than observe and report on the uprising, giving no notable support to the East German population in their protest.) Ulbricht undertook further actions against individuals opposing his rather hardline policies, with the trial and imprisonment of Wolfgang Harich and his group in 1956, and the exclusion of an opposing faction in the Politburo in 1958. Ulbricht thus effectively removed all serious internal opposition to his rather Stalinist brand of socialism – which remained hard-line even after the Communist Party of the Soviet Union officially denounced Stalinism in 1956 (although there were experiments with economic reforms and a degree of liberalisation in policies concerning youth, workers and culture in the period 1963 to 1965).

Meanwhile, further measures of economic reform were undertaken. Agriculture was collectivised in two main phases in 1952–3 and 1959–60. While some concessions were made to consumers in the wake of the 1953 uprising, the emphasis in industrial production continued to be on heavy industry. A series of unrealistic plans were successively pronounced, revised, and abandoned. Despite the brief hopes aroused when West Germany's growth momentarily faltered, it was clear by the beginning of the 1960s that East Germany's centralised economy was not a serious rival for West Germany's material success. Seeing the astonishingly rapid economic growth and new affluence in the west, which was associated not with political repression but relative personal freedom (even the freedom to be apolitical), many East Germans in the 1950s chose to vote with their feet. While the main border with West Germany was closed, it was still possible to cross from East Berlin to West Berlin – with very few possessions, of course, so as not to arouse suspicion – and to leave from there for West Germany. While the number of refugees prepared to abandon their homes each year varied, throughout the 1950s a damaging drain of manpower affected the GDR's economy, as a flood of predominantly skilled younger males left the drab, dispiriting and constraining atmosphere of the GDR to seek a better future in the west.

Plate 40. Soldiers of the East German People's Police stand guard as the Berlin Wall starts to go up, August 1961.

In 1961, radical steps were taken to alter a situation which, following the recent land reform and associated food shortages, had become critical. On the morning of 13 August, Berliners awoke to find the division of their city finalised, with streets crossed by tangles of barbed wire, guarded by soldiers, and more permanent walls of concrete and bricks rapidly being erected. Families and friends were divided by what might have been thousands of miles rather than a few yards. Again, although there were protests from the west, it was clear that western powers were not prepared to risk conflict with the Soviet Union over Berlin: the final, concrete division of the city proceeded unhindered.

Curiously, however, this sealing of the last means of escape perhaps improved conditions for East Germans in the 1960s. This was the decade of the 'scientific-technological revolution', when opportunities for fulfilling careers in the GDR appeared to be opening up. In 1963 the 'New Economic System' was introduced, permitting some decentralisation of economic decision-making, and providing achievement incentives for those with certain technical skills and qualifications. Perhaps because there was no alternative, people started coming to terms with a system which they now simply had to accept. Many had also experienced remarkable social mobility, as a result of educational and social policies and new opportunities. In West Germany, on the other hand, the 1960s saw the rise of movements highly critical of West German materialism, affluence, and unwillingness to confront the past. The economic recession of 1965–6 precipitated the collapse of Erhard's CDU government, the weak successor to Adenauer, and the CDU, under Kurt Georg Kiesinger as Chancellor, went into a 'grand coalition' with the SPD. The student movement in particular articulated a sense of protest and unease, and there was a perceived need for 'extra-parliamentary opposition' with the lack of any real opposition in parliament. Student protest reached a peak in 1967–8, when following the shooting of a student on a demonstration in Berlin a polarisation of popular opinion was fostered by a conservative tabloid press. This period also saw the rise of active right-wing movements, with the highly nationalist NPD gaining representation in several *Land* parliaments, although failing to gain national representation. But in 1969 a new period in West German history was inaugurated when the SPD managed – after considerable post-election bargaining – to form a coalition with the now more liberal FDP, and to become, for the first time in the two decades of the Federal Republic's history, the dominant party of government.

The coming to power of West German SPD Chancellor Willy Brandt, formerly Mayor of Berlin, coincided with an era of detente in superpower relations. It now suited both the USA and the USSR that relations between the two Germanies should be eased; a position that coincided with Brandt's own desire to see an easing of tensions and a facilitation of human contacts between the two Germanies. Brandt's so-called *Ostpolitik* originated in the later 1960s and was continued after the regime change in the GDR where, in 1971, Ulbricht was replaced as Party leader by Erich Honecker. Against considerable domestic opposition from the CDU/CSU, Brandt was able to push through a series of treaties and agreements which culminated in the 'Basic Treaty' between East and West Germany in December 1972. This was ratified (again with opposition) in May 1973. In September 1973 both Germanies were accepted as full members of the United Nations. From then on, the two Germanies formally recognised each other's existence, not as entirely foreign states but in a special relationship (perceived somewhat differently on each side). This was symbolised by the exchange, not of ambassadors, but of 'permanent representatives'. From 1973 to 1989, inner-German relations were concerned less with an apparently receding, almost metaphysical question of potential reunification and rather more with the improvement of relations between the two countries, which were recognised to be separate states but having a unique relationship.

The West German Social Democratic government, in coalition with the FDP, lasted from 1969 to 1982. This period, after Brandt's initial foreign policy successes, was marked by mounting economic problems and domestic difficulties. Energy crises, starting with the oil crisis of 1973, had adverse effects on West Germany's economy, as did the world economic recession of the later 1970s and 1980s. At the same time, the radical movements of the later 1960s dissolved into separate strands: alongside relatively harmless retreatist subcultures there developed the more disturbing terrorist movement led by certain extremists in the 'Red Army Faction' (RAF, also known as the Baader-Meinhof gang after two of its early leaders). After Willy Brandt's resignation as Chancellor in 1974 (following a spy scandal), the more right-wing Helmut Schmidt took over, facing attacks from the left wing of his own party particularly over environmental, nuclear and defence issues. Schmidt also experienced serious difficulties with the SPD's increasingly right-wing coalition partner, the FDP, in attempting to agree budget proposals in the face of rising unemployment and an overstretched welfare state. In 1982 the FDP finally employed the constitutional device of a 'constructive vote of no confidence' in the current Chancellor to switch their parliamentary allegiance to the CDU/CSU. Helmut Kohl of the CDU thus became West Germany's conservative Chancellor by the changed votes of a few members of parliament belonging to a minority party. Experiencing some unease with this situation – as did many West Germans – Kohl made use of the same constitutional device (although engineering loss of the vote) to make possible an early general election in 1983: the outcome of this was in fact to confirm Kohl's government in office. West Germany thus entered a third major political period in its post-war history, with the conservative government following the preceding lengthy periods of Social Democratic rule (1969–82) and conservative rule (1949–69, in the last three years in the Grand Coalition).

Under the leadership of Erich Honecker from 1971 to 1989 East Germany too entered a new stage of development. Following the rapid social transformations and the combined utopianism and repression of the Ulbricht era, Honecker's GDR was marked by an apparent willingness to recognise at least some of the difficulties of the present and to seek longer-term means of resolving sociopolitical problems. While the economy was recentralised in the 1970s, a new and continued emphasis was given to the question of consumer satisfaction and the increased availability of highly desired goods such as television sets and cars. An initial apparent liberalisation in the cultural sphere did not last beyond 1976, when the enforced exile of the critical singer and guitarist Wolf Biermann provoked a storm of protest among many East German intellectuals. Renewed constraint was evident in most cultural spheres in the later 1970s, with the significant exception of the East German Protestant churches, who reached a remarkable agreement with the state in 1978, consolidating their role in East German society and at the same time providing a protected space for the discussion of alternative views. In the 1980s there was further rapprochement between the two Germanies, with improved communications for the populations of the two states, enhanced possibilities for travel to the west by East German citizens, and the historic visit by Erich Honecker to the Federal Republic in 1987. Despite signs of increased repression in the late 1980s, with an ageing political leadership evidently rattled both by the proliferation of dissenting voices at home and the impact of reforming impulses emanating from Gorbachev's Soviet Union, East Germany had apparently matured as a country in which many rather apolitical Germans found it possible to lead an at least passable existence.

The apparent resolution of 'the German question', and the permanence of the division of Germany – and Europe – was suddenly thrown into question when a wave of revolutions swept eastern Europe in 1989–90. In the context of a crumbling Soviet empire, and a dismantling of the post-war settlement of central Europe, the system of communist rule which had held sway in East Germany for forty years was toppled. But before considering the dramatic end of the post-war period, it is worth exploring in more detail certain aspects of the political and socioeconomic systems of the two Germanies in the period up to 1989, and examining the extent to which they had developed from a common past into two very different societies with diverging cultures and identities.

POLITICS IN THE TWO GERMANIES, 1949–89

What accounts for the relative stability of the two Germanies from 1949 to 1989? Part of the answer obviously lies in the changed international system. No longer was Europe a system of powerful, expansive, imperialist states, as in the late nineteenth and early twentieth centuries. Rather, it was divided into western and eastern spheres of influence, under the more global claims to domination of the superpowers, the USA and the USSR. Germany's unleashing of two world wars pulled America into European affairs and, after the Second World War, divided Germany became the pawn and front line of the new Cold War between the leaders of the capitalist and communist worlds. Yet to explain this period of German history in terms purely of a changed international context is not sufficient. Domestic factors too must be invoked to explain the greater stability of communist East Germany than neighbouring Poland or Czechoslovakia in the years before 1989, or the less crisis-prone performance of West German parliamentary democracy than that of post-Fascist Italy. We must start by considering in more detail aspects of the political systems of the two Germanies.

West Germany's democracy (and that of united Germany after 1990) had certain unique constitutional features. The voting system combined proportional representation with 'first-past-the-post' constituency representatives: each voter had two votes, one for a named candidate and one for a party. Votes cast for the former elected constituency representatives in the British manner; votes for the latter entitled parties to seats in parliament, with individuals taken from previously drawn-up party lists, according to the proportion of votes the party received, provided that it was at least 5 per cent of the total. This '5 per cent rule' was designed to ensure that small parties could not easily gain a national platform – as the Nazis did in the Weimar Republic – and that there would not be perpetual difficulties with post-election bargaining among a multiplicity of parties to form unstable coalition governments (again a problem in Weimar democracy). For the most part, these provisions appear to have worked: small parties were progressively absorbed in the 1950s, so that a two-party system, with the smaller FDP as a third party generally holding the balance of power, emerged. There were notable exceptions, such as the rise of the Greens to national representation in the *Bundestag* in the 1980s, and the startling success of the right-wing Republicans in the Berlin city elections of spring 1989 which entitled them to representation in the Upper House, or *Bundesrat*, from 1990.

The Republicans just stayed within permitted limits: there were and still are constitutional restrictions on the nature of parties which are permitted in the Federal Republic – again a provision designed to preclude the proliferation of 'anti-system' parties which so bedevilled Weimar democracy. The right-wing SRP (*Sozialistische Reichspartei*) was banned in 1952, and the Communist Party of Germany (KPD) was outlawed in 1956, on the grounds that their basic aims were hostile to the democratic constitution; but a neo-Nazi party, the NPD, and a reformed German Communist Party (DKP) were permitted in the course of the 1960s. The 1972 'Decree concerning Radicals' (*Radikalenerlass*, also known as the *Berufsverbot*; a 'prohibition on employment', since that was its consequence in certain areas for the people concerned) sought further to protect West German democracy by ensuring that individuals with views, activities or affiliations deemed to be hostile to the constitution were not employed in public service jobs – a wide sector, including not only the civil service in the British sense, but also state employees such as school-teachers, postmen and train-drivers. Many critics argued that this measure, designed to protect democracy, in itself constituted a serious infringement of democratic rights of freedom of speech, discussion and organisation. Improved police surveillance techniques, partly a consequence of terrorist activities in the 1970s, heightened a sense of constraint particularly among university students who feared that being seen on a political demonstration, for example, might harm their future employment prospects.

The West German political system also had other constitutional provisions designed specifically with an eye to the shortcomings of Weimar democracy. The President was given far fewer powers than the *Ersatzkaiser* of Weimar Germany, being a purely ceremonial head of state; furthermore, the President was not to be directly elected by popular vote, but rather indirectly by an electoral college of parliamentarians – a feature reflecting the Allies' mistrust of the Germans, and unwillingness to give the people too much of a voice in their 'democracy' after the war. The device of a 'constructive vote of no confidence' (discussed above, p. 218, with reference to the change from the Schmidt to the Kohl governments) was designed to preclude the perpetual lack of effective government in the Weimar Republic, when successive chancellors were unable to find majority support in parliament and eventually were forced to rely on presidential decrees to promulgate legislation.

However important the constitutional provisions of the Federal Republic, a number of other factors were equally, if not more, important in explaining the stability of West German democracy. One of the most central is undoubtedly the success of the West German economy, on which more in a moment. Other factors have to do with changes in the nature of political parties, and in the relationships between certain economic interest groups and the political system. Obviously, the range of the politically permissible was initially constrained by the Allies after the war, and, as indicated above, was partly determined by constitutional provisions. But the parties themselves developed into rather different sorts of vehicle for political interests than pre-Nazi German parties. On the one hand, the CDU/CSU developed, to adapt a phrase describing the British Labour Party, into a relatively 'broad church' incorporating both Protestants and Catholics, and embracing former Nazis with little hesitation (Adenauer even including them in his cabinet). On the other hand, the SPD radically changed its political colours after its resounding election defeat in 1957, and at its 1959 Bad Godesberg Conference unceremoniously dumped the Marxist-influenced rhetoric it had proudly proclaimed for so many decades. The SPD now sought to compete with the CDU/CSU as an all-embracing *Volkspartei*, appealing to all sectors of the populace, and proposing a moderate management of capitalism with a human face rather than advocating radical socialist transformation. Despite certain specific differences in policy – such as over *Ostpolitik* in the late 1960s and early 1970s, or over the management of economic recession in the 1980s – the two main parties in the Federal Republic converged into moderate alternative managers of a capitalist welfare state. This is in marked contrast to the more volatile oppositions in pre-Nazi Germany. Furthermore, the army, which played a key political role in both Imperial and Weimar Germany, found itself, in its new form since 1956, in a rather different position. It now had to operate under parliamentary control and could not aspire to independent power.

There are similar contrasts between the Weimar and Bonn Republics in respect of the political orientations of economic interest groups. Unlike the Weimar Republic, where certain sectors of business perceived the democratic political system as operating against their economic interests, the particular form of West German corporatism by and large operated in a way perceived as satisfactory by employers. Many policy decisions were developed through processes of behind-the-scenes negotiations among major interest groups, such as, on the employers' side, the Confederation of German Industry, the Federal League of Employers, and the German Chamber of Commerce and Industry, and on the workers' side, the League of German Trade Unions, the German Employees' Union, and the German Federation of Civil Servants, as well as a strong farming lobby. West German corporatism was denounced by some critics as a less than democratic process taking effective decision-making away from the parliamentary arena; by other analysts, it was praised as an efficient means of reaching acceptable and workable policy compromises by means of negotiation among the parties affected prior to the formal legislative process. The fact that the West German economy performed so much better than the Weimar economy is undoubtedly also a major factor in the commitment of economic elites to Bonn democracy.

How far did the West Germans become a nation of committed democrats? It is generally accepted that Allied attempts at denazification and re-education had minimal, and frequently contrary, effects. Evidence on popular opinion in the 1950s reveals widespread political apathy, combined with the persistence of monarchist and right-wing sympathies. Gradually, a pragmatic support developed for a system that appeared to be 'delivering the goods', only slowly developing into a more principled support for a democratic system as such. Many Germans in the 1950s and 1960s put material stability above political freedom, although they also felt that in West Germany they were able to have both, unlike in the East. Political participation for many was limited to the obedient performance of civic duties – turning out to vote in large numbers, compatible also (especially!) with an authoritarian regime. In the 1970s and 1980s more activist orientations emerged, evident in the proliferation of 'citizens' initiative groups' and wider social movements such as feminism and environmentalism, culminating in the formation of the Green Party. Yet it would be a mistake to attempt to characterise 'West German political culture' in a monolithic fashion. There were numerous subcultures, and the persistence and renewal of right-wing movements (such as the Republicans) counter-balanced pressures for the extension of participatory democracy on the left. Political orientations must be seen not simply as a process of 'national re-education', but as a diverse set of changing responses to current circumstances, salient features of which may vary from positive early responses to the postwar economic miracle through to negative responses to tensions concerning foreign workers. Undue complacency about the functioning of a political system is never possible: a wary eye must always be kept on potential dissent and dissatisfaction at the margins.

The pattern of political development in communist East Germany was of course very different. East European communist states have frequently been lumped together by western observers and dismissed as 'totalitarian' one-party states. Less willing to contemplate reform than Hungary or Poland, the GDR was often viewed as particularly rigid. While restrictions on human rights and liberties – such as freedom of expression, freedom of association, freedom to emigrate – cannot be denied, the East German political system in practice was somewhat more complex than is implied by all-purpose labels. To understand the peculiarities of politics in the GDR under Ulbricht and Honecker, it is necessary both to analyse the formal political structure and to consider the dynamics of its functioning.

Despite the formal resemblance between the East and West German constitutions in 1949, real political differences were quite visible and the divergences widened as time went on. The abolition of the *Länder* and the Upper House have been mentioned above. In 1960, on the death of the first President, Wilhelm Pieck, the role of President was replaced with a collective head of state, the *Staatsrat* or Council of State. Other constitutional changes were embodied in the new constitutions of 1968 and 1974, which took account first of the changed sociopolitical realities of life in the GDR, and secondly of its changed international status after *Ostpolitik*. The 1968 constitution enshrined the 'leading role' of the Marxist-Leninist Party, the SED, and hedged many 'bourgeois' freedoms from the original constitution with the serious, indeed fundamental, limitation that all must proceed from the basic tenets of socialism – as defined by the Party. The 1974 constitution sought to develop a 'cultural demarcation', following the easing of physical relations between East and West Germany, attempting to define a specifically 'GDR' national identity and to play down any notions of 'Germany' and all-German links and affinities. It also stressed the close relationship between the GDR and the Soviet Union.

It is frequently assumed that 'party' and 'state' were more or less identical in communist states. While there were two organisational hierarchies, that of the state was assumed to operate at the behest of the leading communist party. This view however, while broadly true, is somewhat oversimplified. Both state and party in the GDR were organised according to the principle of democratic centralism. Ultimate power resided with the Politburo of the SED, and its Secretariat; below this was the rather larger Central Committee; below this was the Party Conference; and then the various lower levels of party organisation in regions, districts and localities. At the bottom were the basic cells, usually organised according to work-place, but also according to place of residence. The SED was a 'mass' as well as a 'cadre' party: in addition to the trained and committed party activists, there was a large number of passive members of the party; in the GDR in the early 1980s, about one in five of the adult working population was a member of the SED. While there were processes of consultation and exchange of views, decisions were taken at the top and had to be carried out at lower levels. In contrast to many other

East European communist parties (for example, Czechoslovakia in 1968), there was little by way of visible factional splits in the SED, after the purges undertaken by Ulbricht in the 1950s, until the revolution of 1989. The relatively monolithic public face of the SED for the best part of the 1960s, 1970s, and 1980s must be seen as a major factor in the GDR's relative political stability in this period. There were, however, different degrees of conformist commitment and private scepticism among lower ranks of the party. With an ageing leadership under Honecker in the late 1980s, and with the succession question being complicated by the reforming leadership of the USSR under Gorbachev, many party members in the regions began at least privately to hope for a change in direction.

The East German state was also organised hierarchically, with the Council of State being the ceremonial head, and the Council of Ministers having governmental power. Among the most important Ministries were those dealing with various aspects of the economy and with defence, and, of course, the Ministry for State Security. The State Security police, or Stasi, grew exponentially over the years, and played a major role in domestic surveillance and attempted repression of opposition. The powers of the Council of State were reduced in relation to the Council of Ministers when Ulbricht retained its chairmanship after losing his position as First Secretary of the Party; but it retained its importance as the formal representative of the GDR, and prominent Party members were also members of the Council of State in order to be able to represent the GDR officially when abroad. The Parliament, or *Volkskammer*, met only infrequently and basically served to ratify and publicise decisions taken at higher levels. Centrally determined decisions and plans were also communicated to regional, district and local governmental levels for implementation. While this account makes clear that the party basically dominated the state apparatus in the GDR political system, it was by no means always a simple matter of identity of party and state. In the 1950s, the SED had to devote considerable energy to adapting state structures to serve the needs of the party, and to bringing bureaucracy into line. Translation of central decisions into policy at the grass-roots remained problematic throughout the GDR's history, although the functionary system began to stabilise in the 1960s and 1970s. Some analysts have suggested

that in the early 1980s, the position was one in which state structures and functionaries to some extent influenced the structure and
goals of the party, helping to set the political agenda and limit political goals to what was deemed to be realistic by the 'experts' in
any given area. Clearly, although the relationship was very close, it
was not one of identity, and the balance varied with different issues
and personalities at different times. A slightly different tension seen
in some communist states, between party and army (as, for example, in early-1980s Poland, or late-1980s Yugoslavia), appeared not
to be present in East Germany, where leaders of the party and the
army appeared to share common goals and enjoy a harmonious
relationship.

The GDR was not formally a one-party state. In addition to the
SED there were the four small parties: the Christian CDU, the Liberal
LDPD, the nationalist NDPD and the farmers' party, the DBD (all
with memberships in the early 1980s hovering around the 100,000
mark, the CDU being the largest). Although these were easily dismissed from the point of view of western pluralism as being simply
puppets of the SED, they did in fact fulfil certain important functions in East German political life. They served as transmission belts
between the SED and different subsections of the populace, translating policies into different subcultural languages, communicating
decisions in special-interest periodicals, for example, as well as chan-
nelling popular reactions and grievances upwards, thus helping to
keep SED leaders in touch with grass-roots opinion. For people who
belonged to these parties, it might be a means of signalling basic
commitment to the GDR without overly compromising on principles; this might have been particularly true for members of the
CDU. The four small parties all had a specified number of seats
allotted to them in the Parliament. The only time there was ever a
vote against a government decision prior to 1989 was in 1972, when
fourteen members of the CDU voted against the Abortion Law. In
addition to the four small parties, the GDR had a number of mass
organisations to encourage the participation of the populace in East
German public life. The largest of these was the trade union organisation, the FDGB, which absorbed almost the entire population of
working age. Also important were the youth organisation (FDJ), the
women's organisation (DFD), the League of Culture (KB), and the

German–Soviet Friendship Society (DSF). The Society for Sport and Technology (GST) was a para-military youth organisation but many other mass organisations served merely to facilitate more mundane leisure pursuits, such as pet care or cacti collection. There were numerous mass organisations in the GDR, and pressures to participate were immense, since career advancement depended not only on talent and merit but was also predicated on at least political conformity, if not active commitment.

East Germany was able, for most of its history until the 1980s, to defuse potentially destabilising political opposition and contain dissent. The June 1953 Uprising was, as indicated above (p. 214), lacking in leadership and overall strategy, as well as external support, and started to collapse even before it was suppressed by force. Individual dissenting Marxist intellectuals – Harich, Havemann, Bahro – failed to gain mass popular followings. Most East Germans appeared resigned to private grumbling rather than public dissent. The 1980s however saw the rapid proliferation of grass-roots dissenting groups, primarily in response to the stationing of nuclear missiles in East and West Europe, but also going beyond specifically peace movement concerns to address issues of human rights and environmental protection. Many of these dissenting voices found space, both metaphorically and literally, for the discussion of unorthodox views under the roof of the East German Protestant churches. The church was the only social institution in East Germany that was not co-ordinated by, and subordinate to, the communist party. After early persecution of Christianity in the 1950s, and a rather uneasy coexistence of church and state in the 1960s and early 1970s, by 1978 a modus vivendi was achieved in which the 'church in socialism' was allotted certain privileges in a new, more harmonious relationship with the state. For a while it appeared as if the church leadership would seek to sustain its position by moderating and containing dissent within acceptable limits, thus effectively playing the role of a safety valve in East German politics. But by the late 1980s it became clear both that there were splits within the church, between grassroots and leaders and among the leaders themselves, and that the discussions of alternative views and the networks of dissenters had proliferated to such an extent that they had outgrown the church's capacity for moderation. Undoubtedly many were also hopeful that the repercussions of Soviet proclamations of *glasnost* might have some real meaning in East Germany. A rattled leadership in the GDR responded to demonstrations by making more forceful use of the State Security Police than had been seen for many years, and by forcing large numbers of dissenters into involuntary exile. While the successful containment of dissent was undoubtedly an important factor in East German political stability in the 1960s and 1970s, the position in the new circumstances of the 1980s was far more volatile. As we shall see, the shaping of dissent by the churches influenced its mode of expression and its political impact in the 1989 revolution; but on its own, domestic dissent would probably not have been able to break the bonds of communism in East Germany.

How far did political culture in East Germany diverge from that of the West? It seems to be the case that, while the East Germans by no means became a nation of committed communists, patterns of political orientation did diverge notably from those evident in West Germany. Many East Germans were prepared to conform in public, but also lived what many considered to be 'perfectly ordinary lives' in private spaces – family, friends, country cottage or allotment – in what was termed a 'niche society' (Gaus). This retreatism, as a response to a relatively intrusive and demanding state, was a rather different phenomenon from the apolitical passivity which was possible for many West German citizens. There was also a certain authoritarianism evident in the GDR, which was arguably less a left-over from the Nazi and pre-Nazi past than a response to current political circumstances. It was hard to learn modes of democratic discussion of differing views, and democratic methods of conflict management, in the context of GDR schools, factories, party or leisure organisations. Similarly, the extensive organisation of every aspect of life militated against a certain form of individualism and enterprise. Generalisations about a 'national' political culture are as unwise in relation to East Germany as to West. However, it is notable that there were marked differences of political attitude to be discerned after forty years of the existence of the two states, with many East Germans by the later 1980s criticising aspects of the functioning, or inadequacy, of their system, but not simply presupposing the superiority of the west. These differences in political patterns were related to marked divergences between the economic and social structures of the two states, to which we now turn.

The most obvious difference between the two Germanies evident to any casual observer in the 1980s was that between their standards of living. West Germany was manifestly a prosperous, westernised, consumer-oriented society, in which sleek, fast cars sped down well-maintained – if often overcrowded – motorways, and where, despite increasing wails about such matters as the 'death of the forests', the general atmosphere was one of cleanliness, a well-maintained environment, and material plenty. East Germany, by contrast, would strike visitors as relatively drab, colourless, polluted by the dirty smoke produced by lignite (brown coal), with small and inferior cars bumping their way over pot-holed, often still cobbled roads (with the exception of the well-maintained motorways from West Germany to West Berlin), with housing generally in a poor state of repair, and the choice in shops severely restricted, offering a limited range of low-quality goods. These appearances partly reflected, and partly also disguised, deeper realities and more complex truths.

Both Germanies in fact experienced what was called, in relation to West Germany in the late 1940s and 1950s, an 'economic miracle'. The phenomenon in West Germany is well known. Starting even before the currency reform in 1948, and given a psychological as well as material boost by the Marshall Aid programme, the German economy took off to achieve phenomenal growth rates in the 1950s. Unemployment, which at the beginning of the decade was relatively high (around 8 per cent) with the influx of refugees and returning POWs, was turned by the end of the decade into a labour shortage. The rapid growth tapered off at the end of the 1950s, so that the performance of the West German economy came broadly into line with that of other western industrial societies in the 1960s. It experienced a small recession in 1966–7, which was effectively dealt with by the economic strategies of the Grand Coalition. West Germany was highly dependent on trade, and on fuel imports, and was therefore adversely affected by the oil crises of 1973 and 1979, as well as the general recession of the later 1970s and 1980s. In the 1980s, the economy's performance was perhaps stagnant in comparison with earlier decades, with unemployment remaining at a relatively high 8–10 per cent, and growth rates at a relatively low 2–3 per cent, but inflation – the main fear of many Germans since the 1920s – being kept at one of the lowest levels in Europe.

Over the post-war period, there were three main phases of government economic policy and approach. The first phase, under conservative government, was master-minded by a former Professor of Economics, Adenauer's Minister Ludwig Erhard, and was characterised by the espousal of neo-liberalism and the 'social market economy'. Understandably wanting to throw off the Nazi heritage of state intervention in the economy, this view held that the state should guarantee or facilitate the conditions for economic growth but refrain from too much intervention and leave as much as possible to market forces. The 'social' qualification indicated a recognition of the need for certain provisions to protect the weakest members of society from the full ravages of unrestricted market forces. Many critics argued that the West German economy was neither 'market' nor 'social'. Inevitably the state intervened in all manner of ways to guide and direct the economy, as well as being quite a considerable employer in its own right. The operations of a free market were further qualified by continuing tendencies towards centralisation in the German economy, despite Allied attempts to split up large concerns and introduce measures against cartels. Decartelisation faced considerable opposition in West Germany, with Erhard's first Bill not being passed, and the 1957 version which was finally passed being so watered down, with so many loopholes, that trends towards concentration in West German industry could continue relatively unabated. Moreover, the policies pursued in the 1950s, of low taxes, high interest rates and profits, low wage increases for workers, a squeeze on domestic credit and the encouragement of investment, not only contributed to the expansion of the economy but also contributed to an increasing gap between rich and poor. Social inequalities were increased by government policies, so that by the 1960s a very small proportion of society held a very large proportion of wealth. Proponents of these policies argued that, since the overall cake was getting so much larger so fast, such inequalities did not really matter; in absolute terms, compared with their own previous positions, all members of society were much better off. For most West Germans in the 1960s, who remembered the 'hunger years' after the war, this was probably infinitely more important than any overall analysis of relative social inequalities.

With the fall of the Erhard government of 1963–6 and the economic recession of 1966–7, government strategy in the Grand Coalition changed to one of neo-Keynesianism, with tax reforms (including what was seen as a fairly high VAT at 11 per cent) and heavy state investment in aspects of the economic infrastructure, particularly motorway construction and the expansion of higher education. The 'Law for the Stabilisation of the Economy and Promotion of Economic Growth' of 1967, and the 'concerted action' between employers and workers (from which in fact the latter withdrew in 1977), facilitated by the state, recognised the importance of state intervention and conscious steering of the economy. The early 1970s, under Social Democratic government, saw an emphasis on research and economic planning, although by the later 1970s faith in planning had given way to a more reactive form of crisis management. With rising unemployment, as well as an unfavourable demographic structure – more pensioners having to be supported by relatively fewer people in work – there were major dissensions in the closing years of the Schmidt government over the balance between taxation and welfare. The more right-wing FDP Economics Minister Lambsdorff could not agree with the more welfare-conscious members on the left of the SPD, contributing to the change of political allegiance and the switch to the CDU-dominated government of Helmut Kohl. Under Kohl, economic policy reverted from neo-Keynesianism to a renewed form of neo-liberalism. It is notable however that Kohl's government in the 1980s did not produce the kind of radical economic restructuring and extensive privatisation programmes favoured by a conservative colleague across the channel, the then British Prime Minister Mrs Thatcher. Moreover, under Kohl, the traditionally good strike record of German workers deteriorated, with rising strains in industrial relations and an increasing number of strikes, provoking legislation attempting to restrict strike action and its effects.

Industrial relations in West Germany were frequently presented in terms of a harmonious 'social partnership' between employers and workers. The trade union structure was relatively streamlined, with one union per factory, simplifying industrial disputes, and one overall trade union organisation, the DGB, representing seventeen member unions, in addition to the organisations for white-collar workers and civil servants. The DGB was not formally affiliated to any political party; the SPD, unlike the British Labour Party, was not historically the 'parliamentary wing of the labour movement'. There were measures of co-determination and workers' representation in industry. These were initially introduced in 1951 and 1952, with co-determination in the coal and steel industries and the formation of works councils for employees to have a voice in certain matters affecting them. Co-determination measures were extended in 1976 to cover all large enterprises of over 1,000 employees. However, against the picture of harmonious industrial relations, it must be pointed out that these pieces of legislation – both in 1951–2 and in 1976 – were only pushed through against considerable opposition on the part of employers, who felt they went too far, and to the disappointment of trade unionists, who felt they did not go far enough.

There was also prevalent a myth that affluent West Germany represented a 'classless' society, with differences of accent and fashion representing regional differences in a still quite diverse federal state rather than differences in class (in contrast to the class connotations of many regional accents in Britain). Undoubtedly, structures of social inequality and their relationship to regional diversity were different in West Germany and Britain, but that does not mean that there were no important class differences in West Germany. A large number of families with the aristocratic 'von' in their names could still be found in leading roles in West German economy and society. Parental status – at all levels in society – tended to be reproduced through the education system. Although there were differences among the *Länder*, there were very few areas which adopted a comprehensive school system, and most operated with a version of the tripartite selective system. The existence of selective schools generally favoured children of middle-class, professional backgrounds, who then proceeded to gain qualifications in higher education, while children from working-class or rural (and often Catholic) backgrounds tended to be held back and condemned at an early age to under-achievement. Educational qualifications in West Germany, despite a series of educational reforms, still tended to legitimate the inheritance of parental social status. Against this, however, may be added a number of qualifications. The economy as a whole shifted from being one in which the majority were employed in industry to one in which white-collar and tertiary, service-sector jobs expanded to overtake blue-collar employment. There was therefore a considerable amount of 'structural' social mobility. Secondly, West Germany provided a very high level of training for young people, so that all sectors of the work-force were comparatively well educated and qualified for their occupation. Women continued to be 'under-achievers' in West German society, with progressively fewer females represented at higher levels of the educational ladder (and a very small percentage indeed becoming, for example, university professors). Those women who were in paid employment outside the home were predominantly to be found in mainly low-status, low-paid, impermanent and often part-time employment, readily laid off in times of recession. Despite governmental efforts and the existence of quite vocal feminist movements among a minority, the still prevailing general assumption was that women should choose between family and career, and that those married women with young children who did go out to work did so out of economic necessity and to the detriment of the children's well-being. Pre-school childcare provision, particularly for the pre-Kindergarten age, was very limited, while the short school day, with afternoons free, made provision for school-age children still difficult in households with working parents.

Finally, the social structure of West Germany was further qualified by the existence of a large 'under-class' of foreign 'guest-workers' (*Gastarbeiter*). The supply of relatively cheap and mobile labour in the form of refugees dried up with the building of the Berlin Wall in 1961, and in a period of labour shortage migrant workers from the Mediterranean countries, particularly Turkey, were attracted into the West German economy in the 1960s. Foreign workers were attractive to West Germany because they had cost nothing to educate, their taxes contributed to West Germany's expanding welfare system, they were predominantly unskilled and non-unionised, and could therefore be employed to do the 'dirty' jobs which Germans did not like to do, as well as being employed on temporary contracts with little respect for workers' rights. With the economic recession of the 1970s and 1980s, the foreign workers – many of whom had not simply stayed to earn high wages for a few years and then returned home, but had rather settled and brought, or founded, families – began to turn into more of a perceived problem. There were problems of rising unemployment, and a series of incentives to get foreign workers to leave Germany was introduced. There were also social problems, with rising racial hostility (evident, for example, in high votes for right-wing parties in local elections in Berlin and Frankfurt in spring 1989), and questions concerning the social integration of immigrants' children, for whom Germany was as much 'home' as an unknown country far away, but whose language and customs were different from those of their German neighbours. Any account of West German society as 'classless' must be seriously blinkered in respect of around one-tenth of the population of late 1980s West Germany.

ECONOMY AND SOCIETY IN THE GDR, 1949–89

Already by 1949 there were major differences between the socio-economic structures of East and West Germany. These differences were to become more marked after the formal foundation of the two Republics.

Collectivisation of agriculture – following the expropriation of estates in the occupation period – proceeded in two main stages in 1952–3 and 1959–60. There were three different types of co-operative, and by the end of the 1960s the bulk of East German agriculture was organised in collective forms in which land, live-stock, machinery and tools were all in common ownership. The 1970s and 1980s saw some changes in the organisation of agri-culture, with increased specialisation – between, for example, fruit-growing, crop-farming, and livestock production – and intermediate levels of organisation to coordinate the production plans of individ-ual enterprises in the light of nationally determined goals. Although not as efficient as West German agriculture (which benefited from a powerful farming lobby as well as the EEC's Common Agricultural Policy), East German agriculture was relatively productive and the

GDR was nearly self-sufficient in basic foodstuffs (although with limited consumer choice, for example in fruit). The contrast between the serried ranks of combine harvesters moving in formation across large collectivised East German fields and the single, often still horse-drawn carts visible across the landscape of peasant Poland was highly striking to any visitor in the 1980s. A further quite important source of supply of, for example, eggs, in East Germany came from the small private plots and allotment gardens which were actually encouraged by the state in the 1980s as a supplement to the main collectivised production.

The organisation of East German industry went through a number of stages. Private ownership of the means of production was squeezed out fairly rapidly, so that the bulk of production was owned either by 'the people' (that is, the state) or in some form of joint ownership with state participation. The 1950s were characterised first by a Stalinist emphasis on heavy industrial production (although some concessions were made to consumerism in the wake of the 1953 Uprising) and secondly by the pronouncement and attempted implementation of a succession of Plans. Central planning was however bedevilled by a variety of problems, including unrealistic goals and a focus on production of quantity without reference to quality or saleability of goods. In 1963, in the climate of new economic ideas in the USSR, the New Economic System was announced, which introduced a measure of decentralisation in the economy, with greater decision-making possible at intermediate levels, and the use of profits and bonus incentives as important levers. Since profits were now important, quality became a consideration and goods had to be saleable. There were a number of problems with the New Economic System (which necessitated three sets of price reforms), including a lack of managerial experience among those now expected to take more responsibility. In 1967 it was amended to become the 'Economic System of Socialism'. However, these experiments were quietly terminated in the late 1960s, in the wake of the Czechoslovakian Prague Spring of 1968, when fears were widespread among Eastern European leaders that political decentralisation and democratisation might be an unwelcome concomitant of economic decentralisation. (It should be noted that in the GDR Ulbricht had made quite sure that the dispersion of economic decision-making was not accompanied by any political democratisation, in contrast to the situation in Czechoslovakia.) In the 1970s, under Honecker, there was a recentralisation of economic planning.

There were a number of changes in the organisation of East German industrial production under Honecker. Following the economic recession of the late 1970s and early 1980s – from which East Germany suffered because of its dependence on trade and fuel imports – there were new attempts at the co-ordination of research, technological development, and production, with more sensitive economic levers at intermediate levels of economic planning, while overall control remained centrally with the Politburo and Council of Ministers.

Despite setbacks and difficulties, the East German economy in fact performed remarkably well. Although wrenched from its natural economic links with the western areas of the former German Reich and forcibly integrated with the less developed economies of the COMECON bloc, and although initially suffering more from dismantling and reparations policies, the East German economy nevertheless rose to attain, by the 1980s, the highest per capita production of the Eastern bloc and to become, according to World Bank figures, the twelfth most important trading nation in the world. It was not particularly favourably endowed with natural resources: it was heavily reliant on the inferior domestic brown coal for energy, and although it moved towards nuclear power the GDR was also reliant on the USSR for oil imports. In contrast to most of the rest of Eastern Europe (with the exception of western Czechoslovakia), the GDR was already an industrialised country before being incorporated in the communist bloc. Traditional strengths included vehicle and machine production, as well as chemicals, optical and electronic enterprises. By the 1980s, there were developments in such areas as microelectronics and computers, although the GDR remained well behind the west and could in the main only hope to export computers within Eastern Europe.

A major, if hidden, source of East German economic strength, in contrast to other COMECON countries, lay in East Germany's special relationship with West Germany. Lack of tariffs and favourable trade and credit agreements rendered the GDR a secret extra member of the EEC. About a third of East German trade was with non-COMECON countries, and of this about a third was with West Germany (i.e. about 8 per cent of the GDR's overall foreign trade). Apart from favourable terms and credits, East Germany thus also secured a reliable source of supplies which helped to avoid certain bottlenecks in production common in East European economies. Moreover, East Germany received a large amount of western hard currency, through the unique links with West Germany, from such matters as West German subvention of motorway access to West Berlin, the payment of road tolls by travellers, and large compulsory currency exchanges for visitors to the GDR, West German support of certain projects (such as the West German churches contributing to the restoration of churches in East Germany, or the equipment in East German church hospitals), the money sent by westerners to their East German friends and relatives, and so on. West German loans on very favourable terms at crucial moments also helped East Germany, which managed to weather the economic crises of the early 1980s somewhat more smoothly than other East European economies. Whatever comments may be made about East Germany's relatively well-educated, skilled and efficient work-force as a factor in East German economic success, the unique relationship with West Germany must not be ignored in any explanation of East Germany's relatively successful economic record.

However, this success, while evident in a range of statistics such as annual growth rates and GNP per capita, also posed something of a puzzle for the western visitor. For the appearance of everyday life in East Germany was somewhat drab and far from the affluence enjoyed by a majority of West German citizens. Standard of living comparisons between the two Germanies indicate improvements on the consumer front, at least in quantitative terms, in East Germany in the 1970s and 1980s. Increasing numbers of East German households possessed televisions, fridges, washing machines and cars – although if one compares in qualitative terms, most Germans in both East and West would have admitted the superiority of a Mercedes or BMW over a Wartburg or Trabant. The problem in the area of consumer durables in the GDR lay not so much in the lack of money – although prices were high relative to average earnings – as in the limited availability of goods, with long waiting lists for new cars, and second-hand cars frequently costing as much as new ones because of their immediate availability. (Privileged members of GDR society were however able to queue-jump, and usually obtained even western cars with ease.) A further problem lay in the stratified system of shopping. While basic necessities of life were available at cheap, subsidised prices, more desirable goods might be obtained at much higher prices, but still in East German currency, in the chains of Exquisit and Delikat shops, or, for western hard currency, in Inter-shops (which were initially only open to western visitors). Effec-tively the existence of the latter divided East Germans between those who had access to western currency and those who did not. What-ever grumblings and criticisms there might be among East Germans (such as that the choice in 'fruit and vegetable' shops was between cabbages and more cabbages), there was no actual want. Employ-ment was guaranteed – even if not appropriate to qualifications – and prices for food and housing were low. Nevertheless, even in the area of food and drink East Germany did not come very well out of comparisons with the west: in the late 1960s, East Germans ate less meat and dairy products than their western relatives; in the 1980s, the increasingly health-conscious West Germans ate less meat and more fruit and vegetables than the East Germans, who, despite having overtaken westerners in meat consumption, still seemed to come out worse in the comparison. One important implication of East German economic performance, combined with periodic con-sumer concessions in moments of political insecurity, was that there was not the material basis of mass popular discontent such as was seen at intervals in Poland. On the other hand, it was not sufficient to deter large numbers of East Germans from fleeing to what they hoped would be a better life in the west when Hungary opened its borders with Austria in the summer of 1989. Nor did it prevent large numbers from taking to the streets and demonstrating in favour of increased freedom of speech, travel, and human rights in the autumn of 1989. 'Bread and circuses' policies could not in the end satisfy desires for a more democratic society.

East Germany's social structure diverged quite notably from that of West Germany. East Germany's population – with fluctuations – remained almost static (in the late 1980s somewhat below the 17 million mark) in contrast to West Germany's population expansion of around 50 per cent since the end of the war (to around 62 million). East Germany's citizens remained residents of medium-sized towns and smaller communities, with a relatively low population density, contrasted with West Germany's higher degree of urbanisation. Inequalities of income were less marked in East Germany than in West Germany: the GDR has been characterised as a 'society of small people', without extremes of wealth or poverty. The negligible private ownership of means of production in the GDR meant that it was, in formal Marxist terms, a 'classless' society. However, it was not a society without privileged elites. In particular, elites in the GDR were primarily political, in contrast to the differing, if overlapping, multiplicity of elites in the Federal Republic of Germany. Yet groups other than the top politicians in the GDR enjoyed certain privileges and comfortable life styles: the GDR was not a society without inequality.

There was greater social mobility in East than West Germany, with early policies of sponsorship of people from under-privileged, working-class and peasant backgrounds. The education system until the late 1960s had the promotion of workers' and peasants' children as one of its specific aims, although in the 1970s this gave way to an emphasis on the sponsorship of talent irrespective of social background. The comprehensive school system in the GDR emphasised the importance of work experience, and there was a range of routes to higher education such that those who did not take the academic route through the upper school (leading to the equivalent of the German *Abitur* or the British A level qualifications) might still gain access to further and higher education in other ways. A prerequisite for social mobility in the GDR, however, was at least political conformity if not active commitment. While educational qualifications were increasingly characteristic of the most privileged group, the political elite, no non-conformist young person would be able to proceed smoothly through the education system whatever his or her talents. Even a 'non-political' subject such as medicine would be closed to young people who stepped too far out of line at school; and often the children of pastors were forced to study theology rather than other vocational subjects of their choice. Opting for alternative military service as a 'building soldier' (*Bausoldat*) or failing to participate satisfactorily in the Free German Youth movement might jeopardise a chosen career.

East German women had a more equal position in society than did West German women, although they were still far from 'emancipated' by the late 1980s. Slightly over 50 per cent of the East German work-force was female, and the normal expectation was that even married women with young children would engage in paid work outside the home. There were very high levels of childcare provision in the GDR, with crèche and kindergarten places and after-school provision for the vast majority of children. There were also very generous maternity leave provisions in the attempt to halt what was in the 1970s a worrying decline in the birth-rate. However, there were criticisms of the quality of life for both working mothers and their children in East Germany, with long hours in the factory (or place of childcare) followed by long hours of domestic housework (or experience of tired, harassed and unhappy parenting). Divorce rates were relatively high (although so too were rates of marriage, perhaps indicating high expectations) and women were financially more independent of their partners than in West Germany. However, women were disproportionately to be found in lower-paid and lower-status jobs, and were represented in declining numbers the higher up any hierarchy one looked (large numbers of teachers, few school heads, for example). They had higher levels of trade union and political party membership than did West German women, but were still not to be found at the pinnacle of politics (with the notable exception of the former Minister of Education, Margot Honecker, wife of Erich Honecker). East German feminism (if one may give such a label to what were in fact diffuse tendencies) changed from an emphasis in the early 1970s on being able to do men's work to a desire in the late 1980s to be able to be different from men, having realised that the former aim simply represented the imposition of a 'double burden' on women in a still unequal, gender-divided society.

It is clear that East Germany did not attain some of its own proclaimed ideological goals, particularly with respect to social equality, not to mention the classical Marxist doctrine concerning the eventual withering away of the state. The latter in fact grew in importance, with an ubiquitous and frequently repressive presence associated with a marked bureaucratisation and inhibition of personal freedoms in all sorts of areas of life. It is nevertheless clear that by the end of the 1980s the two Germanies had diverged into markedly different societies.

How far did the cultures of the two Germanies diverge? Both Germanies, after somewhat faltering starts (with the exception of returning exiles such as Bertolt Brecht) contributed new classics to the German literary heritage: in the Federal Republic, writers such as Günter Grass and Heinrich Böll attained international reputations, while in the GDR Christa Wolf and Stefan Heym are but two of those whose writings were translated and recognised beyond German frontiers. While many of the issues German writers had to deal with in the two Germanies were similar – particularly the question of the Nazi past – their answers were interestingly different; and, over the years, other concerns became increasingly important as East and West German writers confronted current realities in their different societies and sought to advocate ways of thinking and behaving often at odds with prevailing orthodoxies. In East Germany, literature had a heightened political significance; it was also, interestingly, aided by the existence in West Germany of a common language community where East German works could be published and receive a wider circulation – often evading censorship and filtering back into the GDR. At the level of more popular culture, there were similarities and differences: the youth culture of the GDR was more constrained than that in the Federal Republic (although jeans and rock concerts were spreading in the Honecker era). Sport was conventionally held to constitute a major source of East German national pride; but even in this area, there were divisions between elitist sponsorship for the select few, and relatively poor facilities for the masses, whose West German counterparts were far better served by ubiquitous sporting facilities of a high standard. There were even instances of football hooliganism in the GDR (notably against Erich Mielke's Dynamo team in East Berlin: Erich Mielke was Minister for State Security and his unpopularity was reflected in the severely limited number of 'fans' for his team). Differences in patterns of leisure were marked, with a far greater range of facilities and freedom of choice – including foreign travel – in the Federal Republic than in the GDR.

Yet for all their divergences, the two Germanies remained tied by a common historical heritage as well as by a wide range of current interconnections, economic, political and social. While very different, they yet remained related; neither could be considered satisfactorily without reference to the other, giving each of these sovereign states a unique status in the modern world as part of a divided country. However stable each part appeared, the division remained; and the gash across central Europe, resulting from conflicts for which Germans had to bear primary responsibility, was one which caused pain to countless others in non-German countries too.

THE REVOLUTION OF 1989 AND THE UNIFICATION OF GERMANY

In the later 1980s, extraordinary changes began to appear in the system which had held sway in eastern Europe for forty years. An economically weak and politically overstretched Soviet Union was no longer able to sustain massive defence spending on a par with the USA, and was keen to defuse international tensions in order to deal with mounting troubles on the domestic front. Under the reforming leadership of Gorbachev in the Soviet Union, processes of democratisation and economic restructuring were introduced that were to have radical implications for the entire post-war settlement of Europe. Under the non-interventionist eye of a Soviet Union which was relinquishing its hold on the former satellite states of Eastern Europe, processes of political democratisation were allowed to proceed in Poland and Hungary which brought to an end their respective Communist Parties' monopolies on power. Hopes for reform in East Germany under Honecker were disappointed by the increasing repression evident in his last years of power, but attention was focussed on a possible reformist successor.

In the event, the revolution which swept away the old regime in East Germany came initially not from pressures from within, but was sparked by a regime crisis occasioned by changes elsewhere. In the summer of 1989, Hungary – under its new reformist leadership – began to dismantle the fortified boundary with Austria. The Hungarians also chose to waive the East German visa restrictions on travel to the west. Around 220,000 East German holidaymakers were in Hungary in August: perhaps one-tenth of them decided to take the opportunity of the opening of the borders to flee to the west, taking with them only what possessions they had on them. The reception in the west was initially ecstatic: refugee camps were set up to look after the resettlers, offers of work came flooding from German employers, and in a party atmosphere there was talk of 'reunification of the Germans on West German soil'. Other East Germans, seeing the nightly West German television reports, decided to seize the opportunity to make the break too: some left for Hungary via Czechoslovakia, others sought refuge in the West German embassies in Prague and Warsaw. Soon the movement had reached crisis proportions. The staffs of the embassies could no longer deal with the thousands seeking refuge and demanding to leave for the west; the host governments were embarrassed in their relations with both East and West Germany; the West German government began to worry about the capacity of the West German economy and housing situation to absorb the tens of thousands of immigrants; and the East German government was only too well aware that this damaging haemorrhage of citizens amounted to a major crisis, not only affecting the functioning of the economy (as in the 1950s), but also striking at the very heart of the regime's claims to legitimacy. Attempts at containment by closing all the country's borders – not only imprisoning East Germans within Eastern Europe but confining them, as it were, to a form of 'house arrest' in East Germany itself – were clearly impracticable and an admission of failure.

The situation was somewhat complicated by the fragile health of Erich Honecker, who underwent major surgery for a gall-bladder problem in the summer, and who was rumoured to be suffering from cancer (later confirmed). Virtually ignoring the problems of his country, Honecker proceeded with plans to celebrate the GDR's fortieth anniversary in October 1989. Meanwhile, there was a growing movement among a number of groups in the GDR, the largest of which was New Forum, to confront directly and explicitly the problem of *why* so many East Germans wanted to leave, rather than simply attempting to prevent them from leaving. An important feature of these early voices for reform was the rejection of the West German system, and the demand to move forward to some form of humane, non-Stalinist, truly democratic socialism. Voices demanding internal debates with a view to constructive reform of the system became ever more insistent, particularly with the organisation of weekly mass demonstrations in Leipzig, and, on a smaller scale, in other major cities. Initially, there was some fear that such mass demonstrations would simply be suppressed by force (as in China earlier in the year), and it took considerable courage and discipline to come out and demonstrate in a peaceful and organised manner. The role of the church was very important here, with its organisation of non-violent protests, peaceful candle-lit vigils, prayer meetings and discussions. In the event, there was a major turning point on 9 October, when the authorities renounced the use of force to suppress the Leipzig demonstration, and effectively conceded the legitimacy of demands for dialogue. From then on, demonstrations continued to grow.

In the face of these challenges, and prompted by Gorbachev (who had visited the GDR for the rather hollow fortieth anniversary celebrations), the East German leadership attempted to effect what was in the nature of a 'last revolution from above' to ward off the threat of worse disturbances from below and to attempt to regain control of an increasingly untenable situation. At a meeting of the Politburo on 18 October, Honecker was replaced as SED leader by Egon Krenz, a hard-liner who had long been billed as Honecker's 'crown prince'. With unfailingly smiling face, Krenz returned from a brief visit to Moscow (calling in on Poland on the way back) to preside over an initial phase of reform in East Germany. People were less than convinced by the sincerity of this recently converted reformer (with cartoon captions such as 'The shark has pretty teeth, my dear' – a reference to the prominent display in Krenz's smile), and demands for more radical changes continued and grew, with increasing size and confidence of the demonstrations. At the same time, the stream of refugees to the west continued, now taking a much shorter route over the Czech border.

It was clear that the 'Iron Curtain' across Europe was now riddled with holes. The East German leadership's attempt to defuse pressure by announcing very limited travel concessions (four weeks a year, under permit) satisfied no-one. Suddenly, at the end of a press conference on Thursday 9 November, a weary government spokesman admitted that newer, more far-reaching freedoms to travel effectively meant that the Berlin Wall no longer served its former purpose. The effects of the announcement were electric.

West and East Berliners rushed to the Wall; soon even the East German border guards gave up the attempt to stamp permits or issue

Plate 41. A West Berlin pensioner looks on as people hack out
mementoes from the now defunct Berlin Wall.

visas; a euphoric party atmosphere rapidly developed. By midnight, people were dancing on the top of the Wall, helping each other over – in both directions – and drinking bottles of champagne, as Berliners were reunited over what was rapidly becoming merely a piece of concrete, rather than the ultimate boundary of the habitable universe. In the following days and weeks, the borders between the two Germanies and the two parts of Berlin were increasingly opened up, with new crossings being opened and attempts being made to ease the pressure of traffic in both directions. An extraordinary period ensued, in which huge numbers of East Germans rushed to take the opportunity to see what life was really like in the other, forbidden, affluent Germany – and returned home again to the East, laden with bananas, oranges, and what other few goods they could buy with their limited western currency.

The party was not without its hangover. Nor had the 'German problem' simply disappeared with the opening of the borders. Rather, the true dimensions of the question only began to become apparent in the winter of 1989–90. For one thing, the stream of refugees continued to flow at a rate of between 1,000 and 2,000 a day – amounting to between a third and a half a million in a year. Evidently some East Germans still felt they could make a better life for themselves in the west, or did not trust the new leadership to institute satisfactory and far-reaching reforms. The continuing influx of refugees posed very serious problems for the West German economy and infrastructure, as well as provoking a flare-up of social tensions associated with extremist political movements. The welcome was considerably cooler than it had been for the early refugees of the summer. For another, all manner of delicate international issues were at stake, as Chancellor Kohl rather rapidly opened up the question of the unification of the two Germanies. International debate revolved on the changed roles of the Warsaw Pact and NATO in the new circumstances of a democratising Eastern Europe, as well as the question of introducing market elements into Eastern European economies, and the relationship of such changes to the planned programme of integration of the European Community in Western Europe. The German question was one with far wider implications.

In East Germany, processes of domestic political change continued rapidly. Egon Krenz's leadership of the SED was short-lived,
and he was replaced by the young, vigorous and relatively reform-
minded Gregor Gysi. The SED attempted to adopt a new image,
partly by purging the entire old guard leadership – some of whom
were to stand trial on charges of corruption, the extent of which
had shocked the East German public – and partly by adopting a
new tag to its name, adding 'Party of Democratic Socialism' to the
initial 'Socialist Unity Party'. But such changes were less than con-
vincing, and about half the former membership of the SED had left
by mid-January 1990. With a constitutional change to remove the
built-in leading role of the SED in the GDR, elections were called
for 6 May 1990, later brought forward to 18 March. New political parties began to build up their organisations and programmes,
including the New Forum opposition group, Democracy Now, and
Democratic Awakening, as well as the recently founded East German
SPD. The former puppet parties also began to assert their independence: for example, the Liberals had failed to vote for Krenz in his
ratification as leader by the Parliament, and subsequently the Liberals attempted to adopt an independent line. The character of mass
demonstrations began to change, with ever more strident demands
for reunification with West Germany, and with evidence of extreme
right-wing activity (including mobilisation on the part of the West
German Republicans). The East German leadership used evidence
of mounting domestic unrest as a pretext to slow down its disbanding of the hated security police (Stasi) but were eventually forced to
give way on this issue. Nevertheless, talks between the government –
under the leadership of the moderate communist Prime Minister
Hans Modrwo – and opposition groups showed considerable signs
of strain, and by the beginning of 1990 the mood had changed considerably from the early, peaceful days of bloodless revolution in the
autumn of 1989.

By the time of the elections on 18 March, the collapse of the East
German economy and administration was accelerating. Despite the
valiant efforts of the fledgeling East German reform movements,
which lacked both campaigning expertise and basic resources,
the right-wing outcome of the vote was effectively determined by
the entry of the West German political juggernauts. A vote for

the right-wing parties, including the East German CDU – for over forty years a puppet of the Communists, now designated by Kohl to be an acceptable conservative partner in democracy – was seen by many East Germans as the quickest route to acquiring the West German Deutschmark on favourable terms, and ultimately becoming a part of West Germany without having to leave East German soil. Currency union of East and West Germany took effect on 1 July 1990, heralding the end of two separate, sovereign German states. In the event, currency union inaugurated, not economic upswing and equalisation of conditions, but rather mounting unemployment and rising social tensions in the East. The unprecedented experiment of uniting a capitalist and a communist economy, and seeking to adapt the latter to market conditions with loss of protective subsidies and social benefits, was clearly going to produce a rather bumpy ride.

Meanwhile, Gorbachev's Soviet Union was continuing to undergo profound domestic changes and renouncing its claims to domination over Eastern Europe. Kohl took advantage of this possibly brief moment when there was an international 'window of opportunity', and powered the process of political unification at an accelerating rate. Faced with mounting domestic crises and a collapsing coalition government, East German negotiators were in a weak position concerning the conditions for unification. In the end, the East Germans opted for unification as soon as possible after the 'two-plus-four' talks had been completed and ratified by the Conference on Security and Cooperation in Europe. On 3 October 1990, less than a year after the 40th anniversary of the GDR, the GDR was no more. An enlarged Federal Republic had incorporated the five newly constituted East German *Länder*, and, at a solemn unification ceremony, the Germans acknowledged their responsibility for ensuring that their united future would try to learn from the mistakes of their troubled past. Chancellor Kohl reaped his political reward when, in the first general elections to be held in united Germany in December 1990, the ruling conservative-liberal coalition was confirmed in power to preside over the process of unifying in practice what had been so rapidly, and unexpectedly, thrown together over the previous months.

8

The Federal Republic of Germany
since 1990

The enlarged Federal Republic of Germany that emerged on
3 October 1990 as a result of the accession of the five new *Länder*
(federal states) created out of the former GDR was a distinctively
new and somewhat lop-sided entity. It differed considerably from
its West German predecessor, however much the latter had determined the conditions of unification and provided the basic constitutional and institutional framework for the unified Germany. The
differences had to do with an uneven domestic economic, social and
political profile, and with the dramatic changes in the wider international scene consequent on the collapse of communism and the
end of a bi-polar Cold War world. The Berlin Republic represented,
for a range of reasons, a distinctively new stage in German history.

The dislocations of the unprecedented historical experiment of
integrating a collapsed communist state into a successful capitalist
economy in the event proved far greater than the optimists in the
hour of unification had expected. Major and unanticipated costs of
reconstruction fell on West Germans in the form of increased competition for jobs in an era of rising unemployment, and increased
taxation to help fund the modernisation of the East German infrastructure. The old, affluent, relatively self-satisfied West Germany
which could agonise over its own past and proclaim it was the first
'post-national nation' found, too, that it was expected to take a
more proactive role not only on the European, but also on the international, stage. In the short term, as westerners moved in to the
eastern *Länder*, reshaping political and economic structures in their

own image, East Germans found they were subject to even greater immediate dislocations.

The earliest effects of the introduction of a capitalist economy were felt in the spheres of employment and the privatisation of production and property in the eastern *Länder*. With the introduction of western wages and prices, and exposure to world markets and stronger competition, inefficient East German enterprises with grossly outdated equipment and now unsustainably high staffing costs were no longer viable. Unemployment levels rose rapidly and dramatically. With the loss of state-subsidised and enterprise-based child-care facilities, and with the domestic division of labour still based on ingrained assumptions about gender roles, women were particularly badly affected by rising unemployment. So too were people in middle age, who were considered too young to be able to take premature retirement, too old to be able to retrain and develop new skills. On the other hand, for many younger people there were new possibilities for education, training and career development. As far as property was concerned, operating on the principle of restitution rather than compensation, the *Treuhand* organisation was set up to return previously expropriated and GDR 'state-owned' property to former owners or their legal heirs. This opened the way for innumerable property disputes, and the ousting of many East Germans from homes and land which they had inhabited and often improved by immense personal efforts over many years. For a wide range of reasons, a relatively high rate of migration westwards continued, as people left in search of better living and employment conditions in western Germany, and East German population decline continued.

Yet, despite all these immediate economic difficulties with immense personal consequences for those adversely affected, the net result of a decade of investment and rebuilding was the 'sanitisation' of much of (what survived of) East German industry, the renovation of crumbling housing stock, reconstruction of the transport infrastructure, modernisation of communications, and the expansion of western consumer outlets into the East. While eastern Germany in 1990 looked possibly even more decrepit than the Germany of the 1930s, by the early twenty-first century many areas in the former GDR were virtually indistinguishable in appearance from comparable regions of western Germany. Only the occasional crumbling or deserted and half-ruined building among the generally fresh façades of renovated city centres betrayed the very recent character of the transformation; and even smaller towns and villages had generally achieved new plaster and whitewash on the houses, and replacement of cobbled streets by tarmac, to effect a major transformation in physical character. The wartime pock-marks which had survived in the walls of many older buildings since 1945 were rapidly disappearing under the new regime; the bleak housing estates of the socialist new towns were acquiring new amenities; the air was cleansed of brown coal dust and Trabi fumes, as western cars proliferated on the streets.

In the unified Germany's new capital, Berlin, the symbolic centre of gravity shifted eastwards, with the central areas of the formerly drab communist capital around Alexanderplatz and Unter den Linden becoming more lively, more 'the centre' than west Berlin's fading and increasingly tacky consumer parade along the Kurfürstendamm near the Zoo railway station. With the extraordinary building programme all along the previous no-man's strip of the Berlin Wall, even the very traces of division, the empty gash across the city, were disappearing: disappearing under the international skylines of global entertainment industries, brash commercialism and businesses around Potsdamer Platz, under the new architect-designed government centre near the presidential residence of Schloss Bellevue and the revived Reichstag, under the more modest building projects and individual family homes on the former death strip in the outskirts and suburbs such as Griebnitzsee down the S-Bahn line towards Potsdam. Only the odd concrete block from the Wall was left standing here or there as a visual reminder of what once had been. For those who had not experienced it at the time, it was hard to imagine the terror and emotion of the former crossing-point between East and West at the Friedrichstrasse S-Bahn station, where the transformation of bleak waiting areas, secure police cells and border guard offices into shoe-shops, mobile phone and computer outlets, newsagents and grocery stores made the new sanitised version look much like any modern western airport or railway station. Even the former headquarters of the Stasi in Normannenstrasse, where the offices of Stasi chief Erich

Mielke had been opened as a museum, no longer looked quite so forbidding. Thus in Berlin the physical traces of the very recent German Democratic Republic collapsed almost unnoticed into the changing environment, jostling for recognition in historical consciousness alongside the traces of the Third Reich, of Weimar Germany, of Imperial splendours and the more squalid legacies of rapid industrialisation; alongside, too, the more lasting architectural and sculptural heritage of the great age of Berlin in eighteenth-century Prussia. Even for those who knew at first hand what had existed so recently, it required some effort of mental reconstruction – or a trip to an outlying or relatively neglected area – to re-imagine the so recently overthrown past.

The new appearance of the eastern areas of unified Germany nevertheless belied continuing, if slowly fading, differences between eastern and western Germans. These were first thematised in popular parlance by the widely prevalent jokes about 'Ossis' and 'Wessis'; opinion polls and sociological research also served to back up informal observations about the prevalence of competitive individualism among westerners, a stronger community orientation and continued commitment to state provision and welfare support in the East. Marriage and friendship patterns very often sustained a now invisible social and psychological Wall. Controversies over works of literature and film also reflected differences between easterners and westerners, as debates flared up and subsided over works such as Christa Wolf's post-revolutionary publication of *Was bleibt*, a lightly retouched short novel written over a decade earlier, or the attempted 'rendering harmless' of the dictatorship by humorous novels and films such as Brüssig's *Helden wie Wir* ('Heroes like us') and *Sonnenallee* (the name of a street straddling the Wall).

Historical interpretations also took on wider political and moral significance. Curiously, the often overly vitriolic attacks of many West German politicians and much of the western media on what was widely labelled 'the second German dictatorship' led to an almost paradoxical nostalgia among many East Germans for at least some aspects of the repressive state which they had helped to overthrow. The denunciations of the 'totalitarian dictatorship', and the explicit comparisons of the GDR with Nazi Germany, made many ordinary East Germans feel that the authenticity of their own lives and memories was being in some way distorted, even denied. The determination of the new German parliament to investigate the character and consequences of the East German dictatorship led to a long-running parliamentary inquiry (*Enquêtekomission*) in the 1990s, with specialist testimonies and often heated debates, serving to raise tempers even higher over how best to interpret and 'overcome' this recent past. While it proved remarkably difficult to bring individual prominent leaders of the SED regime to trial, the much wider witch-hunt for those who had acted as unofficial informers for the Stasi (*Stasi IMs*), and the loss of professional occupations and prospects for anyone in any way tainted by having been an 'accomplice' of the SED regime, was seen by many as quite disproportionate in comparison with the relatively lenient treatment of 'fellow travellers' (*Mitläufer*) after 1945, following the collapse of the far more evil Nazi regime with its responsibility for organised genocide and world war. The Nazi period too remained the subject of heated debate in the 1990s, with massive public controversies over subjects such as an exhibition demonstrating Wehrmacht involvement in Nazi atrocities, the proposed construction of a Holocaust memorial in Berlin, and the contested thesis of Daniel Jonah Goldhagen that an alleged long-term German mentality of 'eliminationist anti-semitism' provided the key to explaining the Holocaust. The agonies over this now more distant German 'past which will not pass away' (to appropriate an expression coined by Ernst Nolte in the historical controversies of the mid-1980s) merely added an additional layer of complexity to the complications of German history and construction of a new national identity in the unified state.

In the first decade after unification, these economic, social and cultural dislocations had a major impact on the character of German politics. In the early 1990s, the initial major danger seemed to be that of a resurgent right-wing radical nationalism. While in West Germany right-wing parties such as the Republikaner and the DVU (Deutsche Volksunion) had already affected the electoral landscape at regional level in the 1980s, the strains associated with unification appeared to offer fertile stamping grounds for fomenting incipient and pre-existing racial prejudices in eastern areas. Acts of individual racist violence, as well as more coordinated incidents such as the attacks on foreigners in Hoyerswerda and Rostock in eastern Germany, and Solingen and Mölln in western Germany, rose alarmingly in the early years following unification, leading many observers to fear a return to rabid nationalism with the resurrection of some version of a unified nation state. Yet, in contrast to the situation in the 1930s, this grass-roots racism was firmly opposed and dealt with by the government (despite what appeared on occasion to be somewhat tardy responses by members of the local police forces and onlookers), and was explicitly opposed by many among the wider German population, such that early fears of resurgent racism and virulent nationalism in united Germany appeared unfounded. Even the tightly constructed German citizenship laws were revised in the course of the 1990s, making it easier for long-term resident 'guest workers' and their descendants to apply for German citizenship.

The national political landscape was further transformed by the changed character of the electorate. In the eastern *Länder*, the PDS (Party of Democratic Socialism, the successor to the discredited SED) scored notable successes in some areas – and particularly in East Berlin – as a party representing the regional interests of disaffected easterners who felt they were being treated as second-class citizens. And once the transitional electoral provision of 'separate voting pots' for the areas of former West and East Germany had been abolished, after the 1994 General Election, the FDP found that it too had become but a rump western regional party, struggling to reach the 5 per cent electoral threshold with dilution by the new electorate in the eastern *Länder*. Moreover, the CDU 'unification Chancellor', Helmut Kohl, whose own political difficulties in the 1980s had been rescued by the fall of the Wall, came increasingly under critique in the 1990s, once again in relation to somewhat murky scandals concerning party finances. Thus, a historic General Election in 1998 produced a new coalition government of the SPD and the Greens, with Gerhard Schroeder taking over as Chancellor. Despite mounting domestic difficulties, while the CDU cast around for a successor of comparable political stature to Helmut Kohl, Gerhard Schroeder and the 'Red–Green' coalition managed to cling on to power in the General Election of 2002, not least because of a rapidly changing international situation.

Changes in Germany's international context were partly to do with the collapse of the 'Iron Curtain', the rapid transformation of the former communist states of Eastern Europe, and the concomitant moves to both a 'widening' and a 'deepening' of processes of European integration that had already been underway before 1990. The Schengen Agreement rendered travel across the physical borders between participating continental European states almost unnoticeable, with the dismantling of most border controls within this area, and only occasional checks when there were alerts connected with suspicions of smuggling, terrorism, drugs or illegal immigration. The introduction of a new common European currency, the Euro, served not merely to mark the new millennium but also to bring the economies of participating EU states more into line with each other. Some EU states still preserved their distance; most notably Britain, which, despite the new Eurotunnel literally undermining the few kilometres of water which had historically rendered it such a separate island, still retained its distance on both Schengen and the Euro. Unified Germany, along with France, spearheaded moves which to many looked like a push towards ever closer European integration and possibly even some form of incipient federal United States of Europe.

In many respects, these moves were not dissimilar, though on a different scale and in a different world historical context, to the kinds of developments which had taken place within and between the German states of the early nineteenth century. But the parallels perhaps end with the development of a 'Customs Union'. For while a united foreign policy under Prussia in the Franco-Prussian War of 1870 brought about the slightly unwilling 'small German' unification of the Imperial Germany of 1871, there was far from anything resembling unity with respect to a possible united 'European' foreign policy in the early twenty-first century. While in the international crises of the early 1990s (the Gulf War, Kosovo), the recently unified Germany was badly jolted in having to wake up to new international commitments and responsibilities, by the time of the renewed crisis over Iraq a decade later, in 2002–3, the situation was rather different. Schroeder in part succeeded in winning the 2002 election, despite growing economic problems and rising unemployment at home, precisely because he played on the remarkable levels of pacifism among a German population which had learned only too well the historical lessons of two world wars unleashed from German soil. While British Prime Minister Tony Blair was busy resurrecting and strengthening a governmental commitment to the 'special relationship', the 'transatlantic alliance', with the USA, supported to a degree by Spain, Germany stood by the French refusal in principle to unleash what seemed to many a totally unnecessary war against Iraq.

The world at the start of the twenty-first century was a dramatically different place from that of even a few decades earlier. The spectacular terrorist suicide attacks on New York and Washington of 11 September 2001 (or '9/11' as they came to be called) both inaugurated and symbolised a new era of international uncertainty, characterised by fears of fundamentalist terrorism and military instability. The predictable dangers and threats of the old Cold War in a world divided by two superpowers had been replaced by an infinitely more dangerous and unstable multi-polar world, with unpredictable flash-points and new forms of ideological and religious conflict alongside the continuation of long-term patterns of political oppression, inequalities of health and disease, and contrasts between areas of plenty and of famine. In an age of increasing globalisation, the new Germany itself was a land incorporating contrasts, seeking to overcome the internal legacies of the Cold War heritage, and taking up new pacifist and post-nationalist stances informed by its own part in a tortured but now increasingly distant past.

9

Patterns and problems of German history

After this brief summary of the main patterns of German history, we may turn to the wider questions of overall interpretations of the 'peculiarities' of German history.

The problems of German history have frequently been held to lie at least partially in its 'geopolitical location': its position in central Europe, without natural boundaries defining its frontiers, in contrast to the island kingdom of England/Britain. Thus in Germany there was perpetual warfare, and a concomitant militarisation, in contrast to the trading nation of England which substituted a navy and control of the seas for a standing army. But this view is grossly oversimplifying in its lack of consideration of detailed differences in political, economic and social structures (even leaving aside the view of English history it presupposes). The central European location of the German lands is not in itself a particularly illuminating factor in seeking to explain the peculiar paths of German history. The recently popular appeals to Germany's mid-European situation represent merely a superficially meaningful substitute for explanation: they do not in fact take serious exploration of the range of diverse historical factors involved at any time very far. On the other hand, it is also clear that it is an international system with which we have to deal, and that interactions among the different elements jostling for space, position, power and status in central Europe must be taken fully into account in addition to internal factors in any particular region or territory. While the same is in principle true of any 'national' history, the history of the German territories is perhaps peculiarly complex because of the multiplicity of units and their curious interrelations.

One particular peculiarity in the German case has to do with the non-overlapping of certain political entities. This is particularly important in relation to the existence of Habsburg dynastic territories outside the Holy Roman Empire, which gave the Habsburgs a certain independence but at the same time implied problems and interests which were separate from, and potentially at odds with, those of the non-Habsburg territories in the Empire. This non-overlap, while perhaps crucial for the Habsburg power base, probably also contributed to the weakness of the Holy Roman Empire as a central force. At certain key times of conflicts within the Empire, the emperor might be engaged elsewhere and unable to intervene effectively at an early point, providing leeway for the development of dissidence (as in the Reformation period). On the other hand, the all-embracing existence of the Holy Roman Empire was just sufficient to protect the system of states, some of them extremely small, and which, without the protection of the Empire, might well otherwise have been rapidly gobbled up by larger neighbours in a process of territorial aggrandisement in the early modern period. Such processes as were at work did involve the enlargement of certain states at the expense of others (although not all schemes were realised, as for example Austria's failed ambitions for spreading Austrian influence in southern Germany, particularly Bavaria, in the later eighteenth century). The existence of an overarching focus of identification also facilitated the development of alliances and defensive leagues, similarly aiding the protection of the relative independence of smaller territories. It was a curiously symbiotic system that developed, with slowly changing balances between and among the different elements. The problem of non-overlap also connected with that of the existence of Prussian territories outside the Empire – which gave Prussia the possibility of attaining royal sovereignty when Elector Frederick III crowned himself King Frederick I, King in Prussia, in Königsberg, outside the Holy Roman Empire, in 1701. In the nineteenth century, the non-overlapping of territories and political interests, states and supraterritorial organisations, with non-German ethnic groups in some of the German states (notably Austria and Prussia, also Schleswig-Holstein) in areas both within and outside the Confederation, was to become perhaps more problematic, in the era of nationalism and attempts at unification.

However, mention of nationalism and unification leads one to the question of whether the distinctive German combination of decentralisation at the Imperial level and centralisation at the territorial level actually also constituted a problem with respect to state formation. It could well be argued that to view the peculiarities of pre-nineteenth-century German history in this light, considering differences from English and French history as aberrations from a 'normal' pattern of development of a modern nation state, would be quite anachronistic. It would be imposing modern categories and assumptions about the normality of the nation state as the obvious political unit to view German history as a distortion. Had it not been for the rise of competitive nation states in the era of modern industrial capitalism, the earlier German pattern of co-existence of a multitude of smaller, weaker political units within a weak, broader overall framework might have remained at least to some degree viable.

One may nevertheless wonder whether the peculiarities that have been described above in any sense add up to some form of long-term determination of the problems of late nineteenth and twentieth-century German history. As mentioned at the outset, German history is frequently written in a disturbingly teleological fashion, with identification of 'failed revolutions' (Engels pouncing on the Peasants' War for this purpose), 'turning-points where Germany failed to turn' (A. J. P. Taylor's characterisation of 1848), and accusations of 'immaturity' (the German bourgeoisie) and 'belatedness' (the German nation state). Even if one jettisons all the biases and assumptions involved in such notions, one may still, when considering the long-term conditions, circumstances and constraints, as well as the shorter-term patterns of events of more recent German history, be tempted to answer the question of Germany's non-democratic route to modernity with an adaptation of the Irish joke: when asked the best way to Dublin, the Irishman replies to the traveller, 'Well, if I wanted to go there, I wouldn't start from here.' However, there is another game that German historians particularly like to play, apart from the game of 'identify the distortion', and that is 'identify the real break'. The current most favoured candidate for 'real break' is 1945, despite analyses of continuities across the myth of the *Stunde Null* (zero hour). If tempted to play this game in the longer-term context, one might want to argue that in a sense the destructive cycle of 1871–1945 was not ultimately determined by the long-term patterns depicted above, but rather by the short-term manner of small-German unification through Bismarck's policies of 'blood and iron'. An alternative scenario might have involved a more benign form of German federalism developing more gradually in the context of German economic unification in the era of industrialisation. Moreover, it is distinctly unwise to adopt too long-term a determination of history: scholars must be able to account, not only for Germany's path into Nazi dictatorship, but also for its double transformation into very different, communist and democratic capitalist, states in the post-war era, and its new character as an enlarged Federal Republic since 1990.

What of the role of German cultural patterns in political development? These too have often been exaggerated as factors in Germany's 'peculiar' history. German culture has presented an extraordinary range and potential; which features of the cultural heritage were selected, reinterpreted, transformed and adapted for current concerns and endeavours at any given time – and which selections were historically dominant – was more a matter of political and social struggle than of any ethereal intellectual history. The ways in which such processes operated should have become clear again and again in the account presented above.

Every history is a product of the time in which it is written. Nationalist histories in the era of triumphant nationalism were most concerned with the problem of belated unification. Twentieth-century histories written under the shadow of Hitler were more concerned with the roots of malignancy. In the twenty-first century, in an era of increasing European federalism, and sensitivity to the role of smaller political units and grass-roots involvement, as well as new tensions and flash points across a global stage, perspectives begin to shift again. Understanding of what is meant by 'the German problem' changes, and so too does what is of interest – and what appears to be 'peculiar' – in German history. The fascinating richness of the German past should ensure that it will continue to excite interest from a range of perspectives and view-points; and that there will never be any final and ultimately definitive interpretation of its complex patterns, which continue to invite further exploration and debate.

SUGGESTIONS FOR FURTHER READING

The field of German history is controversial and constantly developing. The titles listed below represent a highly selective sample of mostly recent English-language literature on German history, although a few important earlier titles are also included.

The bibliography is roughly divided according to major historical periods, but many works straddle chronological boundaries and some periods and topics are better covered than others. The uneven coverage of topics in different sections of the bibliography in part illustrates imbalances in English-language historiography: works on the modern period, and in particular on Nazism and the Holocaust, have – typically – burst the bounds of proportion in both publishing history and public interest.

Listed in each section is at least one, and preferably more than one, good general guide to the relevant period or key problems. These overviews are marked with an asterisk. Readers who are interested in exploring certain periods and problems in more depth, or pursuing references in less well-trodden fields, may find these works particularly helpful for initial orientation.

MEDIAEVAL GERMANY

B. Arnold, *German Knighthood 1050–1300* (Oxford: Clarendon Press, 1985)
* B. Arnold, *Medieval Germany 500–1300. A Political Interpretation* (Basingstoke: Macmillan, 1997)

B. Arnold, *Princes and Territories in Medieval Germany* (Cambridge: Cambridge University Press, 1991)

* F. R. H. Du Boulay, *Germany in the Later Middle Ages* (London: Athlone Press, 1983)

J. Fleckenstein, *Early Mediaeval Germany* (Oxford: North-Holland, 1978)

H. Fuhrmann, *Germany in the High Middle Ages* (Cambridge: Cambridge University Press, 1986)

J. Gillingham, *The Kingdom of Germany in the High Middle Ages* (London: The Historical Association, 1971)

* A. Haverkamp, *Medieval Germany, 1056–1273* (Oxford: Oxford University Press, 2nd edn, 1992)

J. Leuschner, *Germany in the Later Middle Ages* (Oxford: North-Holland, 1979)

K. Leyser, *Mediaeval Germany and its Neighbours, 900–1250* (London: Hambledon Press, 1982)

EARLY MODERN GERMANY, C. 1500–1800

* R. Asch, *The Thirty Years War: The Holy Roman Empire and Europe, 1618–1648* (Houndmills: Macmillan, 1997)

G. Benecke, *Society and Politics in Germany 1500–1800* (London: Routledge and Kegan Paul, 1974)

O. Büsch, *Military System and Social Life in Old Regime Prussia, 1713–1807: The Beginnings of the Social Militarisation of Prusso-German Society* (Atlantic Highlands, N.J.: Humanities Press, 1997)

E. Cameron, *The European Reformation* (Oxford: Clarendon Press, 1991)

C. Clark, *The Politics of Conversion. Missionary Protestantism and the Jews in Prussia, 1728–1941* (Oxford: Clarendon Press, 1995)

G. Darby, *The Thirty Years War* (London: Hodder and Staughton, 2001)

A. G. Dickens, *The German Nation and Martin Luther* (Glasgow: Collins (Fontana), 1976)

* C. Scott Dixon, *The Reformation in Germany* (Oxford: Blackwell, 2002)

C. Scott Dixon (ed.), *The German Reformation* (Oxford: Blackwell, 1999)

* P. Dwyer (ed.), *The Rise of Prussia, 1700–1830* (Harlow: Pearson, 2000)

K. Friedrich, *The Other Prussia. Royal Prussia, Poland and Liberty, 1569–1772* (Cambridge: Cambridge University Press, 2000)

M. Fulbrook, *Piety and Politics: Religion and the Rise of Absolutism in England, Württemberg and Prussia* (Cambridge: Cambridge University Press, 1983)

* J. Gagliardo, *Germany under the Old Regime, 1600–1790* (London: Longman, 1991)

R. Gawthrop, *Pietism and the Making of Eighteenth-Century Prussia* (Cambridge: Cambridge University Press, 1993)

* M. Hughes, *Early Modern Germany, 1477–1806* (London: Macmillan, 1992)

* C. Ingrao, *The Habsburg Monarchy 1618–1815* (Cambridge: Cambridge University Press, 2nd edn, 2000)

C. Ingrao, *The Hessian Mercenary State* (Cambridge: Cambridge University Press, 1987)

M. Lindemann, *Patriots and Paupers: Hamburg, 1712–1830* (New York: Oxford University Press, 1990)

J. Van Horn Melton, *Absolutism and the Eighteenth-century Origins of Compulsory Schooling in Prussia and Austria* (Cambridge: Cambridge University Press, 1988)

G. Mortimer, *Eyewitness Accounts of the Thirty Years War 1618–48* (Houndmills: Palgrave, 2002)

G. Parker (ed.), *The Thirty Years War* (London: Routledge and Kegan Paul, 1984)

R. Porter and M. Teich (eds.), *The Enlightenment in National Context* (Cambridge: Cambridge University Press, 1981)

M. Raeff, *The Well-ordered Police State* (London: Yale University Press, 1983)

L. Roper, *The Holy Household: Women and Morals in Reformation Augsburg* (Oxford: Oxford University Press, 1989)

* H. M. Scott (ed.), *Enlightened Absolutism: Reform and Reformers in Later Eighteenth-century Europe* (London: Macmillan, 1990)

H. M. Scott (ed.), *The European Nobilities in the Seventeenth and Eighteenth Centuries.* 2 vols. (London: Longman, 1995)

R. W. Scribner, *For the Sake of Simple Folk. Popular Propaganda for the German Reformation* (Oxford: Oxford University Press, 1994)

* R. W. Scribner, *The German Reformation* (London: Macmillan, 1986)

R. W. Scribner (ed. by L. Roper), *Religion and Culture in Germany (1400–1800)* (Leiden, Boston: Brill, 2001)

M. Shennan, *The Rise of Brandenburg-Prussia* (London: Routledge, 1995)

Q. Skinner, *The Foundations of Modern Political Thought: the Age of Reformation*, vol. II (Cambridge: Cambridge University Press, 1996)

J. A. Vann, *The Making of a State: Württemberg 1593–1793* (London: Cornell University Press, 1984)

R. Vierhaus, *Germany in the Age of Absolutism* (Cambridge: Cambridge University Press, 1988)

J. Whaley, *Religious Toleration and Social Change in Hamburg, 1529–1819* (Cambridge: Cambridge University Press, 1984)

P. H. Wilson, *Absolutism in Central Europe* (London: Routledge, 2000)

P. H. Wilson, *German Armies. War and German Politics, 1648–1806* (London: UCL Press, 1998)

P. H. Wilson, *The Holy Roman Empire, 1495–1806* (Basingstoke: Macmillan, 1999)

P. H. Wilson, *War, State and Society in Württemberg, 1677–1793* (Cambridge: Cambridge University Press, 1995)

GERMANY C. 1789–1918

L. Abrams, *Bismarck and the German Empire, 1871–1918* (London: Routledge, 1995)

L. Abrams, *Workers' Culture in Imperial Germany* (London: Routledge, 1992)

L. Abrams and E. Harvey (eds.), *Gender Relations in German History* (London: UCL Press, 1996)

C. Applegate, *A Nation of Provincials: the German Idea of Heimat* (Berkeley, Calif.: University of California Press, 1990)

R. M. Berdahl, *The Politics of the Prussian Nobility: the Development of a Conservative Ideology, 1770–1848* (Princeton, N.J.: Princeton University Press, 1988)

* D. Blackbourn, *History of Germany 1780–1918: the Long Nineteenth Century* (Oxford: Blackwell, 2nd edn, 2003)

D. Blackbourn and G. Eley, *The Peculiarities of German History* (Oxford: Oxford University Press, 1984)

T. C. W. Blanning, *The French Revolution in Germany* (Oxford: Oxford University Press, 1983)

* J. Breuilly, *The Formation of the First German Nation State, 1800–1871* (Basingstoke: Macmillan, 1996)

* J. Breuilly (ed.), *Nineteenth-century Germany: Politics, Culture and Society* (London: Arnold, 2000)

J. Breuilly (ed.), *The State of Germany: the National Idea in the Making, Unmaking and Remaking of a Modern Nation-State* (London: Longman, 1992)

R. Chickering, *Imperial Germany and the Great War, 1914–1918* (Cambridge: Cambridge University Press, 1998)

A. Confino, *The Nation as Local Metaphor: Württemberg, Imperial Germany and National Memory, 1871–1918* (Chapel Hill, N.C.: University of North Carolina Press, 1997)

* G. Craig, *Germany 1866–1945* (Oxford: Oxford University Press, 1981)

U. Daniel, *The War from Within: German Working-Class Women in the First World War* (Oxford: Berg, 1997)

P. Dwyer (ed.), *Modern Prussian History 1830–1947* (Harlow: Pearson, 2001)

R. J. Evans, *Death in Hamburg: Society and Politics in the Cholera Years, 1830–1910* (Oxford: Clarendon Press, 1987)

N. Ferguson, *The Pity of War* (London: Allen Lane, 1998)

U. Frevert, *Women in German History: From Bourgeois Emancipation to Sexual Liberation* (Oxford: Berg, 1989)

M. Levinger, *Enlightened Nationalism: the Transformation of Prussian Political Culture 1804–1848* (Oxford: Oxford University Press, 2000)

* T. Nipperdey, *Germany from Napoleon to Bismarck, 1800–1866* (Princeton, N.J.: Princeton University Press, 1996)

J. N. Retallack, *Germany in the Age of Kaiser Wilhelm II* (Basingstoke: Macmillan, 1996)

H. Schulze, *The Course of German Nationalism. From Frederick the Great to Bismarck, 1763–1867* (Cambridge: Cambridge University Press, 1991)

* J. Sheehan, *German History 1770–1866* (Oxford: Clarendon Press, 1989)

J. Sheehan, *German Liberalism in the Nineteenth Century* (London: Methuen, 1982)

* W. Siemann, *The German Revolution of 1848–49* (Basingstoke: Macmillan, 1998)

B. Simms, *The Impact of Napoleon. Prussian High Politics, Foreign Policy, and the Crisis of the Executive, 1797–1806* (Cambridge: Cambridge University Press, 1997)

* B. Simms, *The Struggle for Mastery in Germany, 1779–1850* (Basingstoke: Macmillan, 1998)

H. W. Smith, *German Nationalism and Religious Conflict* (Princeton, N.J.: Princeton University Press, 1995)

G. Steinmetz, *Regulating the Social: the Welfare State and Local Politics in Imperial Germany* (Princeton, N.J.: Princeton University Press, 1993)

M. Umbach (ed.), *German Federalism: Past, Present and Future* (Basingstoke: Palgrave, 2002)

GERMANY SINCE 1918: GENERAL OVERVIEWS

* V. Berghahn, *Modern Germany* (Cambridge: Cambridge University Press, 2nd edn, 1987)

* W. Carr, *A History of Germany, 1815–1990* (London: Edward Arnold, 4th edn, 1991)

* M. Fulbrook, *History of Germany, 1918–2000: the Divided Nation* (Oxford: Blackwell, 2nd edn, 2002)

* M. Fulbrook (ed.), *Twentieth-century Germany: Politics, Culture and Society* (London: Arnold, 2001)

G. Martel (ed.), *Modern Germany Reconsidered* (London: Routledge, 1992)

GERMANY 1918–1945

The Weimar Republic, 1918–1933

R. Bessel, *Germany after the First World War* (Oxford: Clarendon Press, 1993)

M. Broszat, *Hitler and the Collapse of Weimar Germany* (Leamington Spa: Berg, 1987)

T. Childers, *The Nazi Voter* (Chapel Hill: University of North Carolina Press, 1983)

G. Feldman, *The Great Disorder. Politics, Economics and Society in the German Inflation 1914–1924* (New York: Oxford University Press, 1993)

N. Ferguson, *Paper and Iron. Hamburg Business and German Politics in the Era of Inflation 1897–1927* (Cambridge: Cambridge University Press, 1995)

E. J. Feuchtwanger, *From Weimar to Hitler: Germany 1918–1933* (Basingstoke: Macmillan, 2nd edn, 1995)

C. Fischer, *The Rise of the Nazis* (Manchester: Manchester University Press, 2nd edn, 2002)

H. Heiber, *The Weimar Republic* (Oxford: Blackwell, 1993)

H. James, *The German Slump* (Oxford: Clarendon Press, 1986)

L. E. Jones, *German Liberalism and the Dissolution of the Weimar Party System 1918–1933* (Chapel Hill: University of North Carolina Press, 1988)

I. Kershaw (ed.), *Weimar: Why did German Democracy Fail?* (London: Weidenfeld and Nicolson, 1990)

* E. Kolb, *The Weimar Republic* (London: Unwin Hyman, 1988)

H. Mommsen, *The Rise and Fall of Weimar Democracy* (Chapel Hill: University of North Carolina Press, 1996)

J. Noakes and G. Pridham (eds.), *Nazism*, vol. 1: *Hitler's Rise to Power* (Exeter: Exeter Studies in History, 1983)

* D. Peukert, *The Weimar Republic: the Crisis of Classical Modernity* (London: Allen Lane, 1991)

H. A. Turner, *German Big Business and the Rise of Hitler* (Oxford: Oxford University Press, 1985)

The Third Reich, 1933–1945

G. Aly, *'Final Solution'. Nazi Population Policy and the Murder of the European Jews* (London: Arnold, 1999)

M. Balfour, *Withstanding Hitler* (London: Routledge, 1988)

D. Bankier, *The Germans and the Final Solution: Public Opinion under Nazism* (Oxford: Oxford University Press, 1992)

O. Bartov (ed.), *The Holocaust: Origins, Implementation, Aftermath* (London: Routledge, 2000)

K. D. Bracher, *The German Dictatorship* (Harmondsworth: Penguin, 1975)

M. Broszat, *The Hitler State* (London: Longman, 1981)

C. Browning, *Fateful Months* (New York: Holmes and Meier, revised edn, 1991)

C. Browning, *Nazi Policy, Jewish Workers, German Killers* (Cambridge: Cambridge University Press, 2000)

C. Browning, *Ordinary Men: Reserve Police Battalion 101 and the Final Solution in Poland* (London: HarperCollins, 1992)

C. Browning, *The Path to Genocide* (Cambridge: Cambridge University Press, 1992)

M. Burleigh, *The Third Reich: a New History* (Basingstoke: Macmillan, 2000)

M. Burleigh and W. Wippermann, *The Racial State: Germany 1933–45* (Cambridge: Cambridge University Press, 1991)

P. Burrin, *Hitler and the Jews* (London: Edward Arnold, 1994)

D. Crew (ed.), *Nazism and German Society* (London: Routledge, 1994)

G. Fleming, *Hitler and the Final Solution* (London: Hamish Hamilton, 1985)

N. Frei, *National Socialist Rule in Germany* (Oxford: Blackwell, 1993)

R. Gellately, *Backing Hitler. Consent and Coercion in Nazi Germany* (Oxford: Oxford University Press, 2001)

R. Gellately, *The Gestapo and German Society* (Oxford: Oxford University Press, 1990)

D. Goldhagen, *Hitler's Willing Executioners: Ordinary Germans and the Holocaust* (London: Little, Brown and Co., 1996)

S. Gordon, *Hitler, Germans and the 'Jewish Question'* (Princeton, N.J.: Princeton University Press, 1984)

U. Herbert (ed.), *National Socialist Extermination Policies: Contemporary German Perspectives and Controversies* (Oxford: Berghahn, 2000)

R. Hilberg, *The Destruction of the European Jews*, 3 vols. (New York: Holmes and Meier, 1985)

G. Hirschfeld and L. Kettenacker (eds.), *The Führer-state: Myth and Reality* (Stuttgart: Klett-Cotta, 1981)

I. Kershaw, *Hitler*, vol. I: *Hubris, 1889–1936* (London: Penguin, 1998)

I. Kershaw, *Hitler*, vol. II: *Nemesis, 1936–1945* (London: Penguin, 2000)

I. Kershaw, *Hitler: a Profile in Power* (London: Longman, 1991)

I. Kershaw, *The Hitler Myth* (Oxford: Oxford University Press, 1987)

* I. Kershaw, *The Nazi Dictatorship* (London: Arnold, 4th edn, 2000)

I. Kershaw, *Popular Opinion and Political Dissent in the Third Reich* (Oxford: Clarendon Press, 1983)

C. Leitz (ed.), *The Third Reich* (Oxford: Blackwell, 1999)

M. Marrus, *The Holocaust in History* (London: Weidenfeld and Nicolson, 1988)

T. Mason, *Nazism, Fascism and the Working Class* (Cambridge: Cambridge University Press, 1995)

T. Mason, *Social Policy in the Third Reich* (Oxford: Berg, 1993)

J. Noakes and G. Pridham, *Nazism*, vol. II: *State, Economy and Society, 1933–1939* (Exeter: Exeter Studies in History, 1984)

J. Noakes and G. Pridham, *Nazism*, vol. III: *Foreign Policy, War and Racial Extermination* (Exeter: Exeter Studies in History, 1988)

J. Noakes and G. Pridham, *Nazism*, vol. IV: *The German Home Front in World War II* (Exeter: Exeter Studies in History, 1998)

R. Overy, *The Nazi Economic Recovery* (Cambridge: Cambridge University Press, 2nd edn, 1996)

R. Overy, *War and Economy in the Third Reich* (Oxford: Clarendon Press, 1994)

R. Overy, *Why the Allies Won* (London: Jonathan Cape, 1995)

D. Peukert, *Inside Nazi Germany* (London: Batsford, 1987)

R. Shandley (ed.), *Unwilling Germans? The Goldhagen Debate* (Minneapolis: University of Minnesota Press, 1998)

J. Stephenson, *Women in Nazi Germany* (Harlow: Pearson, 2001)

D. Welch, *The Third Reich. Politics and Propaganda* (London: Routledge, 2nd edn, 2002)

GERMANY SINCE 1945: DIVIDED AND UNIFIED

M. Allinson, *Politics and Popular Opinion in East Germany, 1945–68* (Manchester: Manchester University Press, 2000)

T. Garton Ash, *In Europe's Name* (New York: Random House, 1993)

M. Balfour, *Germany: the Tides of Power* (London: Routledge, 1992)

D. Childs and R. Popplewell, *The Stasi. The East German Intelligence and Security Service* (Basingstoke: Macmillan, 1996)

D. P. Conradt, *The German Polity* (London: Longman, 4th edn, 1989)

* M. Dennis, *The Rise and Fall of the German Democratic Republic, 1945–1990* (Harlow: Pearson, 2000)

L. Edinger, *West German Politics* (New York: Columbia University Press, 1986)

M. Fulbrook, *Anatomy of a Dictatorship: Inside the GDR, 1949–1989* (Oxford: Oxford University Press, 1995)

M. Fulbrook, *German National Identity after the Holocaust* (Cambridge: Polity Press, 1999)

* M. Fulbrook, *Interpretations of the Two Germanies, 1945–1990* (Basingstoke: Macmillan, 2nd edn, 2000)

G.-J. Glaessner, *The Unification Process in Germany* (London: Pinter, 1992)

G.-J. Glaessner and I. Wallace (eds.), *The German Revolution of 1989* (Oxford: Berg, 1992)

A. Glees, *Reinventing Germany* (Oxford: Berg, 1996)

P. Grieder, *The East German Leadership 1946–73: Conflict and Crisis* (Manchester: Manchester University Press, 1999)

K. Jarausch, *The Rush to German Unity* (Oxford: Berghahn, 1994)

K. Jarausch (ed.), *Dictatorship as Experience: Towards a Socio-Cultural History of the GDR* (Oxford: Berghahn, 1999)

K. Jarausch and V. Gransow (eds.), *Uniting Germany: Documents and Debates* (Oxford: Berghahn, 1994)

L. Kettenacker, *Germany since 1945* (Oxford: Oxford University Press, 1997)

C. Kleßmann (ed.), *The Divided Past. Rewriting Post-War German History* (Oxford: Berg, 2001)

J. Kopstein, *The Politics of Economic Decline* (Chapel Hill: University of North Carolina Press, 1997)

A. Kramer, *The West German Economy* (Oxford: Berg, 1991)

K. Larres and P. Panayi (eds.), *The Federal Republic of Germany since 1949: Politics, Society and Economy before and after Unification* (London: Longman, 1996)

C. Maier, *Dissolution* (Princeton, N.J.: Princeton University Press, 1997)

P. Major and J. Osmond (eds.), *The Workers' and Peasants' State: Communism and Society in East Germany under Ulbricht, 1945–71* (Manchester: Manchester University Press, 2002)

A. J. McAdams, *Germany Divided* (Princeton, N.J.: Princeton University Press, 1993)

A. J. McAdams, *Judging the Past in Unified Germany* (Cambridge: Cambridge University Press, 2001)

L. H. McFalls, *Communism's Collapse, Democracy's Demise?* (Basingstoke: Macmillan, 1995)

P. H. Merkl (ed.), *The Federal Republic of Germany at Forty-five: Union without Unity* (Basingstoke: Macmillan, 1995)

N. Naimark, *The Russians in Germany* (Cambridge, Mass.: Harvard University Press, 1995)

* A. J. Nicholls, *The Bonn Republic: West German Democracy, 1945–1990* (London: Longman, 1997)

J. Osmond (ed.), *German Reunification* (Harlow: Longman, 1992)

* P. Pulzer, *German Politics 1945–1995* (Oxford: Oxford University Press, 1995)

C. Ross, *Constructing Socialism at the Grassroots* (Basingstoke: Macmillan, 2000)

* C. Ross, *The East German Dictatorship: Problems and Perspectives in the Interpretation of the GDR* (London: Arnold, 2002)

H. P. Schwarz, *Konrad Adenauer*, 2 vols. (Providence, R.I.: Berghahn, 1995, 1997)

G. Smith, W. Paterson, P. H. Merkl (eds.), *Developments in West German Politics* (Basingstoke: Macmillan, 1989)

G. Smith, W. Paterson, P. H. Merkl, S. Padgett (eds.), *Developments in German Politics* (Basingstoke: Macmillan, 1992)

* G. Smith, W. Paterson, S. Padgett (eds.), *Developments in German Politics 2* (Basingstoke: Macmillan, 1996)

S. Szabo, *The Diplomacy of German Unification* (New York: St Martin's Press, 1992)

H. A. Turner, *Germany from Partition to Reunification* (New Haven, Conn.: Yale University Press, 1992)

P. Zelikow and C. Rice, *Germany Unified and Europe Transformed* (Cambridge, Mass.: Harvard University Press, 1995)

INDEX